Life with Birds

Life with Birds

A Story of Mutual Exploitation

MALCOLM SMITH

Whittles Publishing

Published by
Whittles Publishing Ltd.,
Dunbeath,
Caithness, KW6 6EG,
Scotland, UK

www.whittlespublishing.com

ISBN 978-184995-028-2

Printed by Bell & Bain Ltd., Glasgow

For my soulmate, my support and inspiration. And for my growing family in the hope that they might be interested.

CONTENTS

PREFACE

An early morning jog in a city park. A lunchtime break from the office. A drive through rush hour traffic. A leisurely weekend walk along your local river or through a favourite wood perhaps.

You may not notice them – or you might care not to – but, wherever you are, birds will be there too. Maybe just a city pigeon picking up a few crumbs on a pavement. Some sparrows chirping on a nearby building. A robin beside you as you work in your garden. The noisy, grating calls of a crow or seagull on a rooftop. Or the cadenzas of early morning birdsong from nearby trees.

From the earliest days of human existence, birds have tagged along with us. They still do. They raid our crops for some easy eats. They use nooks and crannies in our buildings to nest. Sometimes they even help clear up our garbage. And they are a reminder, even in the most built-up environments we create, that a natural world still exists.

We have long exploited birds. Think how often we eat them, chicken especially; turkey at Christmas or at Thanksgiving. Eggs, mostly from chickens – boiled, scrambled, easy-over fried or as an ingredient of our cakes and many other foods – are a dietary mainstay. And we are snug on many a winter's night because duvets full of feathers keep us warm while we sleep.

Birds have long inspired our art, from early Neolithic drawings to Van Gogh's foreboding depiction of rooks against a stormy sky painted just hours before his untimely suicide. They inspire much of our music, too, both classical and pop. They feature on a surprising number of postage stamps and who isn't familiar with a local called 'The Swan' or some other pub named after a bird.

Wherever we have chosen to live, from isolated farms to the bustle of city centres, birds have joined us there. And many of them have adapted amazingly well to our changing lifestyles.

A surprising number have set up home in our largest cities. House Crows squawk in the noisy sprawl of Mumbai. Cormorants fly up and down the River Thames through the centre of London. American Robins feed on the White House lawns. Smart-looking Tree Sparrows – countryside birds across Europe – ply the pavements of Bangkok alongside arguably the most vehicle-congested roads in the world. Turkey Vultures nest on the high rises in Mexico City. And in dusty Timbuktu on the edge of the mighty Sahara, sand-coloured Barn Owls perch at night on identically coloured buildings ready to pounce on a passing rodent.

But do we know why certain birds, not others, have adapted to city life? And is it possible to predict which ones might yet do so? The simple answer is no. With hindsight it might have been possible to predict that Peregrines would set up home in cities. After all, our high-rise buildings provide them with 'cliffs' to nest on and plenty of prey such as city pigeons to kill. But ravens haven't become city slickers even though they, too, nest mainly on cliffs and eat a broad diet including almost anything they can scavenge.

It might just be that some birds are innately more adaptable than others. We know a lot about the behaviour and the ecology of very many species but perhaps still not enough to understand the intimate detail of their requirements and the degree to which they can adapt to new circumstances and new opportunities.

The first humans were hunter-gatherers and, with skill and perseverance, they learnt to trap and kill birds for food. Eggs were easier to obtain, especially if the birds nested in colonies and on the ground. Many wild birds are still trapped and killed for food, sometimes illegally. In certain cultures the kill has been transformed into a social event as anyone participating in a grouse shoot on a Scottish moor will testify. In others, a meaty wild bird, or some bird eggs, are still a necessity to add some variety to a desperately poor diet and a torrid existence.

Today, in most developed countries, the majority of our bird meat is 'farmed', often in controversial intensive units housing very large numbers of long since domesticated birds such as chickens, turkeys and ducks. Many people eat them every day – portions which come in clean, sealed packs our ancestors would never recognise. With increasing affluence, and greater concern about animal welfare, more and more of these domesticated meats – and the vast number of chicken eggs we consume – are being produced from birds kept in less confined, more humane conditions.

But domestication brings other problems. The close proximity between the birds and their keepers can have frightening consequences. Bird flu, transferred from poultry to farm workers, is proving to be one of the deadliest influenza viruses ever identified. It may yet mutate to become the basis for a pandemic that could kill millions of people worldwide.

In the past, countries have gone to war over birds and their outcomes still cause diplomatic tensions. Without birds – more correctly their feathers – one of the deadliest weapons of war ever invented, as destructive in its day as the machine gun in its own time, could not have inflicted the terrible human carnage that it did. It was the longbow and its deadly arrows would have been useless without their feather fletching.

Over the millennia, we have used birds for sending messages and for warning miners of dangerous gases. Many birds have religious and symbolic significance; European Goldfinches, perhaps because of their scarlet faces, symbolise Christ's passion. Doves have long symbolised peace. We use their images in advertising and branding, from Swan Vestas matches and Penguin books to Guinness's toucan.

We are entranced by their beauty. Birds such as peacocks have long been captured and confined to adorn stately gardens, while many people keep canaries, parrots and other birds in cages for their often exquisite colours and to appreciate their songs and mimicry. But human greed to possess ever more exotic birds has spawned a huge illegal trade in many that jeopardises the survival of some of the rarest species in the world.

This exploitation isn't all one way. Birds exploit us too. They exploit our homes to make theirs. The earliest-known buildings provided new breeding places for swallows and for what were, originally, wild pigeons that became semi-domesticated in our towns and cities. The world over, birds such as gulls and kites exploit our detritus at refuse tips or in our streets. An array of stately, wading birds like egrets and herons make copious use of rice paddies for the insects and frogs they nurture to retrieve an even easier meal.

Other birds steal our food from the croplands we have created, whether it's Wood Pigeons raiding fields of peas in Britain, flocks of smartly plumaged Cedar Waxwings devouring a Florida farmer's blueberries or starlings making a meal of ripening grapes in Australia. They can be phenomenally destructive. A poor African farmer's livelihood can be devastated in an hour if sparrow-sized quelea finches – often tens of thousands of them – descend on his millet crop like an ominous locust cloud. And ask an Australian sunflower farmer what he thinks of the flocks of albeit beautifully coloured cockatoos stripping his flower heads of seed … and stand well back for his reply!

Very rarely, exploitation can bring mutual advantage to birds and to people! In the centre of Mumbai, the vultures, today replaced by kites, that consume the Parsi dead – a fundamental part of their Zoroastrian religion – get an easy meal. And some tribesmen in the Kenyan bushlands still use birds called honeyguides to lead them, sometimes a kilometre or two through scrub and forest, to wild beehives. The honeyguide locates the hive, the human gatherer opens it up to extract the honey … and the bird gets rewarded with a handout of a piece of the sweet comb.

In the past much of our exploitation of birds has been enormously destructive. Some of it still is. Our killing sprees, albeit for food, took the Wild Turkeys of North America to the brink of extinction and extirpated the once super-abundant Passenger Pigeon. Some practices like cockfighting, commonplace in some countries, are repugnant to many people and evoke strong emotions akin to those provoked by bullfighting.

Our exploitation of birds, though, isn't always what it might seem. Provided that Scottish moorlands continue to be managed to raise unnaturally high numbers of Red Grouse, there will always be a 'Glorious Twelfth' and more grouse than could ever exist naturally. And pheasants would still be confined to their Southeast Asian homeland if they had not been introduced to much of the world to adorn gardens and villas and to be killed for food.

The purpose of this book is to describe a wide range of fascinating examples of mankind's long association with birds around the world, some historic, others present day. It tells the story of our exploitation of birds – and of their continued exploitation of us. Our life with birds – and theirs with us – is something which has long fascinated me wherever I have been in the world.

But it isn't my intention here to mention every recorded association between birds and people; that would occupy more than one volume. Some individual topics – birds in art for instance; the use of carrier pigeons; the history of cockfighting – could each have a book written about them. Some already have!

Instead, I've tried to use the most interesting, intriguing – as well as the more commonplace – examples of birds and people getting along with each other, of us exploiting them and, equally, their exploitation of us for living space and an easy meal. If you, the reader, believe that, in places, I should have used better examples, you might well be correct. The judgements of what to include, and what to omit, have often proved difficult.

What this book doesn't do is to rehearse our more indirect impact on birds; the way we farm the land, the way we exploit forests, the way we fish our seas and oceans. And, of course, the way we are artificially warming our world because of the carbon dioxide and other emissions our society produces.

Nor does it dwell on the impact of many of the animals – rats, cats, pigs and others – people have taken with them, either purposely or accidentally, when they have colonised new lands and islands, the kinds of introductions that have frequently had a catastrophic impact on the birds, and many other animals, that naturally existed in such places.

I have tried studiously not to take any moral or ethical position in dealing with traditions or practices which some people might find repugnant and cruel, at least to western, more affluent sensibilities. My intention has been to provide a factual summary of such topics as cockfighting and animal sacrifice which, in the countries where such practices continue, they are viewed very differently.

The arguments that those participating in such practices use to justify them is, I hope, balanced with a view from some of those who deplore them. If I have not struck an acceptable balance, and my prejudices show through, the fault is solely mine. I leave it to you, the reader, to make up your own mind about these often complex relationships.

Throughout I have endeavoured to use the most up-to-date, internationally recognised names for birds authorised by the International Ornithological Congress. As knowledge of different species increases and an understanding of how they fit into different families changes, so do their names. To British readers, some of this might seem rather unnecessary; the familiar swallow, for instance, becomes the barn swallow. But there are 89 different swallows and martins in the world so calling one of them 'the swallow' would be downright confusing to many potential readers!

ACKNOWLEDGEMENTS

This book would not have been possible without considerable help from a huge range of people across an inevitably large range of subjects, from rice growing in Southeast Asia to the living conditions in medieval London; from eiderdown collecting in Iceland to the implication of vultures disappearing in India for the Parsi community there.

I have tried to be assiduous in recording the help that I received along the way. To anyone I have inadvertently missed, please accept my apologies. My thanks go to the following:

Khalfan Butti Alqubaisi in the United Arab Emirates for information on falconry and for his photography; Karol Bailey of Holly Tree Farm near Knutsford in Cheshire, UK for explaining free range, organic bird rearing; Eric Bajart for photography; Oli Ben (Olafur Benedikksson) of Dün & Fidur in Reykjavik for showing me finished eiderdown duvets; David Bills of the Royal Pigeon Racing Association; Larry Blakely, Emeritus Professor of Biological Sciences at Cal Poly Pomona in California for his help in selecting bird-inspired classical music; M and Mme Blanc at Domaine de Paulon, Le Sambuc in the Camargue, France for their help in explaining European organic rice farming; Luca Borghesio of BirdLife International for his considerable help in discussions with Robert Lentaaya who provided much insight into the relationship between honeyguides and tribesmen of his Ndorobo people in northern Kenya, and Paul Kariuki Ndang'ang'a, Species Programme Manager for Africa for BirdLife International in Nairobi.

Chris Bowden of the RSPB for keeping me updated about the plight of vultures across the Indian subcontinent; Paul Burke of www.firstpeople.us for photography of a Native American chief; my old friend Peter Bye for his insights into pub names; John Cannon of Roughway Farm near Tonbridge, Kent, UK for his knowledge of fruit and cobnut growing; Tomás Castelazo for photography; Alessandro Catenazzi for photography; Louise Chambers of the Purple Martin Conservation Association in the US; Dr Sansanee Choowaew, Programme Director for Natural Resource Management in the Faculty of Environment and Resource Studies, Mahidol University, Bangkok (for her knowledge of rice paddies); John Clark, formerly Senior Curator (Medieval) in the Department of Early London History and Collections at the Museum of London for his help with living conditions in medieval London and contemporary references to red kites; Jeremy Coote, Joint Head of Collections, Pitt Rivers Museum, University of Oxford; and Giles Deacon for photography.

Robbie Douglas Miller for his help in understanding grouse moor management and allowing me to participate in a grouse shoot on his Scottish estate; fashion designer Giles Deacon for use of a photograph; Ed Drewitt of Bristol's City Museum and Art Gallery for information about city-living peregrines; Nancy Egloff, Historian at the Jamestown-Yorktown Foundation at Williamsburg, Virginia, US; Jonathan Elphick for his advice and guidance on bird artists; Nick Fairhall and the Guinness Collectors Club for the image of Guinness's toucan on a playing card; Kim Forrester, editor of *Cage & Aviary Birds*; Flagstaffotos for photography; Dr Nick Fox, Director of International Wildlife Consultants (UK) Ltd for advice on Middle East falconry; Sam Glover of PETA (People for the

Ethical Treatment of Animals) UK; David Hammerson, owner of Eversleigh Farm Shop Ltd in Wiltshire for information on gulls' eggs; Bonnie Hanbury-Calliotte in Elizabeth City, North Carolina about garden bird feeding; Thorvaldur Haroldson, his family and friends for introducing me to the technique of collecting eiderdown on the fabulous islands in the Breidofjordur off Iceland's west coast; Dr Chris Healey of Clifton Creek, Victoria, Australia for his knowledge of bird plume use in New Guinea; Dr Tim Healey of Melbourne and Dr Mick Poole of Perth for helping direct me to information on crop damage by birds in Australia; Kristóf Hecker, Conservation Officer of the International Council for Game and Wildlife Conservation based in Hungary; Katherine Howard, a Threatened Species Network Regional Manager for WWF in Australia.

Graeme Jeffrey of the Centenary Archers Club in Brisbane, Australia for the use of his internet compilation of historical events involving archers; Helga Jóhannesdóttir of the Icelandic Farmers Association who provided much guidance about eider 'farming'; Mrs Margaret Johns of Medway, Kent for her experience of cage-bird keeping; Tony Juniper for advice on Spix's macaw; Robert Lancione for photography; Florian Leppla, Campaigner at the League Against Cruel Sports; Dr Randall Lockwood, Senior Vice President at the American Society for the Prevention of Cruelty to Animals, and ASPCA Special Investigator Mark MacDonald; Barbara Allen Loucks and staff of the New York State Department of Environmental Conservation Endangered Species Unit and for use of photography; Grahame Madge and John Clare at the RSPB in the UK; Bobby Maisnam and Mike McDonough for photography; Nanette Mickle and family for their hospitality and information on purple martin nesting at Woodbridge, Washington, DC; Patrick Morel, President of the Belgian Falconers Association, and Carlo Verbiot, for showing me the intricacies of falconry in practice; Craig Nash for photography; Natural History Museum, London for use of photography; Ross Newham, Principal Communications Manager at Defra, London for his help in obtaining information about birds as crop pests; Gary Norman, in charge of the wild turkey restoration programme for the Virginia Department of Game and Inland Fisheries in the US; Gavin and Linda Perry of the B'darra Estate winery on the Mornington Peninsula, South Australia; Dr Alan Pipe of the Museum of London Archaeology for compiling information on excavated bird bones in London; Björk Þorleifsdóttir of Fuglavernd, the Icelandic Society for the Protection of Birds; Alastair Rae for photography; Steve Richards of *British Homing World*, David Higgins, its Regional Secretary in northwest England and Mrs Jeannette Taylor of Failsworth, Manchester for showing me her racing pigeon loft.

Leigh Riley at Defra for helping to unravel UK poultry statistics; Ignasi Ripoll, RietVell's Manager in the Ebro Delta, Spain for explaining organic rice paddy management; Paul Robinson of the UK's Hawk Board; Eibhlin Roche, Guinness Archivist at Guinness's Dublin headquarters; Dr Phillip Round, Assistant Professor at the Department of Biology at Mahidol University, Bangkok for discussions about rice paddy birds in Southeast Asia; Sue Royale of Dunhan Massey Home Farm in Cheshire; Nicolas Sadoul, ornithologist at the Station Biologique de la Tour du Valat, Le Sambuc, Arles, France; Kjell Scharning, who operates the website, www.birdtheme.org, for information on birds on postage stamps; my good friend Gabriel Sierra, with whom I have spent many happy hours watching birds in Spain, for photography; Dr Klara Spandl of the Oxford Archaeological Unit and John McCann, both experts on dovecotes; Richard Thomas of TRAFFIC's Cambridge, UK headquarters for his enormous help and invaluable advice on CITES and the illegal bird trade and Chris Shepherd and Panjit Tansom of TRAFFIC's Southeast Asia office; Dr Des Thompson, Policy and Advice Manager at Scottish Natural Heritage, for his advice on grouse moor management; Mark Tibbott, Operations Manager (Wales) for the Mines Rescue Service Ltd for his recollections and advice about coalmine canaries; Mike Toms, David Glue and Graham Appleton at the British Trust for Ornithology in the UK; Colin Tudge, biologist and author; John Tully of Westbury on Trym for his unfailingly cheerful advice about urban birds and for his knowledge of city pigeons; Will Unger, Field Manager for Oregon Berry Picking at Portland, Oregon, US; Ami Vitale for her collaboration over the years and her, as always, brilliant photography; Vicki Watkins of Fauna Wildlife Rescue in South Wales for information on pigeon deterrence; Phil West for his encyclopaedic field knowledge of wild turkeys in Virginia; Dave Wheeler of the Abbotsbury Swannery in Dorset for explaining modern-day use of swan quills; Peter Williams, Marketing Communications Manager for Corus Strip Products, Port Talbot, South Wales; and Simon Williams, Head of Operational Services for Cardiff and The Vale Health Board.

1

A free lunch

The world over, birds have always been exploited by us as a source of free food. Many
still are. Sometimes, though, our exploitation has proved
disastrous for the birds concerned.

Crossing the wide expanse of the James River by ferry on the eastern fringe of the state of Virginia and looking at the forests on the bank ahead – autumn-tinted in a plethora of rust, orange and olive-green – it's not difficult to imagine how relieved the first English settlers must have been when they saw this verdant, forested landscape 400 years ago. At first sight, it doesn't look as if it has changed very much.

Jamestown, the first permanent community in what would eventually become the United States of America, was established here on the banks of the James River near the coast of Virginia in 1607. The settlers had crossed the vast Atlantic in three small wooden ships and set about building their homes in a strange land.

They soon started trading with the local forest-dwelling Powhatan Indians. In exchange for trinkets the settlers had brought with them from England, the Powhatans provided them with plenty of wild-caught food and cultivated crops. There was no shortage in the shallow seas and the forests around.

In addition to the deer, fish and vegetables they obtained in this way was a large, wild-caught ground bird the early settlers believed was some bigger version of guineafowl that they were more used to back home. Soon they would rename them: turkeys.

Wild Turkeys were common birds in the extensive forests right across the American continent. And they were good eating. But their forest homes were disappearing. In 1600, US forests covered about 430 million acres. Today there are about 20 million acres. Soon the settlers were shooting turkeys themselves, not only for their own eating but to sell at market where they were a popular buy. Settler numbers started increasing fast. By 1790, there were 4 million. The land they needed for farming was cleared more and more rapidly.

Inland from these growing Virginia communities was the rest of the American continent, stretching an incredible two to three thousand miles west – vast open spaces where no white man had been. And vast space is what this burgeoning population desperately needed.

Little over two centuries ago, pioneering Europeans set out west from the towns and villages they had built along the east coast. In the already colonised eastern states, from Massachusetts in the northeast down to the Carolinas in the southeast, settlement by more and more Europeans had already caused massive changes to the local landscape and wildlife. Huge swathes of the native red and white oak, beech and pine forests had been felled for timber and to clear land for farming.

And as their horse-pulled wagon trains headed west, trying – not always successfully – to avoid attacks from Native American Indians who had colonised this land aeons before, it wasn't only bison on the great open plains that the settlers hunted in vast numbers. It was Wild Turkeys in the extensive forests too.

Difficult though it is to accept today, the settlers were convinced that they were destined, even divinely ordained, to expand across this vast continent and populate it. Native Indians, long established across much of the land, were simply in the way. Bison were there to be hunted. And so was the turkey!

'By the turn of the 20th century, the extensive forests of Virginia were gone', says Gary Norman, who leads the Wild Turkey reinstatement project for Virginia's Department of Game and Inland Fisheries (DGIF). 'They had disappeared from two-thirds of the state and their populations were probably at their lowest from 1880 to 1910.'

According to the National Wild Turkey Federation, the birds lived originally in what are now 39 US states and the Canadian province of Ontario, maybe 10 million of them altogether. As the settlers pushed west, turkeys died out. Connecticut lost them by 1813. Vermont held out until 1842. By 1920, this huge bird had been extirpated in 18 of the original 39 states and Ontario. Elsewhere, few populations survived. Forest felling and shooting had done its worst.

Wild Turkeys are large, the males – known as toms – 1.2 metres in length and the females – hens – nearly a metre. More slender than domesticated birds, the toms are strikingly colourful with their bronze and blue plumage … though hardly beautiful. The hens are duller. Displaying males are a sight to behold. With tails fanned upright, puffed out chests and drooping wings, they strut about on spring mornings to impress the local hens. In spite of their size, though, turkeys are often quite difficult to spot.

'It's impossible to find them if you walk off-track into a forest', comments Phil West, a turkey expert and wildlife biologist for DGIF in Virginia I meet near the quiet little community of Providence Forge about 50 km east of the Virginia capital, Richmond. 'They'll hear you coming way before you see anything. And even though they roost at night high up in a tree, they're real hard to spot in spite of their size. They're easier to spot in fields where they often feed near the edges of forests.'

'They sure are hard to hunt too. You have to get into a forest you know they're in before first light. Then settle down and mimic the calls of the hens to attract a tom. If you're lucky, he'll come along looking. You don't shoot until they are, say, 30 yards away', adds Phil.

So how did the Powhatans do it centuries back without guns? Nancy Egloff, the historian at the Jamestown-Yorktown Foundation at Williamsburg, Virginia, thinks that they probably also used calls to entice the turkeys. Then they perhaps killed them with a spear throw or a bow and arrows.

Reinstating turkeys in the wild has taken decades and has proved far from straightforward. Early laws established in the first few decades of the 20th century helped reduce hunting pressure and protect dwindling wildlife. But the first attempt at recovery, starting in the 1920s, used turkeys reared in game farms and released into suitable habitat. They failed to survive because they contracted diseases in confined rearing pens and because they had not learnt as young birds how to avoid predators and search for wild food. Millions of dollars and two or three decades were wasted.

'After 1955, Wild Turkeys were captured in traps baited with grain or by firing rocket-propelled nets over them, then transferred to areas with suitable habitat', says Gary Norman. 'By 1993 nearly 900 wild birds were relocated in Virginia this way', he adds.

Very slowly this translocation of Wild Turkeys has worked. Today there are estimated to be around 7 million US-wide. Hunting under licence is commonplace once more. Regulations vary from state to state but they all restrict the number that can be shot. Research has found that more turkeys die of natural causes, mostly through being taken by foxes and bobcats. Most states allow hunting on Thanksgiving Day in November when Americans (and Canadians) traditionally give thanks for their safe deliverance. So more and more families once again are sitting down to a meal of wild, rather than farm-raised, turkey on that special day.

It's unlikely that a bird that is revered by so many people in today's US – and remembered as a part of the original struggle the early settlers endured to found their country – will be allowed to get into such dire circumstances ever again.

It's too late, though, for some other birds. The incredible story of the demise of the Passenger Pigeon, once the most common US bird, is barely believable. Around 3–5 billion of them lived on the continent at the time the Europeans discovered America; there are claims that they represented up to 40 per cent of all land birds living in the US! They lived in enormous flocks, so large that some would take several hours to pass and contain millions of birds. Theirs was the bird version of the huge buffalo herds that roamed the prairies.

A nomadic bird, in summer PassengerPigeons lived in forests throughout North America east of the Rocky Mountains and in much of Canada. In winter, many moved to the southern US and occasionally as far as Mexico and Cuba, exploiting seasonally available beech mast, acorns and chestnuts. It's because of all this moving from place to place that French settlers in North America christened them '*pigeon de passage*'. So Passenger Pigeons they became!

Adult Passenger Pigeons were about 38 cm long, larger than the Mourning Dove (to which they were most similar) found throughout today's US and a little smaller than the more plump Wood Pigeon found commonly across Europe. They were colourful, graceful, fast and manoeuvrable in flight and they really were at least as attractive as any species of pigeon in the world today, possibly more so.

Passenger Pigeons were extremely social birds. The flocks spent much of their time scouting for food, and information sharing between the birds was likely to have required flocks of a certain critical size to survive.

Their migration, in massive flocks, was a spectacle without parallel. The famous American ornithologist John James Audubon recorded a flock in 1813 over Kentucky that he estimated to contain over a billion birds. 'The sky', he said, 'was black with birds for three days.'

John Muir, the Scottish-born American naturalist, author and early advocate of the preservation of US wilderness, wrote in 1913 about the passenger pigeon:

> I have seen flocks streaming south in the fall so large that they were flowing over from horizon to horizon in an almost continuous stream all day long, at the rate of forty or fifty miles an hour, like a mighty river in the sky, widening, contracting, descending like falls and cataracts, and rising suddenly here and there in huge ragged masses like high splashing spray.

There was safety in large flocks. When one established itself in an area, the number of local animal predators – wolves, foxes, weasels and hawks – was so small compared with the total number

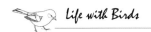

of pigeons that little damage would be inflicted on the flock as a whole. The problem was that this colonial way of life was poorly suited to coexistence with people when they arrived and began to hunt them! Their technique of survival had been based on mass tactics. Very soon, mass tactics were to be their downfall.

An individual forest nesting site may have covered many thousands of acres and the birds were so congested that hundreds of nests could be counted in each tree. One such nesting area in Wisconsin was reported to cover 850 square miles, and the number of birds nesting there was estimated to be around 136 million!

With the birds massed like this, it was easy for people to slaughter them in such great numbers that there were not enough left to successfully reproduce the species. As the flocks dwindled in size, with the resulting breakdown of their social structure, the Passenger Pigeon was doomed. A trade even developed in live birds so that they could be used as targets in New York shooting galleries, veritable sitting ducks, a practice not banned until 1907.

Just as forest clearance fuelled the demise of the Wild Turkey, the widespread clearance of the hardwood forests which provided the pigeon's food must have reduced their breeding numbers too.

So the pigeons turned to the grain fields planted by settling farmers. Not a clever move! Predictably, the flocks caused serious damage and the farmers retaliated by shooting the birds and using them as a source of meat. Competitions were held; in one, 30,000 pigeon corpses were needed to claim a prize! But there were so many pigeons that not even this seemed to seriously diminish their numbers.

What finally did for them was the proliferation of the US telegraph system which enabled information about the location of nesting colonies to be passed quickly to hunters, coupled with the growing railroad network that could transport young live birds to market for food. Pigeon meat was sold as a cheap food for slaves and the poor in the 19th century resulting in hunting on a massive scale. While mature pigeon meat was dark and tough, the flesh of young birds was good eating.

All sorts of horrendous ways of attracting, then killing, the pigeons were devised. Alcohol-soaked grain intoxicated the birds and made them easier to kill. Smoky, sulphurous fires were set under nesting trees to drive them from their nests. Another method was to blind a bird by sewing its eyes shut using a needle and thread. This bird's feet would be attached to the end of a stick and it would flutter its wings, attracting the attention of others flying overhead. When the flock landed near this decoy bird, nets would trap them and the hunters would crush their heads between their thumb and forefinger.

'In 1805 I saw schooners loaded in bulk with pigeons caught up the Hudson river coming in to the wharf at New York when the birds sold for a cent a piece', recorded Audubon in his famous book *Birds of America*, first published between 1827 and 1838. 'I knew a man in Pennsylvania who caught and killed upwards of 500 dozens in a clap-net in one day, sweeping sometimes twenty dozens or more at a single haul', he wrote.

Accounts of their slaughter make harrowing reading. Audubon recorded one such affair in forests in Kentucky:

Suddenly there burst forth a general cry of 'Here they come!' The noise which they made, though yet distant, reminded me of a hard gale at sea. As the birds arrived and passed over me, I felt a current of air that surprised me. Thousands were soon knocked down by the pole-men. The birds continued to pour in. The fires were lighted, and a magnificent, as well as wonderful and almost terrifying, sight presented itself.

The Pigeons, arriving by thousands, alighted everywhere, one above another, until solid masses were formed on the branches all round. Here and there the perches gave way under the weight with a crash, and, falling to the ground, destroyed hundreds of the birds beneath, forcing down the dense groups with which every stick was loaded.

It was a scene of uproar and confusion. I found it quite useless to speak, or even to shout to those persons who were nearest to me.

The uproar continued the whole night … Towards the approach of day, the noise in some measure subsided: long before objects were distinguishable, the Pigeons began to move off in a direction quite different from that in which they had arrived the evening before, and at sunrise all that were able to fly had disappeared.

It was then that the authors of all this devastation began their entry amongst the dead, the dying, and the mangled. The Pigeons were picked up and piled in heaps, until each had as many as he could possibly dispose of, when the hogs were let loose to feed on the remainder.

The pigeons declined steadily through the 19th century as the trade in young birds for eating blossomed. Attempts in the mid 1800s to pass protective laws to stem the slaughter got nowhere. Many politicians argued against such a need. In any case, it was too little too late. By 1896, there was just one flock of maybe a quarter of a million left. When word got around that they were nesting in the Great Lakes area, there was no stopping the hunters. Callously, as they knew perfectly well that this was the last wild flock, sport hunters went out and shot the lot.

Attempts to revive the species by breeding the surviving captive birds were not successful. The Passenger Pigeon was a colonial and gregarious bird and needed large numbers to breed. They soon weakened and died. A few individuals lingered on into the first months of the 20th century. In 1900 the final wild bird was shot by a 14-year-old farm boy in Ohio who apparently saw it eating his corn. It was stuffed, named 'Buttons' (its embalmer used them for eyes) and sent to the Ohio Historical Society in Columbus where it is still on display today.

At 1 p.m. on 1 September 1914, 29-year-old Martha fell off her perch in Cincinnati Zoo, Ohio and expired. She was the last of them. Martha's body was frozen in ice and sent to the Smithsonian Institution in Washington, DC. She is no longer on public display.

Disentangling the impact of hunting birds to eat, for sport or to obtain decorations like feathers from the impact of the destruction of their habitat and the introduction of new predators is very difficult. Rarely does just one of these factors account entirely for a bird's extinction. Nevertheless, hunting since the start of the 17th century has probably been the main or sole factor in the extinction of at least seven different birds worldwide.

Others had faded away even earlier! The ten species of massive, flightless moas – in appearance like overgrown emus, the largest 12 feet tall – inhabited New Zealand but were killed off for their meat and eggs by the Maoris before 1500. They may have become extinct in little more than a century and with them perished the giant Haast's Eagle, the largest known bird of prey, that hunted these massive ground birds.

The world over, though, there are far more birds, from various species of ducks and geese, to pheasant, snipe and quail, seabirds like puffins and even tiny birds like finches and larks, that are killed, cooked and eaten for food. Today, most of them are not killed on the scale that many had been in the past but several have declined in number, at least partly because of the carnage they have suffered.

Les Beletsky, in his enthralling *Birds of the World* (Collins, 2006), reckons that about 365 of the 1,180 threatened species of birds in the world (there are about 9,750 species in total) are under threat because of continued hunting for food. That might be a lot but it's a lot less than the numbers under threat because of destruction or degradation of their habitats. Other wild birds, hunted for food rather more sustainably, are holding their own.

In New Guinea and Australia, cassowaries (large, shy, dark-coloured, flightless ground birds) are hunted primarily to eat although their decline in some places is more down to habitat loss and road kills. In Central and South America, tinamous (chicken-sized, generally brown-coloured ground birds) are commonly hunted in their forests. Tinamou meat is considered tender and tasty even though it looks odd – kind of translucent and greenish in appearance! All the same, tinamous remain reasonably common.

Europe-wide, pigeons – plump Common Wood Pigeons especially but smaller Stock Doves and European Turtle Doves too – have always been good eating. So, too, have partridge, quail and pheasant, and grouse on the hills and moors, many of them taken in the past on privately owned estates by so-called poachers who were in many cases poor people desperate to feed their families.

Common Quail – ground birds the size of Song Thrushes – used to be shot in vast numbers or caught in nets on migration between Africa and Europe. There are 19th century records, for instance, of 100,000 taken in one day near Naples. They were commonplace at markets across Europe, and their numbers fell.

Not until after 1937, when regulation of hunting began in the Mediterranean, did their populations start rising again. Quail are avidly hunted today in many countries and often feature, sometimes expensively, on restaurant menus. A good proportion that are eaten now, though, are farm-reared.

Northern Bobwhites, a quail of open woodland found across the central and eastern US, have in past centuries been hunted for food to such an extent that their numbers have fallen considerably. The same happened to the two species of larger grouse-like prairie-chickens in the Midwest US states, though habitat destruction was a factor in their decline too.

In Britain through at least the Middle Ages, birds such as cranes and spoonbills – breeding more commonly then on still extensive wetlands – were hunted and eaten. Bitterns (skulking, brown, heron relatives) were popular too, being listed in the London poultry markets of the time. Birds of dense reedbeds, they must have been hard to find and catch, probably the reason why they were expensive to buy and well outside what a humble peasant could afford.

There was much munching of small birds too. At the end of the 19th century, for instance, shepherds on the Sussex Downs were supplementing their meagre income by trapping skylarks (now called Eurasian Skylarks) in nets. Tens of thousands a day were sold through Leadenhall Market, then London's main poultry market, most of them arriving by train. Contemporary accounts recall whole train wagons full of them!

From the netting places in southern England, many more larks were exported to France, always a good market for edible birds! Most were toasted as a gourmet delight. In the Victorian era, their popularity waned and eating larks became more confined to special occasions such as the opening of the Forth Railway Bridge in Scotland in 1890. A pie containing a reputed 300 larks was served for the occasion!

In Britain sparrows were commonly eaten too, until World War II. The birds were often caught by netting them where they roosted the night or where several pairs were nesting. Generally only the breast meat was eaten (there isn't much else on a sparrow), often sliced off with a penknife – a sliver about the size of a small finger – and a large number of them cooked to provide an apparently tasty meal. Others, though, were eaten whole! A sparrow pie containing a hundred of the tiny things was served on 16 January 1967 at The Rose Inn at Peldon near Colchester. People caught blackbirds and thrushes to eat too – rather larger, meatier birds compared with sparrows.

For centuries in countries around the Mediterranean, a huge range of small and larger birds have been caught in nets, shot, enticed into traps by putting out caged birds as decoys or caught by bird-lime, a sticky substance applied to twigs. The killing has lessened over the last century with more wildlife protection laws and because increased affluence means that fewer people need wild birds to supplement their diet.

But not all small birds eaten in Mediterranean countries are trapped locally. A consignment from China of nearly 2 million frozen sparrows was seized by customs in Rotterdam in 1993 en route for Italy and another of well over a million plucked and frozen sparrows was confiscated by customs in Antwerp in 1997. Presumably they were all, or mainly, China's commonest sparrow, the Tree Sparrow.

For many years the island of Malta has had an unenviable reputation for bird killing on an enormous scale. Although it joined the European Union (EU) in 2004, it was not until September 2009 that the Mediterranean island state was forced by the European Court of Justice to comply with EU bird protection law!

While the shooting of small migrating birds has been banned there only since 2008, early in 2010 Maltese hunters tried to persuade their government to defy international bird protection laws and the European Court of Justice by again permitting the spring shooting of quail and turtle dove. The Royal Society for the Protection of Birds (RSPB), BirdLife International and BirdLife Malta objected on the basis that any relaxation would result in the deaths of many more birds and provide a 'smokescreen' for illegal hunters targeting other species migrating over the island.

Hunting in autumn, though, is still allowed for certain birds on Malta so it is not surprising that conservationists across Europe remain concerned about the illegal hunting of protected species, including birds of prey and herons, and a lack of police enforcement on the island. Much of the island remains what might be politely called bandit country.

In Cyprus, too, hundreds of thousands of small birds are caught each year in nets, or trapped with sticky bird-lime, as they migrate south in autumn and north in spring. Many of them end up in ambelopoulia, a dish of pickled or boiled songbirds served in some Cypriot restaurants. All of this is illegal, but few people – including the police – take any action. Since the entrails of the birds are not removed (it isn't cost effective to do so) the consumer is encouraged to swallow the birds whole.

Cypriots and the Maltese, though, don't need to eat wild birds in order to keep body and soul together! But in some developing countries, wild-caught food remains a vital part of everyday diet.

In the north of Mali, one of the world's poorest countries, the seasonal floodwaters of the mighty Niger river provide a bountiful supply of fish, water plants for cattle fodder and irrigation for rice growing. They also attract huge numbers of birds including many species of heron, egret, duck and smaller wading birds. Any of them, potentially, are valuable sources of protein particularly in poor flood years when water levels are too low to support many fish or for crop growing. At such times of drought, starvation haunts the human population of this sub-Saharan country.

According to Leo Zwarts and his co-authors in *Living on the Edge: Wetlands and Birds in a Changing Sahel* (KNNV Publishing, 2009), shooting birds is too expensive for most Africans so "a bewildering variety of cheap catching devices have been developed using discarded fish nets and tubes, hook lines, traps, catapults and slings".

In the Niger floodplain, small clay tablets with an array of little nylon loops are laid in shallow water and vegetation to ensnare small birds while larger tablets are used to trap herons, bitterns and other bigger ones. As the waters recede at the end of the flood season, feeding birds concentrate up in what remains and are easy prey. Harvesting of birds for food might not otherwise deplete their populations if loss of habitat as the human population grows and tree felling to supply firewood weren't also reducing their numbers. As a result, several species of birds are declining and are likely to be delpeted even more.

It is only relatively recently in most developed countries that killing birds out of necessity has stopped.

Rook pie was popular in Britain in the past, and not that long ago. It was made, as you might guess, with well-grown young rooks, those crow-like birds that feed mostly on open fields and nest in noisy tree colonies. An old Somerset recipe, published in *Farmers Weekly* in 1940 at the height of World War II austerity, says that rooks should be skinned and only the breast and legs used because the rest is bitter!

Elegant Mute Swans, together with Great Bustards (a large ground-living bird extinct in Britain since the mid 1800s and now reintroduced), were used as the centrepiece of many a royal banquet. They had long been prized for their taste, even by the ancient Greeks.

The art historian Sir Roy Strong, in his *Feast: A History of Grand Eating* (Harcourt, 2003), relates what he considers the best and most complete account of a late medieval banquet. It was a dinner given by Gaston IV, Count of Foix, at Tours, France in 1457. It was staged in honour of royal representatives from Hungary and was attended by perhaps 300 people seated at 12 tables bedecked with silver plates. Unusually, says Strong, it describes what food they were served, and birds figured high on the menu.

The seven courses included '*grands pates de chapons* [capons, which are neutered cockerels], *jambons de sanglier* [hams of wild boar] followed by ragouts of game: pheasants, partridges, rabbits, peacocks, bustards, wild geese, swans and various river birds like herons, not to mention venison'. What the account fails to mention, though, is the subsequent indigestion!

When George Neville was enthroned as Archbishop of York in 1465, some 60 cooks prepared a banquet which included vast numbers of birds. There were 400 swans, the same number of plovers, a hundred dozen quail, thousands of ducks, 400 woodcock (snipe-like forest birds), a hundred curlews, even 200 bitterns amongst a surfeit of fish, deer and much else. Let's hope they were all sick.

Many birds popular at such extravagant banquets were protected for the Crown – cranes and swans for instance. Others, such as herons in certain designated places, could in the Middle Ages legally be killed by freemen (those who owned land in return for services to the King). The hoi polloi had to do without and woe betide a hungry peasant who tried to snaffle a heron. Fines were the least punishment; in Scotland you could lose your right hand!

Eating birds like herons and swans might seem like a medieval practice but not so long ago it was still fashionable in England. Stefan Buczacki in his *Fauna Britannica* (Hamlyn, 2002) recounts a story of someone being taken as a child by her mother to Whiteley's department store in London where they ate roast swan (which apparently tasted like duck) in the store's restaurant. The year? 1950.

A single swan in the 14th century cost between three and four shillings (15–20 pence) but that was equivalent to a month's wages for a labourer.

Oxford and Cambridge colleges were once famous for their feasts that invariably included swan, obtained from their nearby rivers of course. Buczacki quotes what he refers to as one of the more repeatable of Cambridge limericks:

> *There was a young man of St John's*
> *Who thought to make love to the swans*
> *The college porter*
> *Said 'Please take my daughter'*
> *The swans are reserved for the dons.*

The tradition of swan upping on the River Thames west of London dates from early medieval times when the monarch claimed ownership of all swans because they were a key part of upmarket banquets and feasts. The annual summertime 'upping' is done from boats; the swans are caught, marked and examined for injuries (they sometimes get snagged by fishing hooks) before being released. Nowadays, they aren't eaten!

As in most countries, wild duck were killed by the thousand in Britain. Mallard were the most commonly killed because they were usually the most abundant. In parts of Britain where wetlands were extensive, duck decoys (from the Dutch meaning 'duck cage') were used, from the 17th century well into the 19th century when there were about 200 of them. Many were in East Anglia in places such as the Broads.

Consisting of a series of nets tapering to a narrow trap so that the unfortunate ducks couldn't get back out, the decoy was incredibly effective. One decoy at Ashby, Lincolnshire between 1833 and 1867 caught nearly 96,000 ducks which were sent to London markets for sale. In due course, with the rising popularity of the gun and the drainage of duck-rich marshes, most decoys fell out of use.

One of the strangest culinary obsessions in the world, though, must be that of ortolan-eating. Ortolans are pretty buntings, peach, grey and brown birds hardly bigger than sparrows. They are rare in Britain but widespread over much of continental Europe, and the French, especially the Gascons, have long considered them a delicacy.

Captured alive, force-fed grain, then drowned in Armagnac, they are – or were – roasted whole and eaten that way, bones and all, while the diner draped his head with a linen napkin apparently to preserve the precious aromas and, some believe, to hide from God! Seemingly, Ortolans are rather crunchy with the texture and flavour of hazelnuts. The birds have long been in substantial decline in France although this is probably not due to their culinary use.

Since 1997 it has been illegal to capture or sell them in France, but not to eat them! How effectively these measures are enforced is anyone's guess, and gourmands talk discreetly about restaurants where they can still be eaten if the customer and restaurateur know each other well. François Mitterrand (1916–1996), the former French president, notoriously ate an Ortolan at his 'last

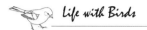

supper' while terminally ill with prostate cancer, concealing his head beneath a napkin in the traditional manner.

Today, wild birds are rarely essential for human survival in developed countries. In the past, though, especially on remote islands, they certainly were.

The islands of St Kilda – Hirta, Soay and Boreray – in an isolated position more than 60 km west of the Outer Hebrides off Scotland's west coast and located in the teeth of any Atlantic gale, were inhabited for at least two millennia. The population was probably never more than 180. It was, without doubt, a tough place to live and the last inhabitants left in 1930 after a succession of crop failures and deaths from disease.

Now owned by the National Trust for Scotland (NTS) and a World Heritage Site, the islands are a breeding ground for many important seabirds including the world's largest colony of Northern Gannets, perhaps 130,000 pairs of Atlantic Puffins and huge numbers of Northern Fulmars.

The St Kildans didn't fish because of the heavy seas and unpredictable weather. Instead, their mainstay was the profusion of island birds, especially gannets and fulmars but also shearwaters, puffins and others too. These they harvested as eggs and young birds; both were eaten fresh and cured to see them through the long autumn and winter when the seabirds had left to feed out over the sea, coming to land only to breed.

Many of these seabirds nested in huge colonies on the ledges of massive, often vertical, sea cliffs. So the St Kildan men became expert climbers and rope users. They even developed prehensile, divergent toes to help them grip the slippery rock as well as extra strong ankles to take the strain. They climbed barefoot. According to the Mountaineering Council of Scotland, boys as young as three were encouraged to climb the outside walls of their stone houses to train, a forerunner of today's artificial climbing walls!

Atlantic Puffins nest in small burrows on gentler slopes so their nests were far easier to raid for chicks and eggs. The islanders also caught adult puffins in flight using fowling rods, a snare consisting of a single noose or jaw attached to a long pole.

Information catalogued by the NTS suggests that, at one time, each inhabitant of St Kilda ate 115 Northern Fulmars every year. They mainly took the fat young birds just before they were ready to leave their nests, taking in total maybe 12,000 a season. Variously described as tasting musty, rancid or 'like paper', the flesh was apparently less palatable than the eggs.

The naturalist Richard Kearton visited St Kilda in 1896 and later wrote about eating puffins there: 'They are plucked, split open like kippers, cured and hung up to dry on strings stretched across the cottages; and whenever a native feels hungry he simply pulls one down from the line, flings it on the fire to grill and forthwith has his lunch.'

However, not all coastal communities and fishermen at sea had the common sense to manage their seabird resource in the way the St Kildans did. What happened to the Great Auk, a flightless seabird found originally in huge numbers on remote rocky islands off eastern Canada, Greenland, Iceland, Norway, Ireland, northern Russia and Great Britain, is a salutary lesson.

Black and white in colour, standing up to 85 cm tall and weighing in at around 5 kg, it looked like a penguin but was really more closely related to guillemots (known as common murres in the

US) and razorbills. Excellent swimmers agile at catching fish and crabs, but slow walkers on land, they had long lost their ability to fly. And with few predators on the islands they inhabited, they had no reason to escape or fear humans.

From at least the 8th century onwards the great auk was hunted avidly for its meat, its eggs, and its feathers. Large, tasty and abundant, the birds were caught in ever increasing numbers by local fishermen and later by European seal hunters and ocean fishermen, being sought after as a welcome change of diet from the salted meat carried on board. With no concept of a sustainable hunt in anyone's mind, by 1700 the Great Auk was in substantial decline.

Records of how they were literally herded like sheep across gangplanks into fishing boats, clubbed to death and cooked or salted are commonplace. Around 1785, a new trade began. After being clubbed to death they were thrown into vats of boiling water to loosen their feathers which were sold for stuffing bedding. The islands had no wood for fires to heat the water so dead auks were used, their fat fuelling the fires! On tiny Funk Island off Newfoundland where large numbers of Great Auks nested, the blackened, bone-filled patches of soil still visible are the legacy of these very fires.

It was in July 1840 on Stac an Armin on St Kilda that the last Great Auk in the British Isles was caught. Islanders had tied it up and kept it alive for three days, and then killed it by beating it with a stick, apparently because they believed it to be a witch.

The last population in the world lived on Geirfuglasker, a volcanic rock with high cliffs, inaccessible to humans, off the south coast of Iceland. In 1830 the rock disappeared underwater during volcanic eruptions and the birds moved to the nearby island of Eldey which was, unfortunately, accessible on one side to boats.

Standing amongst the moss-covered chunks of solidified lava on the rugged Reykjanes Peninsula near the little town of Grindavik in southwest Iceland, Eldey island – about 16 km away – is clearly visible, shaped like a rocky plug. Eldey, though, has a nasty secret.

Here it was that the very last pair of Great Auks in the world nested. They were killed there by local fishermen on 3 July 1844, the adults strangled and their eggs smashed with a kick of a boot in one of the most notorious acts of wildlife vandalism ever. Looking at the island today, it's difficult to imagine that it was just here that one of the world's animals, and an abundant one at that, was killed off for ever.

Atlantic Puffins are now protected in Britain but in Iceland they can legally be captured in hand-held nets as they fly in to land. Perhaps as many as a couple of hundred thousand a year are killed to eat. Strong tasting, and almost the colour of beef but very tender with a gamey taste that's slightly fishy, they're eaten mainly at home in coastal villages. Usually smoked, they can be boiled, stuffed, roasted or salted.

Puffin is on the menu in some traditional Icelandic restaurants; the Lækjarbrekka on Reykjavik's Laugavegur, the capital's main shopping street, for instance, had 'fresh salad with smoked and cured puffin' and a main course of 'marinated fried breast of puffin with malt sauce' when I walked past.

With a worldwide population of at least 6 million – half of them breeding in Iceland – it's very unlikely that the Icelanders' eating habits are having any impact on puffin numbers. All the same, the Icelandic government has banned puffin hunting, at least temporarily, in places where the birds are suffering from food shortages due to a lack of sand eels, a small fish they depend on for food.

In many other island communities the world over, a limited number of wild seabirds and their eggs are still caught for food. This is hardly ever a necessity but rather a continuation of a traditional practice that was central to the survival of their forefathers, and is usually done in a much more controlled way.

Typical is the Inuit hunt of Little Auks in northwest Greenland. These seabirds, not much bigger than starlings, are caught in flight in large, hand-held nets. With a world population of maybe 30 million, the Inuit hunt isn't affecting little auk numbers, but other seabirds killed for food in Greenland are declining.

Pacific islanders often take seabirds to add variety to their diet. On the Mariana Islands about 2,000 km southeast of Japan, for instance, Brown Noddies – small dark seabirds related to terns – breed in large numbers. The islanders take some of their eggs and chicks, and occasionally adults too, but the noddies are thriving. And the Maori of Stewart Island/Rakiura, off the south of New Zealand, continue to harvest the chicks of the Sooty Shearwater as they have done for centuries using traditional methods but now they work with the University of Otago in studying the bird's populations.

A limited annual cull of the young – called gugas – of the Northern Gannet, otherwise a protected bird, still takes place on Suileisgeir, a small barren island with craggy cliffs more than 60 km northwest of Lewis, the largest of the Outer Hebrides. It's a centuries-old tradition and the only surviving gannet hunt in Britain.

The method of catching the gugas has changed little and men still go down the steep cliff-faces on ropes to trap the birds. They are caught using a long fowling rod with an iron jaw fixed at the end which is put around the bird's neck and pulled closed by a rope, very like the way puffins were caught on St Kilda.

Gugas are much in demand locally for eating. They are scrubbed clean with washing soda, placed in a pot and boiled, the boiling repeated three times with fresh water to reduce their salt content. Their meat has a salty and fishy flavour. It is, indeed, an acquired taste.

In the past, a supply of seabirds has saved the life of many a shipwrecked sailor – and even passengers. In 1875, for instance, Florence Wordsworth and other passengers were bound from London to New Zealand aboard the *Strathmore* when it was wrecked on the aptly named Isles of the Apostles in the southern Indian Ocean. Florence's account refers to surviving their seven-month ordeal thanks to seabirds, albatrosses especially, which apparently were excellent to eat and kept them alive.

In 1916, Ernest Shackleton and his five companions got to South Georgia island in the South Atlantic following a desperate 800 mile, gale-hit lifeboat trek after their ship, *Endurance*, had been crushed by ice. And what did they find to eat? Albatrosses! The youngsters were 'fat and lusty' Shackleton recorded; 'what a stew it was!' Once again, mighty albatrosses had doubled up as emergency human food.

Other birds have saved human lives, too, but have not survived the slaughter themselves! The Wake Island Rail, a flightless, dark grey-brown bird with striking narrow white bars on its belly, breast and flanks and related to birds like coots and moorhens, was the sole native land bird on the Pacific island of Wake, a small and very isolated coral atoll now occupied by the US Air Force.

In 1903 it was known to be numerous on Wake. It lived in scrub and fed on molluscs, insects and worms. Since its habitat offered no fresh water, it is assumed that the bird was able to exist by getting the water it needed from its food. Not all rails live in wet habitats, though most do. Seemingly, the bird was quick to run for cover if it was disturbed so it wasn't as confiding as the poor old Great Auk!

No one had ever much bothered with it, until 1944 when the Japanese forces who had occupied the island since 1941 became cut off from their supply route. The soldiers were starving and, apart from seafood, there was nothing else to eat. The last surviving rail was killed in 1945 by the soldiers, an indirect effect of World War II.

Sometimes, birds were eaten by explorers to keep them alive on their expeditions in conditions we undoubtedly wouldn't even contemplate today. One such was Charles Edward Douglas (1840–1916), a Scot who became a land surveyor and artist in New Zealand where he surveyed some of the most difficult terrain in the country and suffered regular privations. In his notes he records eating kiwis, those chicken-sized, brown and flightless birds that became the country's national symbol:

> I have very little to say regarding this bird, as I have only seen two of them, and being pushed with hunger, I ate the pair of them, under the circumstances I would have eaten the last of the Dodos. It is all very well for science, lifting up its hands in horror … but let science tramp through the Westland bush or swamps, for two or three days without food, and find out what hunger is.

Penguins on islands in the Southern Oceans proved all too easy to catch for food. One of the earliest accounts is from 1578 by John Winter. Winter was sailing with the explorer and part-time pirate Sir Francis Drake near the southern tip of South America when they landed on the island of Santa Magdalena. They only stayed one day but killed plenty of birds he had never seen before: '[their] flesh is not unlike a fat goose in England; they have no wings … they walk so upright that a farre off man would take them to be little children'. Today there are about 60,000 pairs of Magellanic Penguins breeding there. And nobody eats them.

Penguins soon became standard fare for sailors. Scurvy and hunger haunted many a long voyage and fresh penguin meat – from birds usually clubbed to death in their breeding colonies – probably saved many human lives. But tens of thousands of the birds were slaughtered.

It might be commonly used, but few people probably know what the phrase 'as dead as a dodo' refers to. The curiously named Dodo, known only from the island of Mauritius in the Indian Ocean, was another flightless bird. It was possibly named after its pigeon-like call or from a mispronunciation of Portuguese or Dutch words used to describe the birds (usually rudely!). Contemporary drawings suggest they were large, plump and covered in plenty of meat. What's more, they nested on the ground and couldn't fly – a rather fatal combination if there are hungry people about. And there were!

First mentioned by a Dutchman, Vice-Admiral Wybrand van Warwijck, who visited the island in 1598, various accounts from the time give mixed reports about Dodo meat, some describing it as tasty, others as nasty and tough. And although there are scattered reports of mass killings of Dodos for provisioning of ships for long voyages, archaeological investigations have found scant evidence of excessive hunting of the birds, overturning the long-standing notion that the Dodo was hunted to extinction for food. This was probably only one of several contributing factors.

There are records of mass kills due to flash floods on the island, and settlers arriving around 1600 brought with them other animals that had not existed on the island before – dogs, cats, pigs and rats – which plundered the Dodo nests.

It was last described living wild by Benjamin Harry, chief mate on the *Berkley Castle*, around 1680 but the Dodo was extinct before 1700, just a century after it was first discovered. For a long time, the bird was forgotten …

… until, that is, it featured as a character in Lewis Carroll's *Alice's Adventures in Wonderland* (1865). The Dodo is a caricature of the author, whose real name was Charles Dodgson. A popular but unsubstantiated belief is that Dodgson chose it because of his stammer, which would cause him to accidentally introduce himself as 'Do-do-dodgson'. With the popularity of the book, the Dodo became a well-known and easily recognisable icon of extinction.

So are all birds edible? Probably yes, and a very wide range have been eaten at some time or place. Attempts to assess the palatability of different species have found that, very generally, the more brightly coloured a bird is, the less palatable it is. The birds considered the tastiest to eat – quail, grouse, partridge, woodcock and so on – are all fairly subdued in colour. The same seems to apply to birds' eggs; the more brightly coloured they are, the less palatable they usually are. If ever you are marooned somewhere, it's a useful fact to keep in mind!

Birds' eggs, of course, are more nutritious, weight for weight, than bird meat because their contents nurture the developing embryo inside. What's more, while fresh eggs are prone to breakage, once they are hard-boiled they can be stored and kept for long periods before they are eaten, a practice that was once commonplace on many an isolated island. On St Kilda seabird eggs were preserved in peat ash, which gave them an astringent taste.

Gulls' eggs are both reasonably large and reasonably accessible because gulls usually nest on the ground at the seashore, at lakesides, or among sand dunes. What's more, gulls have the advantage that each pair usually lays three or four eggs compared with most cliff-nesting seabirds laying one! And they will re-lay if their eggs are taken, offering the advantage of a more sustained food supply.

Until the 1930s, around 300,000 Black-headed Gulls' eggs were sold at Leadenhall Market in London each year. Egg collecting, from common and rare birds alike, was then commonplace though more as a hobby than as a necessity. The practice has since been banned by law in many countries, at least for birds other than a small number of pests like carrion crows and magpies, though some illegal collection – rather like stamp collecting but harmful to rare species – by a few determined individuals still goes on.

Gulls' eggs, though, are still popular for eating today.

'We sell about four to five thousand a year', comments David Hammerson of Everleigh Farm Shops Ltd based in Wiltshire. 'They're about the size of a small chicken egg, blue-green in colour with black blotches. They're all Black-headed Gull eggs. We have to have a special licence to sell them and the collector we buy from, likewise, has a collecting licence from Natural England. He collects from sites on the south coast of England.'

The idea is to take no more than one egg per day per nest so that the birds keep laying until the collectors stop taking them. The gulls don't start incubating until they have a complete clutch, usually three.

Retailing at £4 each or more, gulls' eggs are these days not eaten by the least well off or communities confined to offshore islands as they were historically. They've gone upmarket. They are now a staple of top restaurants such as Wiltons, Le Gavroche and The Ivy plus gentlemen's clubs such as White's and Boodle's.

The eggs are traditionally eaten hard-boiled with celery salt, but as they have become increasingly fashionable, chefs have begun to experiment more. At Le Gavroche in central London, this year, they will be served poached, either with artichokes, smoked salmon and caviar, or with chicken, truffles and foie gras.

Emmanuel Landré, the restaurant's manager, said: 'It is a very, very popular food. It makes a huge impact. I had never heard about it when I was in France. There are very strict regulations governing it. We have been serving seagulls' eggs for 40 years and I don't see why we should change.'

But change is undoubtedly coming!

There are currently about 25 registered collectors in the UK who have a traditional claim to take wild Black-headed Gulls' eggs and to sell them for human consumption even though the gull, along with almost all of Britain's birds, is a protected species. They can collect from 1 April to 15 May and there are six main collecting areas. They take somewhere around 40,000 eggs a year. The licences will eventually cease as the registered collectors give up or die.

Black-headed Gulls in Britain are declining, though not rapidly, and there are currently about 150,000 pairs. The slow decline might be due to a whole range of issues including predation by foxes and mink and it's unlikely that licensed egg collecting is hugely damaging. Europe-wide there are somewhere between 1 and 2 million pairs and their numbers overall have increased since the late 19th century, before which gull eggs were much more widely collected. Nevertheless, most conservationists would like to see the practice ended.

Many different kinds of birds' eggs were collected for food in the past. They still are in many poorer countries where bird protection is virtually unknown and where people are glad to get any nutritious food for free.

Birds' nests are an altogether different dining experience. One type of nest, in particular, is among the most expensive animal product eaten by people anywhere in the world. Bird's nest soup has been a Chinese delicacy since the T'ang dynasty (AD 618–907).

Unlike most birds' nests, those of the insect-eating Edible-nest Swiftlet and black-nest swiftlet, sparrow-sized birds of Southeast Asia, are not composed of twigs or grasses or made of mud. Instead, the male swiftlets make them out of their own saliva, fashioning a small, shallow cup cemented to a cave wall. Six centimetres across, they are usually white and somewhat translucent.

They are rich in nutrients and, once cleaned of any feathers and faeces, are thought to convey health benefits when they are eaten dissolved in an often spicy chicken broth. Hong Kong is the hub of the international trade (where a bowl of the gelatinous mix costs up to $100) and many nests are exported to the US. A kilogram of swiftlet nests can fetch up to $10,000.

These swiftlet nests are harvested traditionally using incredible climbing skills in high-ceiling caves in Borneo, on the roof of which the birds cement their nests in dense clusters. The harvesters climb bamboo poles and scaffolding held in place by rattan ropes and use very long bamboo poles fitted with a kind of hoe on the end to scrape the nests off the roof. Each pole also carries a candle to help the harvester see in the dark cave. The nests are gathered as they fall.

Large concrete nesting houses have now been built, or existing buildings converted for the purpose – sometimes successfully, sometimes not – in several Southeast Asian countries like Indonesia and Thailand to encourage swiftlets to nest where they can be more easily accessed. In

Borneo alone about a thousand buildings are estimated to have been put over to, or specially built for, swiftlet nesting. In these the nests are often harvested three times a year, supposedly once the youngsters have been reared. This means that hazardous collecting in caves, which many young people are reluctant to take on, will almost certainly die out.

Nesting houses might sound like a good idea but they bring their own problems. Rapacious collectors after quick profits are taking nests and discarding eggs and young swiftlets, seemingly oblivious to any notion of safeguarding their long-term profits … or the birds. Some swiftlet populations such as those in the Andaman and Nicobar Islands in the Bay of Bengal have been harvested extensively and the birds there are critically threatened.

Because these little swiftlets are so common right across Southeast Asia, conservationists aren't too worried yet. But if the bird's nest soup market continues to grow, who knows whether their decline could become as rapid as that of America's Wild Turkey two centuries back. And then you might rightly wonder if we will ever learn the obvious lesson.

While hunting birds for food was in the past often a necessity to allow people to eat some meat – and still is in many poor countries – today's wild bird hunting has often transformed itself from a necessity into a sport. But sport involving birds comes in many different guises, as the next chapter will show.

2

A sporting chance

A great many birds get killed in the name of sport, something many people find
repugnant. But, surprisingly perhaps, some birds do remarkably well out of its
continuation, their populations bolstered to levels that would never naturally be attained.

It's late August in the rolling Lammermuir Hills in southern Scotland and the heather moorland all around me is in flower, clothing the gentle slopes in an ethereal purple haze. There are areas of lush green too, rushy wet streamsides and grassy banks, all of it appearing slightly translucent in the rain that shows no sign of easing.

I'm standing with Robbie Douglas Miller who owns 3,000 acres of this velvet moorland and we're watching the occasional mountain hare (the ones that have a white coat in winter) zooming past, their extra long ears almost flapping in the breeze as they run.

Apart from the rain which, mercifully, is keeping the irritating biting midges away, there's hardly a sound to be heard. Behind us the moor slopes down to a shallow, boggy valley where rushes, cotton grass and mosses take over from the heather. In front of us is a short upslope of heather to the nearby skyline.

Over this slope, though, it's all activity. But we can't hear it nor see it. A line of maybe ten men, all clad in full waterproofs and swishing noisy plastic flags low over the heather as they walk towards us, is getting closer.

Suddenly, the silence is broken as several shotguns punch the moist air, reverberating from the five foot deep shooting butts that pairs of us are standing in, only our heads – and shotguns – visible to the birds that are skimming low in flight past us, mostly in small groups of between five and ten birds, their wings whirring like mechanical toys. They are Red Grouse and they are getting killed! Some of them anyway.

Today there are seven or eight guns, all friends of Douglas Miller's. And each time the beaters – the line of local men employed for the day to walk with their flags to disturb the grouse – do a drive of birds towards the shooting butts, somewhere around 30 grouse get killed. But the odds are stacked against the guns! Most seem to get away.

Red Grouse aren't large birds. Like small chickens in size, they are a rich chocolate brown with attractive white-feathered legs. They fly fast, 80 km/hour and more, and it isn't predictable where they will suddenly appear in front of you low over the vegetation; you might get a second or two to aim, and a shotgun is only effective over a range of about 30 metres. To shoot red grouse you have to be a very good shot indeed!

I'd met Douglas Miller that morning near the rather oddly named Horseupcleugh, a farm in the eastern Lammermuir Hills. Here were gathered about 40 people, a motley collection turned out for

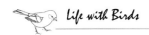

a day's grouse shooting. Around a dozen were beaters. Several others were 'pickers-up' with their dogs – retrievers or springer spaniels – whose main task was to find the dead grouse that had fallen into the heather and collect them up. The beaters and pickers-up, all local men or workers from adjacent estates, were paid just £35 for their day's work.

'We shoot here probably four times in a season', says Douglas Miller. 'We don't usually start on the 12th August [the so-called Glorious Twelfth] because not all the year's young grouse are mature enough by then. And we don't normally shoot towards the season's end [10 December]. On a very good day I suppose we'll shoot about 200 grouse, but that's probably the tops.'

The Duke of Westminster's Littledale and Abbeystead estates in the Forest of Bowland in northwest England still hold the British record for the largest number of grouse shot on a single day. On 12 August 1915, no fewer than 2,929 grouse were shot by eight guns.

'We charge per brace shot [a brace is two birds] or we charge per day irrespective of how good the gun is [a "gun" is the person doing the shooting]. Say £150 per brace. So, if he shoots 50 brace in the day, it costs him £7,500.' Some moors charge well in excess of this. It isn't a sport for anyone short of the readies.

Most of the grouse shot are sold to game dealers who sell on to restaurants and hotels. 'I sell most of mine to a local dealer and I'll probably get £5 a bird. Some of those we shoot today will be in London restaurants tomorrow night. They'll go by train or are flown south.'

In the 2009 season, Rules in Covent Garden, established in 1798 and reputedly London's oldest restaurant, had Red Grouse on its menu, served traditionally with game chips, redcurrant and bread sauce, for £27.50.

But running a grouse moor doesn't come cheap. Parts of the moor are burnt in the autumn, usually in small patches or strips in order to diversify the age of the heather, leaving some old and more mature while replenishing with new growth where the land is burnt. That requires people to carefully control the burning so that it doesn't get out of hand.

There are access tracks to repair, the shooting butts – lined with wooden planks – to maintain and many other tasks including, controversially, predators to kill. It's all managed by the keeper who has to be paid for and provided with a home and an all-terrain vehicle so that he can get these jobs done.

'The keeper traps or shoots crows, foxes, stoats and weasels', says Douglas Miller. 'If we didn't, then we'd hardly have a grouse population because they'd take most of the eggs and chicks.'

It's certainly true that numbers of Red Grouse are artificially high on these managed upland heather moors because the whole system is designed to benefit them. The habitat is manipulated to provide a range of heather ages. Young heather shoots provide food; mature heather provides shelter and nesting spots under cover; clearings provide places for the young birds to sun themselves in. Most of their natural predators are either eliminated or much reduced and are replaced pretty well with a new one … men with guns.

As a result of the control of many of the moor's natural predators, other species that like this kind of habitat do well too. Birds such as Golden Plover and Curlew breed here, and mountain hares usually prosper.

'I come up here to the open moor on a spring day sometimes just to sit and it's simply wonderful', comments Douglas Miller. 'There are Skylarks in song, Golden Plover, Curlew and Lapwing calling. Plenty of Red Grouse of course. It's idyllic.'

Grouse moors are expensive to buy, maybe £10 million for a small one, multiples of that for a large one! Most are owned by what is still regarded as the 'aristocracy' and may have been in the same family for generations, or they're owned by wealthy Middle Eastern Arabs or city bankers. They are not a paying proposition but they have prestige value. A day's shoot is as much a social event as a sporting one and the more traditional shoots will picnic in style at lunchtime before resuming in the afternoon.

But grouse moors do bring employment to very rural and often isolated places where jobs are usually few and far between, including benefits, albeit very seasonal ones, for local hotels, shops and garages. According to a 2009 report from the Game & Wildlife Conservation Trust, grouse shooting is estimated to be worth £30 million a year to the Scottish economy and supports 940 full-time jobs.

In total there are estimated to be about 460 grouse moors in the UK covering between 1 and 2 million hectares of moorland, mostly in Scotland. For the moorland to be economic, Red Grouse densities have to be more than 60 birds in a square kilometre. With densities like that, most of the birds could not survive a winter, especially a cold and prolonged one. If they weren't shot many of them would simply starve to death.

Organised grouse shoots – with beaters and pickers-up and the other adornments – are a fairly recent phenomenon, having begun around the middle of the 19th century. In 1825 there are no records of Scottish grouse moors being let for shooting and, by 1837, just eight were available! The building of the railway north – by 1863 it had reached Inverness – combined with the invention of the breech-loading shotgun in 1847 (lighter and quicker to load) made organised grouse shoots on 'remote' moors a real possibility.

But the numbers of Red Grouse on these moors can go up and down like a yo-yo according to Dr David Baines of the Game & Wildlife Conservation Trust.

'Red Grouse can suffer huge population crashes due to a parasitic gut threadworm they carry naturally. In order to maintain our grouse stocks, counter-intuitively, shooting older birds on the moor is a good way of controlling the disease as they often have very heavy worm burdens that will infect the younger ones. Climate warming has provided better conditions for the worm to flourish', says Baines.

Grouse moor management is very controversial, with many conservationists claiming that gamekeepers often illegally kill birds of prey like Golden Eagle and Hen Harrier (now called the Northern Hen Harrier) which take grouse as well as more common predators like foxes. There have been prosecutions but the practice continues because of the pressure on a gamekeeper to achieve high grouse numbers, satisfy those shooting and, ultimately, keep his job.

Proving why some of these impressive birds of prey are surprisingly absent over large areas of Scotland where the habitat is ideal for them is difficult. Other than persecution from gamekeepers, it's mightily difficult to understand why they are not there or to conjure up any other explanation.

But what would happen to all this heather moorland if grouse shooting was not the main use of the land? Professor Des Thompson, Policy and Advice Manager at Scottish Natural Heritage, the Scottish government's conservation advisers, and an expert on Scottish hills and mountains, is very clear.

'People need to realise that moors managed for grouse are unnatural because the way the land is grazed by sheep and burnt in patches stops scrub and woodland taking over as it would naturally.

Grouse shooting generates substantial income, and it's unlikely that other uses of the moors could match that. In terms of wildlife, well-managed grouse moors have a rich diversity of plants and animals, birds included, so long as birds of prey aren't persecuted and, ideally, if some areas are allowed to develop some scrub and trees', he says.

There are also many voices raised against grouse shooting because it is perceived by some as cruel. League Against Cruel Sports Chief Executive Douglas Batchelor is one of several critics.

'It is utterly ridiculous to label an industry which depends on the mass slaughter of wildlife for entertainment purposes as glorious. Barbaric and immoral would be far more appropriate under these circumstances', he says.

The world over, a vast range of other birds are shot for sport and, sometimes, for food. And provided that the shooting is controlled and responsible, it usually has no discernible impact on their numbers. It's all too easy to forget that most birds raise an excess of youngsters during a breeding season. For most ducks it might be, say, five youngsters. Some smaller birds, like many of the common garden birds, might rear eight or ten.

It doesn't take a mathematical genius to work out that, if all these survived, after a few years we would be knee-deep in birds. Clearly we are not. Vast numbers of them die of starvation in their first winter or are picked off by birds of prey and domestic cats. The strongest, the fittest survive. So it's not surprising that many people who shoot birds claim, probably correctly, that most of the birds they kill would die anyway.

In 2006 a group of shooting organisations commissioned Public and Corporate Economic Consultants to provide an independent assessment of the economic value of wild animal shooting in the UK. The assessment concluded that 480,000 people shoot live animals, mostly birds, that the sport provided the equivalent of 70,000 full-time jobs and that it generated about £1.6 billion for the UK economy.

Bird shooting varies enormously. It might be the occasional pot-shot at a Wood Pigeon or a highly organised pheasant or partridge shoot or wildfowlers shooting ducks, geese and a limited number of wading birds like fast-flying snipe at wetlands or estuaries.

In the UK it's a very organised sport, with strict controls over the seasons in which shooting for different birds is legal and over the particular species that can legally be shot.

But it has its critics. The League Against Cruel Sports, for instance, lists a host of reasons for campaigning against it. These include that game birds like pheasants are reared in cruel, confined conditions; that 40 per cent of pheasants and 90 per cent of partridges used in the UK are imported from Europe and suffer immensely during transport; that gamekeepers snare, trap, poison and bludgeon wild predators including protected species and domestic pets in an effort to protect game birds; that inexperienced shooters are granted gun licences in the UK leading to bird wounding and a lingering death; and that vast numbers of dead birds are actually dumped as waste.

Many shooters – currently around 130,000 – are members of the British Association for Shooting and Conservation (BASC), either as individuals or through affiliated clubs. This organisation has a strong reputation for ensuring good habitat to support flourishing populations of birds and other wildlife and, thereby, promoting sustainable shooting. It also promotes responsible shooting behaviour, setting out guidance on types of shotguns, the differing laws and seasons for different parts of the UK, the use of dogs to retrieve shot birds and so on.

In the UK, Wood Pigeons, because they are pests of farm crops (see Chapter 8), can be shot year-round, and very large numbers are. But still they increase, and have become frequent garden visitors too!

Pheasant shooting is particularly popular. The birds are large (twice as bulky as a red grouse), slower getting up into the air and often fly at no more than 60 km/hour, so they're easier to shoot.

The Common Pheasant, the attractive, long-tailed male with his golden-brown plumage and red wattles on his face, is among the most recognisable of any bird in the UK. But it certainly isn't British! Native to Asia, pheasants have long been bred in captivity and released in very many countries around the world as a game bird to be shot! They were first brought to Britain in the 10th century, perhaps earlier by the Romans, but were first recorded as being eaten at Waltham Abbey in Essex just before the Battle of Hastings in 1066 and it's probable that the invading Normans, once they got well established in Britain, imported even more of the colourful birds.

Something like 30–50 million of them are reared and released each year on British shooting estates and, if they get away without being shot, many won't survive a cold winter. The 'best' estates can charge about £2,000 per gun per day and many events are set up for corporate hospitality (though when the economy takes a nose-dive such corporate jollies are often the first 'extra' to be cut out by most companies).

Certainly, prodigious numbers can be shot in a day. King George V shot over a thousand pheasants out of a total bag of 3,937 over a six-day period in December 1913, a total which still stands as the British record.

Birds of wetlands and damp pasture – Common Snipe, and similar-looking, woodland-living Eurasian Woodcock – are very much smaller, take to the air at the last minute in a sudden swoosh and then fly fast, often zigzagging as they go. Not surprisingly, they are very much harder to shoot. In the past, it was often more common to put up nets across woodland rides to catch the elusive woodcocks as they scooted past. Today, outside the breeding season, both species are sometimes shot for the table.

In the US where shooting game birds and other animals is a passion – though strictly controlled by state laws – most Common Pheasants are wild-born though in some states captive-reared and released birds make up much of the population. The pheasant is often seen as the premier game bird and some states derive significant revenue from pheasant hunting.

The so-called aristocrats of American game bird shooting, though, are the Northern Bobwhite, a brown and black speckled quail like a small partridge, and the prettier Scaled Quail, bluish grey with an obvious white crest on its head. They hide on the ground (a result of being preyed on by coyotes, foxes, raccoons and hawks) and burst into flight amazingly suddenly, often at close range – so they are harder to shoot! Most of the hunting is on private ranches, particularly in the southern US, and, because habitat loss has led to their decline, they are sometimes bred in large numbers for release.

It was on such a hunting visit in 2006 to the 20,000 hectare Armstrong Ranch in Texas' remote Rio Grande River Valley that the then US Vice-President Dick Cheney missed a quail but shot the Texas Republican lawyer Harry Whittington in the face. It caused huge political embarrassment and a festival of lampooning in the media.

Shooting pheasant, quail or partridge for sport is one thing. Shooting thousands, probably hundreds of thousands, of birds, from small thrushes to large eagles, as they migrate across the Mediterranean in spring and autumn, is another. If nothing else, most of the birds concerned are protected Europe-wide. Or supposedly they are.

Because these birds migrate in large numbers at predictable times of year, and often stop for a rest at predictable sites, hunters in countries such as Malta, Italy, Cyprus and across North Africa wait for them like a chain of ambushes with guns, nets, traps or lime-sticks. Laws are often flagrantly ignored and the police slow to act or ineffectual.

Martin Hellicar, BirdLife Cyprus's representative, said at Christmas 2009: 'At this time of year, robins and other birds, such as thrushes, escape harsh conditions further north in Europe and travel to the island for the winter. Sadly many of these birds will be travelling to their deaths, particularly in the trapping hotbeds of Famagusta, Larnaca and the British Sovereign Base Area of Dhekalia.' It is hardly sport.

A study in autumn 2009 by the charity revealed that 700,000 birds had been trapped and killed illegally, that net use was up by over one-third compared with the autumn of 2008 and bird-lime use was also on the rise. The organisation believes that the total number of birds trapped in Cyprus each autumn may exceed 1 million and that the Cypriot government is failing to take action.

This supposedly 'sport' hunting is widespread, and the number of migratory birds hunted is thought to be rising as a result of people's increased leisure time and disposable income, easier access to guns, cheaper ammunition and increased availability of four-wheel drive vehicles. Education initiatives, some promoted by the EU, and several by conservation non-governmental organisations (NGOs), are underway to try to limit the killing but the hunting mentality is deeply embedded in local and historic traditions. It isn't going to change quickly.

The Society for the Protection of Nature (SPNL) in the Lebanon, for instance, found that in a four-month period in 2005, some 1,780 storks, cranes and pelicans and 3,640 birds of prey were shot or trapped in the main hunting localities in that country alone. However, they point out that reliable information was impossible to obtain since hunting in Lebanon at this time was officially banned, although the hunting law didn't seem to restrict either dealers in guns and traps nor dead bird sales to restaurants and markets.

'Hunters think that migratory birds have large populations and contribute no value to the ecosystem, so migratory species are more vulnerable to hunting than local species', said Bassima Khatib, SPNL Assistant Director General at the time.

Estimates by national hunters' organisations of the numbers of hunters include up to 1,000 in Palestine; 11,400 in Tunisia; more than 40,000 in Morocco; 92,000 in Algeria; around 60,000 in Lebanon; 500,000 in Syria; and at least 10,000 in Egypt. Some are registered; many are not.

Sometimes uncontrolled hunting can threaten the very survival of already depleted populations of birds. In 2009 a hunter in Saudi Arabia shot and killed a Northern Bald Ibis, one of the rarest birds in the world with just over 200 left in the wild, mostly in Morocco. Glossy black with blood-red faces, legs and curved beaks, they are roughly the size of a goose and hard to mistake for anything else! The bird he killed was one of now four struggling to survive in Syria. Others have disappeared in recent years as they migrate to Ethiopia for winter, crossing parts of the southern Middle East where illegal hunting might well have put paid to them too.

There is, though, another much more bloodthirsty pursuit, long banned in most western countries – not everyone would describe it as a sport – which in places is said to be intimately bound up with religion and tradition. In some countries it involves considerable amounts of betting and even, sometimes, violent crime.

Cockfighting is a blood sport in which two cockerels, or roosters as they are known in the US, which have been specifically bred for their aggression, are encouraged to fight each other, often to the death or 'at best' to the point of serious injury. In some countries it's traditional to fit sharp metal spurs or blades to the fighting cocks' legs, seemingly to cause even more injury. In other countries, Thailand for instance, spurs are banned.

After a bout, which can last for less than a minute or as much as half an hour, if the loser isn't dead, its injuries – commonly punctured lungs, broken bones and pierced eyes according to the Humane Society of the United States – are frequently severe enough to have to end its misery.

Cockfighting originated in Southeast Asia and China about 2000 BC and remains a common spectacle in some of those countries today. Building on the natural aggression between hormone-charged male junglefowl – the ancestors of today's cockerels and chickens – it soon became popular in ancient Greece, Rome and western Europe.

In the 1st century AD, Julius Caesar probably introduced it into England, where, by the 16th century, it was flourishing. During the time of King Henry VIII, cockfights were held at Whitehall Palace. The game became a national sport and exclusive schools were required to teach students the details of cockfighting such as breeding and conditioning of the birds.

Dr Barry Peachey in his book *The Cockfighters* (Beech Publishing, 1993) quotes a letter dated 12 June 1365 from King Edward III to the Sheriffs of London, in which he called upon them to ban a variety of sports including cockfighting in order to encourage the male population to practise archery for the defence of the realm instead. It seems to have made little difference.

At the very height of its popularity, even the clergy encouraged it. Churchyards and the inside of churches were sometimes used as fighting arenas. The sport declined in England during the 17th century and was banned in England and Wales in 1835, and in Scotland in 1895, as more and more people found it repugnant.

By the early 1800s it had spread across the US where presidents George Washington, Thomas Jefferson, Andrew Jackson and Abraham Lincoln became devotees. It was socially acceptable. 'Gentlemen' were encouraged to keep a flock of gamecocks and to be an expert on the sport and it wasn't until the US Civil War that it started to decline. By the late 1800s public opinion was changing and bans were being introduced. Today it's illegal in all 50 US states although Louisiana banned it as recently as 2008. It's still legal in some overseas US territories, Puerto Rico, the US Virgin Islands and Guam for instance.

'Cockfighting is generally given a relatively low priority for law enforcement but this is changing as it's realised that, in addition to illegal fighting, the activity is often associated with illegal drug sales, illegal weapons possession, illegal alcohol sales, assaults, prostitution and other crimes', says Dr Randall Lockwood, Senior Vice President at the American Society for the Prevention of Cruelty to Animals (ASPCA). 'Cockfights are increasingly seen as a good opportunity for police to find many people with outstanding warrants wanted for a variety of crimes.'

'It's more common in parts of the country with large Hispanic communities, particularly the Southeast [Florida, Georgia, South Carolina] and in Texas, but there have been arrests in almost every state. Cockfighting is more common in California, Oregon and Washington State because they have large Asian communities', he adds.

There is no centralised tracking of cockfighting arrests by US law enforcement authorities. But a website, www.pet-abuse.com, tracks cases of animal cruelty including US cockfight raids and lists 80 in 2008, 74 in 2007 and 77 in 2006. Fines vary from state to state. Since 2007, the transfer of birds or fighting implements across state lines has been a federal offence with possible fines up to $250,000. State fines are generally between $5,000 and $15,000 but they can be higher.

One of the biggest law enforcement busts in recent years in the US was in 2005 at Del Rio, Tennessee when 144 people were arrested, more than 300 cockerels had to be destroyed and $40,000 in cash was confiscated.

'Cockfighting occurs in all sorts of communities and among all sorts of people', comments ASPCA Special Investigator Mark MacDonald. 'People in New York City can sometimes even buy a box seat, like you would for sports. Bets can range from a few hundred to thousands of dollars. You have to know someone to enter a fight. That's where the undercover part comes in', he says.

In July 2007 police in Sydney, Australia broke up a cockfighting ring and rescued a flock of birds worth almost $1 million, or nearly $6,000 each. They discovered 170 roosters in cages. Seven were so badly injured they needed emergency veterinary treatment. A 40-year-old man was arrested at the property and charged with serious cruelty to animals, possessing items used to train animals to fight, six counts of failing to provide proper veterinary care and four counts of failing to prevent animal cruelty.

The Royal Society for the Prevention of Cruelty to Animals (RSPCA) is sure that cockfighting remains quite prevalent in the UK, but it's very hard to obtain evidence for prosecutions. In 2005 the ringleader of a cockfight in Chichester, Hampshire was jailed and fined together with nine others who received smaller fines. And in 2009, three men in Bishop Auckland were fined after a cockfight was seemingly broken up after a tip-off.

In countries where cockfighting is still practised, including a few villages in northern France (although in most of France it's illegal) and in Mexico, Puerto Rico, Haiti and most Southeast Asian countries, some venues have circular cockfighting pits with tiered seating while others are often just a bit of waste ground near a road, the spectators gathering around to form a circular fighting arena.

There have been fears about cockfights helping to spread bird flu and the practice was recently banned in Thailand – where there are an estimated 15 million fighting cocks – though only temporarily and it was soon reinstated after an enormous public outcry. Cockfighting is big business in Thailand. A fighting bird can cost up to a few hundred thousand Baht (several thousand pounds sterling) while bets at licensed cockpits start at 5,000 Baht (£93).

It's not a pretty spectacle, the cockerels lunging at each other with sudden thrusts of their sharp claws or beak. It's hard to see which one is in the ascendancy, which one the loser until, that is, one constantly backs off or is bleeding and injured. When there's an obvious winner, the fight is generally stopped. Rarely are cockerels killed. It's an aggressive, bloody spectacle that contrasts sharply with the perhaps unexpectedly lavish attention the owners of the birds confer on their fighting charges.

Where cockfighting is bound up closely with tradition and culture, in the Dominican Republic for instance, breeders spare no expense in preparing their cockerels for competition. In some cases they are treated better than family members, receiving specially prepared meals, vitamins, massages and baths in preparation for what could be very lucrative fights.

Rather as with bullfighting in Spain, outsiders to the cockfighting 'culture' seem either baffled or disgusted by the sport, while insiders accentuate not the bloodiness of it all, but the beauty and the drama that accompanies the fights. The 'culture', though, often seems more about a considerable amount of betting on the fight's outcome rather than any more deeply held spiritual values!

Falconry – using trained birds of prey like falcons and hawks to hunt other birds or small animals – is also a very ancient tradition and one that uses the natural hunting and killing behaviour of these often spectacular birds. It was originally a way of getting meat; the birds were trained to kill their prey without eating it themselves! More recently, and particularly in the west and the Middle East, falconry has developed as a sport rather than a way to get a meal.

Near Sart Risbart Incourt village not far from Namur in Belgium, I'm with Patrick Morel and Carlo Verbiot, a couple of the 200 or so falconers in Belgium, as they fly their Peregrines at partridges their dogs put to flight from the extensive areas of farm crops in the rolling countryside around us.

We fail to spot any partridges that these impressive and elegant birds of prey can hunt this autumn afternoon, in spite of the dogs bounding through the crops searching for any to flush out. One of the Peregrines flies high above us, circling and waiting for a bird the dogs might send up, the faint jingle of the tiny bells attached to its legs helping us locate it.

Then a pigeon, maybe a stray racing pigeon or a wild Wood Pigeon, happens to fly past and the Peregrine spots it in an instant. A sudden turn in the pigeon's direction, a super-fast plunge through the blue autumn sky and this interceptor jet fighter of the bird world is giving chase. The pigeon's life is about to end. We lose sight of them as they track like bullets across the sky in the direction of a farm.

We jump in Patrick's vehicle and speed down a rough track to the farmyard where the Peregrine is on top of the now dead pigeon, perched in a shower of feathers as it plucks what it regards as its meal and starts to eat the hapless bird. Patrick and Carlo smooth over the sudden death with the surprised farmer and we are on our way.

'We rent the right to hunt over this farmland with our falcons from several farmers in the area', comments Patrick, the President of the Belgian Falconers and a former President of the International Association for Falconry and the Conservation of Birds of Prey. 'It can cost between 10 and 15 euros (£9 to £13.50) per hectare per year so it isn't a cheap sport. But the farmers particularly welcome us if we hunt some crows and magpies which are farm pests', he adds.

Falconry is an ancient and highly skilled sport. It appears to have been practised in China by 2000 BC, in Japan by 600 BC or earlier and probably at an equally early date in India, Arabia, Persia and Syria, in all of which it is still practised today. It might have an equally long ancestry in North Africa too. There are claims that it might be much older still, maybe practised as early as 6000–4000 BC in Mongolia, Egypt and possibly Asia, though there is no real proof.

According to Marco Polo (1254–1324), the famous Italian trader and explorer, Kublai Khan – leader of the huge Mongol empire in Asia in the 13th century – while on journeys in his kingdom took with him 10,000 falconers split up into small groups who hunted with Gyrfalcons, Peregrine and Saker Falcons plus, apparently, many vultures too. How they ever found enough birds and small animals to hunt is hard to imagine.

Falconry was probably introduced into England from the continent in about AD 860 after reaching continental Europe maybe 400 years earlier from the East when the Huns and others invaded, bringing falconry with them. From then until the middle of the 17th century falconry was hugely popular in the UK, as popular as golf is today!

The narrow, often cobbled roads and cul de sacs with small houses that run behind main streets in much of London – the 'mews' – were originally built to house falcons belonging to gentry living in the adjacent main houses. Today, mews houses are pricey bijou homes and most of their occupants are probably totally unaware that they live in former bird barns!

Stringent laws and enactments, notably in the reigns of William the Conqueror, Edward III, Henry VIII and Elizabeth I, were passed from time to time and a hierarchy of hunting birds to accord with the status of the practitioners was developed. For instance, royalty of the times were to use Gyrfalcons, large, light-coloured falcons; earls used the Peregrine; yeomen the Goshawk; priests the smaller Sparrowhawk; and a knave or servant, the useless Kestrel which could catch a small mouse … at best!

Just about anyone who was anyone during this time dabbled in falconry. The Bayeux tapestry depicts King Harold of England taking a falcon and hounds on his visit to William of Normandy some time before the Norman invasion in 1066 and all that. The two are known to have practised falconry together during this meeting, and William brought with him Flemish falconers when he conquered England. It was something that kings did! Likewise, when he invaded France at the start of the so-called Hundred Years War, Edward III (1312–1377) reputedly took with him in his army 30 falconers on horseback to hunt with every day. Battles were presumably fitted in between.

About the middle of the 17th century, though, falconry in Britain began to decline. Access to open land was being restricted by its enclosure with hedges, and guns, which could kill things with less effort than a falcon, were being introduced. London mews were left without their falcons and were put over to stabling horses instead!

Today, according to a recent review (*Falconry in the United Kingdom: An Audit of the Current Position* by Nick Fox and Jim Chick for the Hawk Board, 2007), there are up to 5,000 falconers in the UK out of no fewer than five times that number who keep and/or breed birds of prey. An incredible 45 million people go to watch falconry displays each year, most of them paying to do so. Three thousand full-time equivalent jobs in the UK now depend on falconry or falcon displays.

Falconers use a range of birds of prey that they train with huge amounts of skill and patience, a process that can take years. It is not a sport for casual involvement and falconry jargon takes some effort to understand. Falcons such as the fast-flying Peregrine or the much larger Saker Falcon, a brown bird more common in Eastern Europe and Asia, and hawks such as the large, grey-barred Goshawk, buzzards and even eagles can be trained and used to hunt.

Northern Goshawks have re-established themselves in Britain since the 1950s largely because of escapes from falconers! Today there might be 500 pairs of these large, woodland-breeding hawks. Because they hunt small and medium-sized birds and mammals including grouse, rabbits and hares, goshawks are often persecuted by gamekeepers. This is why most of their nesting sites are kept secret and why they were wiped out in Britain by gamekeepers and egg collectors in the late 19th and early 20th centuries.

In Britain, though, many falconers in the last 30 years have been using chestnut-brown Harris Hawks, birds of the southern US and parts of South America. They are now the most popular hawks in the west for hunting rabbits and small birds because they are the easiest to train and the most social. While Harris Hawks don't seem to have set up in the wild in the UK, or not yet anyway, Eurasian Eagle-Owls, arguably the largest owl in the world, have!

Large, mottled brown and cream owls with a characteristic pair of head tufts, Eurasian Eagle-Owls stand up to 75 cm tall and can kill hares, foxes or even young deer. They are found across much of Europe and North Africa but don't occur in Britain naturally. Several pairs are now breeding, mainly in northern England, and what they might decide to kill is anyone's guess. They could well prove more of a liability than an asset.

Any birds of prey which falconers in the west use today have to be bred in captivity and licensed. Gone are the days when they could be taken from nests and reared for the sport. Falconers in the UK can, however, hunt any birds they fancy even though all wild birds are, in theory, protected. They have a special licence to do so.

But controls of any description are absent in some countries of the 60–70 in which falconry is a modern-day sport. In the Middle East, falconry has long been an important part of Arab culture. The United Arab Emirates (UAE) reportedly spends more than $27 million annually towards the protection and conservation of wild falcons and has set up several state-of-the-art falcon hospitals in Dubai and Abu Dhabi. There are breeding farms in the Emirates and Saudi Arabia but, in the past, birds of prey have often been taken from nests.

There is evidence that the illegal trade continues as Middle Eastern falconers are prepared to pay large sums for certain prized birds. According to TRAFFIC, the wildlife trade monitoring network, in 2008 traffic police from Milkovo District in Kamchatka in the Russian far northeast stopped a truck carrying 38 illegally captured Gyrfalcons, the large, mainly white falcons that inhabit the Arctic north. Under Russian law, the possession of a Gyrfalcon from Kamchatka carries a fine of RUB250,000 (£5,200) so, if convicted, those arrested could face a total fine of RUB9.5 million (£199,000).

'This is the biggest such case recorded in recent years', said Alexey Vaisman, Senior Programme Officer with TRAFFIC Europe-Russia, adding that he expected a criminal investigation to reveal where the birds were being taken. Following veterinary inspection, three of the birds were kept for treatment but the other 35 birds were released. According to local ornithologists, as many as 100 Gyrfalcons (which are protected internationally) are smuggled from Kamchatka each year, and overall numbers in the region have dwindled from 3,500 to 500 pairs.

According to BirdLife International, falconry in the Middle East – together with habitat loss caused by overgrazing by goats and sheep – has contributed to the massive decline in once common birds of prey such as the desert-living Macqueen's Bustard, a medium-sized, brown, cream and white ground bird.

Over its Middle East and western Asian range, it has declined by at least 25 per cent in the last two decades alone. Its close relative in North Africa, the similar-looking Houbara Bustard, may have suffered even more. Captive breeding centres for these bustards have been established in Morocco, the UAE, Kazakhstan and Saudi Arabia but there's an obvious need to get the amount of falconry in step with the abundance of the birds they hunt to safeguard any future they have.

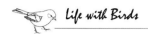

Khalfan Butti Alqubaisi, a keen falconer based in Abu Dhabi in the UAE, doesn't agree that there's a problem. 'We hunt mainly with Gyrfalcons or gyrs crossed with peregrines and they kill Macqueen's Bustards, Stone Curlews [long-legged, sandy-coloured ground birds larger than Lap-wings] and rabbits. But we have plenty of bustards because there are rearing farms that release them into the desert', he says.

The largest, and arguably the most impressive, birds used in falconry are eagles. The huge Golden Eagle, which stands nearly a metre tall on a falconer's arm, is the speciality of Kazakhstan and Kyrgyzstan but is flown in few other countries because these birds need large open spaces to hunt and because of public reaction in populated areas.

There are few sights more impressive than a Kazakh horseman, clad in a thick leather tunic, riding out after the first snowfall of autumn, his eagle standing on the horse, ready to take flight and swoop after a Blue Hare or Steppe Fox. The eagles have pride of place in Kazakh families, living by the front door of their wooden homes.

Many conservationists are critical of falconry. During the passage of the 1981 Wildlife & Countryside Act in Britain, successful efforts were made by the RSPB and other lobby groups to have all captive birds of prey native to the UK ringed and government-registered, with DNA-testing to verify birds' origins as a back-up. After a centuries-old but informal existence in Britain, the sport of falconry was finally given formal legal status in Great Britain by the act which, at the same time, outlawed any capturing of wild birds of prey.

In 2008, however, the UK government reduced the protection given to several birds of prey whose populations were not under threat. John Clare, an RSPB spokesman, says that the Society is concerned that removing birds like peregrines from nests may start up anew.

Does falconry have any impact on the birds it hunts and kills? Conservationists in the UK think not. And falconry kills a tiny fraction of the numbers of birds killed by domestic cats. If a falcon or hawk is allowed to eat its prey, the bird soon stops hunting. It doesn't need to expend the energy so it sits still wherever it perches. It's 'fed up' – the origin of the much-used phrase!

Today, falconers are often in demand in or near cities to help control pest birds and animals around waste landfill sites, at commercial buildings and at airports – for instance at Toronto City Hall where they are used in an effort to control the city's gull and pigeon population or at high-rise luxury hotels in Dubai where city pigeons aren't wanted. Inevitably, though, controversy rages, with some people wanting to protect 'their' pigeons against the perceived ravages of these birds of prey.

Occasionally, the tables get turned, as in the summer of 2009, when Morgan Pitts, a Brooklyn, New York resident, witnessed a gang of pigeons chasing and pecking at a Peregrine chick on a street. Pitts rushed in and rescued the baby predator, which had either been abandoned by its mother or fallen from its nest somewhere high on a skyscraper above!

Now, breathe a sigh of relief that there is one sport using birds that doesn't set out to kill them. Indeed, those participating in it desperately want to see their birds alive time and again. And as quickly as possible too.

Around 45,000 people in the UK take part in what has always been considered a sport of the so-called working classes or, at any rate, of people far removed from those who shoot grouse. It's pigeon racing and, in an organised form, it's been popular in the UK for over a hundred years.

Though its origins in the Far East are ancient, it achieved a great deal of popularity in Belgium in the mid 19th century. The pigeon fanciers (that's the rather odd name for people who keep pigeons) of Belgium were so taken with the hobby that they began to develop pigeons specially bred for fast flight and long endurance. From Belgium the modern version of the sport, and the pigeons which were bred by the Flemish fanciers, made their way to most parts of the world. In Britain, the first organised race was in 1881 and the sport gained rapid popularity in the industrial areas where it was known as 'poor man's horse racing'.

These days it's enjoyed by people from more varied social backgrounds than those typified by the British newspaper cartoon, working class *Andy Capp*! Even the Queen has a loft, at Sandringham, where she continues a long line of royal participation going back to her great grandfather. The Queen is also the patron of the Royal Pigeon Racing Association (RPRA), the governing body of the sport in Britain which was established in 1897 and currently has more than 54,000 members. China has the most fanciers, maybe 300,000. According to the RPRA's David Bills, pigeon racing remains popular in Germany, Belgium and Poland too.

Jeannette Taylor has been keeping racing pigeons in a large wood-built loft in her back garden in Failsworth, a suburb of Manchester, since 1996.

'Mine are all racers, several different varieties, and I breed them too. We have about 150, sometimes more, and I'm putting some in a race pretty well every week during the season, that's from April to September because it's the better weather', says Mrs Taylor.

'We've got 28 members in the Failsworth Club and we mostly race ours against all the clubs in the Oldham Federation. The furthest inland race is just over 200 miles [320 km] from Portland on the south coast and the longest we do is back from northern France, that's 500 miles [800 km] and they're back in about three days.'

Mrs Taylor confirms that you need to be dedicated and not work-shy to keep pigeons. And it's not cheap, what with buying feed and medication, an outlay of about £450 for the electronic timing system used to record their return from a race, buying the breeding birds to start off, transporting birds to the release points for the races and so on.

Not that prize money is enough to make you dizzy either!

'My pigeons have won some trophies but the prize money might be £5 or so in one of our local Federation races. The big money is in the national and international races, probably thousands then', she adds.

Oddly, perhaps, South Africa is the home of the richest race in the world, the Sun City Million Dollar Pigeon Race, which often pits more than 4,000 birds from 25 countries against each other for a share of $1.3 million in prize money. The winner can expect to pocket US$200,000.

Sun City's race sees birds from across the world air-freighted to South Africa as youngsters, months before the race, then trained to orientate to a single loft. On race day, after being released 550 km out in the South African countryside, the birds all fly back to the same destination.

Traditionally for a race a small, uniquely numbered rubber band was placed around the pigeon's leg, and the birds to be raced put in a basket and transported by road with others to the release location. Released at a fixed time, the pigeons flew back to their respective home lofts. When a pigeon returned home, the fancier removed the rubber ring and placed it in a special timing clock to record its arrival time. These days, it's more usual to use electronic timing like Jeannette Taylor does.

A plastic ring with an electronic chip in it is attached to the bird's leg. When the pigeon arrives back at the loft it passes over a sensor pad which records the time it 'clocked in', a bit like going through the checkout at a supermarket!

Because the home lofts are all in different places, the race winner is calculated by dividing the distance from the liberation site to the loft by the time it has taken the pigeon to fly home. The bird with the fastest speed is the winner.

Pigeons can cover astonishing distances at speeds in excess of 95 km/hour, and top racers can cover 800 km in one day. The pigeons use a combination (as do all migrating birds) of their natural ability to home and navigational skills using an 'in-built' magnetic compass, the position of the sun by day, landmarks and their sense of smell. A racing pigeon will compete until it is about six years old then a fancier will retire the pigeon to breeding duties.

Young pigeons are usually trained progressively for at least six months before being allowed to compete in a race. A racing pigeon's initial training involves familiarising it with the loft and its surroundings and training it to know the various features of its home, including how to get in! After a few weeks of this, the young birds are allowed outside for the first time, usually before they can fly strongly to prevent an overzealous pigeon flying away before it can find its way back home. As the birds grow older, they become stronger and smarter and are therefore allowed to fly further and further away from their home loft.

Training methods are as varied as the pigeons themselves and many fanciers are reluctant to reveal details. One of the most popular systems is widowhood. This uses 'motivation' to try to give the bird a sense of urgency on race day. The use of widowhood is usually begun by first allowing the racer to raise a chick in their nestbox. After the chick is weaned the female pigeon is removed and often the nestbox is closed off so that from then on the only time these birds are allowed to see their mate or enter the nestbox is upon returning from training or a race.

As well as losing their way or suffering from exhaustion during a race, racing pigeons face another natural hazard. Mention Peregrines to most pigeon racers and they are apt to get incandescent with rage. To these killer birds of prey, one pigeon is much like any other. And all are good eating. As a result, some pigeon fanciers have killed Peregrines, leading to several prosecutions. Conservationists argue that the Peregrines were around long before racing pigeons and that they are a natural hazard the pigeons must learn to avoid. Such arguments, often fuelled by deeply held opinions, are set to continue, probably indefinitely!

Using pigeons' homing instincts and developing that into pigeon racing may have evolved, at least in some parts of the world, from keeping pigeons in structures like dovecotes to provide a source of food in the shape of the youngsters or squabs. The adult birds would fly out each day to find food, often travelling some distance if it was scarce, but always returning to their home dovecote at night.

Some animal welfare groups are critical of pigeon racers killing off poorly performing birds. If they regularly get lost or they're slow to return home, the birds are of little value and considered useless for breeding. Jeannette Taylor acknowledges that some owners do bump off these poor performers. She prefers to give them away to anyone starting out on pigeon-keeping. It seems a lot more kindly and it reduces their start-up costs.

Racing pigeons that 'home' to their lofts aren't the only sort of pigeons kept for sporting competitions. Around 5,000 people in the UK keep 'tipplers'. These usually look very much like racing pigeons but are bred for endurance, staying up in the air for long periods – frequently more than 15 hours (with competition winners breaking the 20-hour barrier) – before they need to land at their loft for food and water. They are the endurance athletes of the pigeon world but their origins aren't at all clear.

They are likely to have been bred from 'tumblers', another kind of domesticated pigeon, bred for its ability to roll over backwards in flight and tumble from side to side. It's a bit of airborne gymnastics that is thought to have developed to help them escape from hungry Peregrines dashing after them in flight. If it was such a useful escape mechanism, though, you might well wonder why all pigeons didn't learn it.

Tipplers are a peculiarly British 'invention', the first ones seemingly bred in Congleton and Macclesfield in Cheshire in the mid 1840s, though possibly earlier. The aim of the old-time breeders was to perfect the graceful action of their wings – 'butterfly action' – and it is the ease and grace with which the wings are used that enable tipplers to stay flying.

In sports not involving birds in any way, a medley of teams – soccer, rugby, American football and others – have taken their names from birds … and certainly not all of them to convey a sense of speed or agility as you might expect. The Arizona Cardinals, founded in 1898, are an American football team based in Tempe, Arizona named after the striking scarlet and black Northern Cardinal found across much of the US. The Sydney Roosters, founded in 1908, are one of the most successful clubs in Australian rugby league. And the Swansea Ospreys, formed in 2003 from existing teams, is a rugby union side in South Wales. That's South Wales, UK.

Birdsong, and even the calls of some birds, has inspired a kind of sport that has sprung up in several parts of the world. In the ten ASEAN countries in Southeast Asia, there's an annual Zebra Dove cooing contest which has developed because of the popularity of such regional and local competitions.

These small, brown and pink, heavily barred doves have a soft, staccato, cooing call, and the competitions – which attract international entrants – are held to find the ones with the most impressive coos! In any year there might be over a thousand doves entered, in various categories – not an easy task for the judges. To many an untrained ear, one coo sounds very much like another!

In Thailand, where (as in several Southeast Asian countries) caged bird-keeping is very popular, there are other, more traditional bird-singing competitions involving a wide selection of caged birds admired for their songs – so-called Golden Voice Competitions. The birds are judged against criteria such as loudness, complexity and special notes.

But such enterprise isn't restricted to Southeast Asia. Local bird-singing competitions are held in some parts of the US too.

At Piedmont High School in the town of Piedmont, not far from San Francisco in California, a spoof competition takes place each year. In 2009 the school held its 44th Annual Bird Calling Contest. This one doesn't use real birds, though; these are students taking to the stage to imitate the Double-crested Cormorant, the Acorn Woodpecker, the Jackass Penguin or whatever they dress up as and call like. The winners invariably get national TV coverage!

So some wild birds have become the centrepiece of a range of very different sporting activities, some of which are undoubtedly controversial. As a result, these birds have become extremely familiar to those who participate in the sport or help rear birds in captivity to supply it.

But a smaller number of birds have become familiar to a very much larger number of people the world over because they have been domesticated on a massive scale to satisfy the demands for cheaper meat obtained far more easily than it ever could by killing wild birds. Domestication, then, is the subject of the next chapter.

3
Domestic bliss

Domesticating birds like chickens and turkeys has long provided us with a guaranteed – and cheap – food supply. But welfare concerns are challenging our bird rearing factories to provide a kinder life for the birds we exploit. And some frightening health risks are looming.

It's difficult to make progress walking along the narrow, dusty and rather shabby Sharia el-Birka street in Luxor, the ancient Thebes, on the east side of the majestic River Nile in Egypt. The street is crowded with people, mainly locals, buying almost anything from river fish and sheep's intestines to vegetables and fruit, as well as items such as rope, fabric, clothes and freshly baked bread from the hundreds of merchants with their ramshackle stalls on either side.

It's noisy, amazingly colourful, full of smells in the warm spring sunshine and incredibly vibrant. Along with Luxor's much better-known ancient Egyptian temples, museums and such wonders of the world as the Valley of the Kings, this old souk is something not to be missed. The lifestyle of most of the merchants and farmers selling their produce – and many of the customers buying them – has probably not changed a great deal for centuries.

It's easy along Sharia el-Birka to find birds for sale. Live chickens are cramped in wooden crates and baskets. You can buy them this way or you can buy whole chickens, plucked and ready to cook. Or pieces of chicken meat. All with complimentary flies that alight constantly on any dead animal parts in the warmth.

There are pigeons for sale too – adult-size young pigeons (known as squabs) that are good eating because their flesh is tender, rich and dark. Like the chickens, they are also cramped in baskets or small wooden crates, many of them exposed to the increasingly warm sun.

Sitting in the sunshine, some of the women who have raised these birds and are trying to sell them are obviously concerned that their charges might dehydrate. Oblivious to any health hazard, they periodically take a mouthful of water from a bottle, hold the hapless pigeon with its beak touching their mouth, prise its beak open and squirt some water into its throat!

Domesticated pigeons, and probably domesticated chickens and geese too, have doubtless been sold in this and other markets like it in Egypt for millennia. The oldest records of wild pigeons being bred in captivity, presumably originally for food, are on cuneiform tablets (a form of writing used in ancient times in much of the Middle East) from Mesopotamia (roughly modern-day Iraq) dating from 3000 BC or earlier. You can find them, too, in Egyptian hieroglyphics, a writing system first used in ancient Egypt at about the same time or a little later.

Pigeons have been domesticated in Britain since before Roman times, as they were across Europe. And they were of huge importance as food. Wander around many a village in Britain and you might well come across a small, round, square or rectangular building, frequently in a pretty bad state of repair. Located in a farmyard maybe. Close to a stately home. Or even behind a garden wall. They are dovecotes, formerly in everyday use for housing pigeons. And virtually all of them have fallen into disrepair.

But dovecotes weren't constructed in order for the doves they harboured to prettify the villages they were built in, flying in and out with flourish, circling the houses to general admiration from the inhabitants. Far from it!

Dovecotes, introduced to Britain by the Normans in the 11th century, were a living food chest, brimming with young pigeons whose necks would be snapped and who would then be plucked, cooked and eaten. Young pigeons were very good eating. And they were free. Mrs Beeton recommended that the birds were broiled, roasted, stewed or cooked in a pie with their feet sticking out, presumably so that whoever ate it knew what they were getting.

According to John McCann, a historian who has made a particular study of dovecotes, 'the Romans mainly used pigeon lofts high in other buildings but there was a larger type, round with a domed roof, and having an aperture at the apex for the pigeons to enter'.

'This type was perpetuated in the first English dovecotes of which the earliest surviving ones date from the 14th century, though earlier ones have been excavated in a collapsed condition. The only access for the pigeons was a round hole at the apex which was the source of daylight and ventilation. The small entrance right at the top helped prevent snakes and other vermin from getting in. The nest holes were fitted into the interior walls from floor to roof like a series of narrow shelves. This basic design travelled from Rome to France and on to England', adds McCann.

'Dovecotes certainly weren't confined to Britain. They were widely used in the Middle East, northern Africa and across Europe apart from the Scandinavian countries and Switzerland', comments Dr Klara Spandl of the Oxford Archaeological Unit and another dovecote expert.

The users of early dovecotes were mainly concerned about their pigeons being killed by birds of prey but also the threat of polecats and martens which could climb the corners of some dovecotes, enter at the eaves and prey on the pigeons and their eggs.

Standing in the large yard at Dunham Massey Home Farm in Cheshire, today a National Trust property, Sue Royle (who with her husband Geoff tenants the award-winning, pedigree beef cattle farm) tells me that the rather ornate brick-built dovecote dominating the centre of their yard is a listed building. Octagonal in shape with a wind vane crowning a cupola on its slate roof, it was built in the early 19th century. A few feral pigeons loaf around the farm buildings; some sit on the dovecote roof and get inside.

Internally, it's replete from floor to roof with brick-made nesting boxes, each one something like 20 cm square. This is where hundreds of pairs of pigeons were encouraged to nest. And the floor is where piles of their droppings would heap up to be periodically cleaned out and used as fertiliser. In the 16th and 17th centuries, saltpetre was extracted from it to produce gunpowder!

Most English dovecotes were designed to have between 300 and 1,000 nesting boxes built into the inside walls but larger ones are known. One at Culham in Oxfordshire has places for 3,000 birds and could almost be mistaken for a small house. But a house without windows.

Until the middle of the 18th century, rats weren't a problem for pigeon-keepers, for the simple reason that the only rats in Britain were black rats, a fruit- and seed-eating species which did no harm to livestock. Only when brown rats were introduced to Britain in the 18th century on ships bringing goods into port did dovecotes begin to suffer rat attacks.

At this point it is probably worth pausing to explain the difference between doves and pigeons. To bird experts there is none! To many people, though, the name 'dove' is associated more with the smarter end of pigeondom, the classy white birds for example, while 'pigeons' are what pick up crumbs on city pavements or raid a farmer's crop.

According to Les Beletsky in his excellent *Birds of the World* (Collins, 2006), there are 308 different living species of pigeons and doves, one of the most successful bird families in the world. Beletsky reckons that the smaller species are usually called doves and the larger ones pigeons, but adds that there is a good deal of overlap. So, please take your pick.

Dovecotes sound better than pigeoncotes which is, anyway, more difficult to pronounce. In France they have long been called *colombiers* and, more recently, *pigeonniers*!

'The right to build a dovecote was traditionally reserved to the lord of the manor – that's why many are associated with stately homes – and presumably resented by tenant farmers because the birds could eat their weight of corn in a day, the tenants' corn', comments Klara Spandl. 'Probably the largest number were built between 1650 and the late 18th century when corn was relatively cheap and abundant. By then, tenants were allowed to build their own dovecotes with their landlord's permission.'

'By the time the young pigeons [known as squabs] were almost fully grown, they were nearly as large as the parent birds but their flying muscles had never been used. So their meat was very tender and was much prized as a delicacy. Squabs could be roasted on spits or baked with other delicacies. As dovecotes were always associated with a luxurious way of life, their eating came to symbolise high social status – or high social aspirations', says McCann.

'Large quantities of young pigeons could be harvested from the dovecote for eating during April and May, then the supply dipped until August, September and October, when most young pigeons were produced. The few squabs produced in winter [when few pigeons would have bred] could be sold for very high prices, a delicacy out of season.'

'For example, in 1634 the Earl of Salisbury paid four times the normal price for winter squabs but the earl was one of the richest men in England. Most of the wealthy householders who could afford to keep a dovecote had to be content with what it could produce, and accepted that pigeons were not available between November and Easter', he adds.

The mature pigeons weren't eaten. At least, not by the well off. But they were sometimes given to employees even though their meat was often as tough as old boots!

Later, dovecotes went into decline. Some experts like Klara Spandl blame the humble turnip! Growing these root crops, introduced from Holland and Belgium during the late 17th century, allowed more farm animals to be kept overwinter. And that meant a supply of meat – larger meat – year-round. Dove or pigeon meat might just have fallen out of fashion too.

John McCann, though, discounts the turnip theory because, he says, the number of dovecotes in Britain continued to rise from the 17th century, reaching its peak in the late 18th century. Instead, he blames the French Revolutionary Wars (1793–1802) and the Napoleonic Wars that followed almost immediately until 1815. They pushed up the price of wheat enormously. Pigeons, many of them from the numerous dovecotes, love nothing better than cereal grain so dovecotes soon ceased to be a matter of pride and became socially unacceptable. Many were demolished. Others were allowed to fall derelict.

After the wars there was a partial revival, but it didn't last. By the middle of the 19th century other developments in farming, and changes in the law, had effectively put an end to dovecotes.

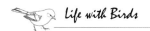

A few, however, have been built in recent years, albeit to try to keep city pigeons off particular buildings! In July 2000, the London Borough of Barking & Dagenham opened a dovecote in Barking Park hoping that it would take birds off the roofs of a neighbouring public convenience and houses. Other dovecotes, with the same purpose, have been built by Malvern Hills District Council in Worcestershire, Heath Park Hospital in Cardiff, and Nottingham City Hospital.

Recognising an ancient dovecote isn't as easy as it might sound either. When I eventually found the oldest recorded dovecote in Britain, in a farmyard in the village of Garway in Herefordshire, I thought at first that it was some kind of fortified tower – more like a surviving part of a former castle. Built, or possibly repaired, in 1326 (the date is on it), round and squat, it's a dumpy tower shape built entirely of stone and rather austere with no pretty features.

'The more flamboyant ones were mainly built on estates in the 17th to 19th century; some occupy the upper floors of three-storied towers containing summer houses in the lower floors. Some later ones were disguised as castellated towers in the gothic revival style or as Grecian temples in classical taste. Dovecotes have been found on top of granaries, above piggeries and hen-houses, even mortuaries and privies', says Klara Spandl.

Building a dovecote is one thing. But how do you get the pigeons to establish themselves in it? Apparently, there's little that doves or pigeons like better than a dark, dry spot in which to nest. So the rows of snug, dark nesting boxes built into the internal walls were immediately attractive. Whitewashing the inside walls of the dovecote apparently helped too, because doves are attracted to white surfaces.

Assuming that a dovecote proved popular with the birds, harvesting their eggs and chicks for food was easy enough. From the floor inside the dovecote it was possible to reach many of the lower nesting boxes. To get to the higher ones, the buildings had a revolving wooden pole in the centre. This had arms against which ladders could be attached, allowing whoever harvested the squabs to get to any of the boxes from top to bottom.

Today, pigeon dishes feature commonly in traditional cuisines in Africa, Asia, many European countries (France and Spain particularly) and Latin America. In Europe especially, much of the restaurant pigeon is wild-shot Wood Pigeon. In other countries, it's often domesticated pigeon squabs raised on farms.

Rules in Covent Garden, London – established by Thomas Rule in 1798 – serves traditional British food including 'roast squab pigeon with summer cabbage and smoked Cumbrian ham', priced at £22.50 in the summer of 2009.

Some birds have rather presented themselves as a potential food supply by choosing to nest in our houses and outbuildings. The ubiquitous House Sparrow is a good example, nesting among the straw, reed or other material formerly used to thatch the roofs of buildings (and still used in many developing countries) or in nooks and crannies in brick or stonework. One full-grown sparrow might not make much of a meal, but a nest-full does.

And it wasn't long before people started to make sparrow nest-raiding easier by supplying the chirpy little birds with nesting places they couldn't resist. Enter the 'sparrow pot', a kind of primitive domestication to make the trusting birds available as food without having to catch them in the wild.

The earliest sparrow pots have been found in Holland. Known since the early 16th century, they were unglazed earthenware pots, slightly smaller than a rugby ball, hung on house walls. They had a small entrance hole for the birds and a larger hole for a human hand at the back where the pot nudged against the wall.

They were common in Holland and Britain; according to Denis Summers-Smith, the world's leading sparrow expert, in his *On Sparrows and Man* (The Thersby Group, 2005), sparrow pie was a common rural dish in Britain until World War I.

Summers-Smith was told of a former practice on Malta (the Maltese have something of a passion for eating small birds) of cutting out cavities in stone building blocks built into the walls of houses. Dating back perhaps several hundred years, they might have been used to collect young birds for use as cage birds (though the pathetic song of a House Sparrow in a cage would surely have driven people demented) or, more likely, for food. Some of these 'sparrow walls' numbered a hundred or more cavities, a bit like a dovecote turned inside out.

Primitive hunters presumably discovered a very long time ago that it might be easier to try to capture some of the wild animals – birds included – that they chased with spears and other weapons, or trapped, and then try to breed them and restrict their movements so they couldn't get away. It would make life an awful lot easier, something the human race is generally very good at.

Slowly, a newly domesticated animal becomes used to getting fed and restrained. And as they bred them, people selected the more docile ones to continue with, getting rid of any aggressive birds so that they didn't pass on their aggressive nature. But the aim of domestication hasn't only been to supply food more easily. It's also been to obtain valuable commodities such as wool or feathers and, in the case of larger mammals like oxen, to help with physically hard work.

Obviously not all of this domestication started at the same time or in the same place. Most experts seem to think that dogs, goats and sheep were the first domesticated animals, possibly during the Mesolithic period (about 11,000–5000 BC) when most people were still hunters. Others are much more recent; the rabbit in the Middle Ages and sugar beet as a sugar-yielding farm crop in the 19th century.

The chicken was probably the earliest domesticated bird. Experts at the University of Adelaide and Flinders University of South Australia reckon that they were domesticated well before 6000 BC and were established by then in China; that they were domesticated in India about 2000 BC and introduced to Japan via Korea sometime between 300 BC and AD 300. They were brought to Europe from China via Russia by 700 BC and their images have been found on coins in the Roman city of Ephesus in modern-day Turkey.

Not everyone agrees with these dates! Some experts think their domestication began even earlier. Dr David Sherman, Director of the Massachusetts Department of Agricultural Resources, for instance, reckons that recent evidence suggests their domestication was underway in Vietnam over 10,000 years ago. That's around 8000 BC.

Chickens were derived by selective breeding from the Red Junglefowl that lives wild in the forests of much of Southeast Asia and the Grey Junglefowl which is more confined to India. They still live there; Grey Junglefowl are gorgeous, the males having black plumage spotted with grey and long, lyre-shaped tails. The Red Junglefowl males are colourful with red head 'combs', rusty-orange necks and bouffant tail feathers, the females much more drab. A pair looks much like the cockerels (known in the US as roosters) and hens that are available as some domesticated chicken varieties today. Walking around villages in Thailand, it's often difficult to tell that the farm birds are domestic varieties at all because they often look so much like wild Red Junglefowl.

Seed and insect eaters, sometimes even taking a small mouse, they feed almost entirely on the ground by grubbing about but, in spite of the male's striking colours, they are often difficult to spot in the scrub and woodland they inhabit. Domestic chickens feed in the same way.

Domestication of chickens for food might initially have been less important than providing male birds for cockfighting (see Chapter 2) or for ritualistic sacrifice (see Chapter 12). But the Romans, always on the lookout for a tasty meal, certainly saw its food value and developed a domestic poultry industry using specialised breeds.

After the Roman Empire's collapse, unbelievably it wasn't until the 19th century that a domesticated poultry industry was re-established in the western world. Today there are literally hundreds of registered domesticated chicken breeds of all shapes and sizes, with often rather sonorous names such as Bearded d'Uccle, Nankin, Lakenvelder or North Holland Blue.

The very limited number of breeds or types used in mass chicken production (bred specially for highly productive lives) are reared by the tens of thousands in huge factory-like buildings where the birds never see daylight and where their environment, their feeding and everything else is strictly controlled. Fast – and cheap – production of eggs and meat is the objective.

Chickens reared intensively for meat have an incredibly short life, generally only six weeks before slaughter. Fifty years ago, it took them three times as long to reach maturity; the acceleration is due to improved breeding and more nutritious feeds. Hens of special laying breeds, of which the most common is the White Leghorn, may produce as many as 300 eggs a year. A century ago it was more like eighty.

After 12 months, the hen's egg-laying ability starts to decline and in Europe commercial laying hens are then slaughtered and used in baby foods, pet foods, pies and other processed foods. In the US they survive until the end of their second year so the US is the place to be if you're a factory-farmed chicken and wish to have (or maybe endure) a longer life.

Males of egg-laying breeds are, of course, of no use. So only female chicks are kept. Vast numbers of male chicks are killed when they're less than three days old, by gassing, being thrown into a macerating machine, having their necks quickly snapped, being buried alive or by electrocution. Not surprisingly, the issue is controversial, subject to a great deal of criticism by animal rights organisations, and the cause of many consumers shunning intensively produced chicken eggs. The male birds can't be grown on for chicken meat because modern egg-laying varieties produce little body muscle!

Today, chickens are the most common and widespread domesticated animal, with perhaps 24 billion in the world at any one time. That's more chickens than any other bird. In 2008 more than 9 billion were slaughtered for food in the US alone according to the US Department of Agriculture.

But intensive poultry rearing, as with the intensive rearing of any livestock, is slowly but surely going out of fashion in the more affluent west. Animal welfare concerns have spearheaded an increasing consumer requirement for meat – and eggs – from animals reared in something akin to natural surroundings, with more room to move and at least part of their short lives spent outdoors.

Karol Bailey has been rearing turkeys, chickens and geese free range for 23 years. When I visited her farm near Knutsford in Cheshire she had hundreds of week-old goslings (young geese) penned in a warm, wood-shavings filled run inside a large modern farm building. Pale brown and very attractive to look at as they ran about, they were, she said, a Danish hybrid reared especially for the table. It takes eight months to rear them ready to eat in such free range conditions.

'They'll be able to go out and graze in the pastures on the farm as soon as they are old enough, once they are about four weeks. If I let them out too soon, crows might kill a few and they can also suffer from sunburn because their feathers aren't well developed. They get fed with a food ration consisting of wheat, soya, minerals and vitamins plus whatever they find themselves in the fields', she says.

'We don't inoculate them at all. But it costs more to rear the birds like this of course; more labour, the cost of the land they have access to, they consume more food and so on. So a 10 lb [22 kg] weight goose from me costs about £55. If you want one that's intensively reared, you can get one for maybe £15 to £25. We kill them here and prepare them for sale ourselves. We do the whole job. You get the quality, the real taste and the freshness you pay for', adds Karol. And, from what I saw, you get the assurance that they have led a reasonably natural life.

According to the British Egg Industry Council, in 2009 we consumed 11 billion chicken eggs. Not all of these were eaten boiled, scrambled or fried of course. Many were eaten in various food products, cakes especially. It's a market worth around £844 million a year.

Fifty-five per cent of these eggs came from cage-reared, often called battery-reared, chickens; 41 per cent from free range birds. To be categorised as free-range, the hens must have continuous outdoor daytime access. Battery hens are kept in cages so they can move about very little. A much smaller number (producing four per cent of British eggs) are called barn reared, a kind of in-between system in which hens are free to move around the shed floor but are pretty densely packed. They can't go outside.

Some supermarkets stopped selling battery/cage-reared hen's eggs a few years ago and others are following the trend. Many food producers that use large numbers of eggs demand free range ones too. And while some research has been contradictory, expert opinion concludes that free range eggs are more nutritious to eat.

In Britain, we are eating fewer eggs overall. According to Government statistics, British households bought, on average, 3.7 eggs per person per week in 1974. Today it's down to two per person per week, much of the reduction due to less home cooking of cakes and other egg-containing foods. Consequently, egg production has fallen, from 1,075 million dozen to 755 million dozen over roughly the same time and the number of laying hens has declined too.

Chicken meat sales in Britain, on the other hand, continue to rise. The average household purchase of uncooked whole chickens and chicken pieces per person per week was 115 g in 1974 and 178 g in 2007. With its comparatively low fat content, chicken is regarded as a healthy alternative to most red meat. But the main factor might be its cheapness!

Chickens, turkeys, ducks and geese are the best-known birds that have long been domesticated to provide a readily available source of food. In western countries it tends to be the breast meat that's most desired followed by the legs ('drumsticks') while, in other parts of the world, rather different parts of such birds are often considered as delicacies. In much of China, for instance, goose and chicken feet – often cooked in a sweet and sour sauce – are considered a delicacy.

Other birds have been domesticated too. Guineafowl is one, but also partridge, pheasant and tiny quail. Ostriches are another, probably the most dangerous to handle in any confined space but a healthy source of low fat meat. Emus and rheas (even larger than emus), too, are farmed in Australia and a few other countries for their meat as well as their leather, oil and feathers.

Domestic ducks are mostly derived from the common or garden Mallard (the males with the green heads), a species found naturally around much of the world. Probably first domesticated in China or Southeast Asia thousands of years ago, there are records in Roman times of eggs being taken from wild mallard and the ducks reared in captivity after being hatched by domestic hens.

Today there are many duck varieties derived originally from wild mallards and some of their names – like Aylesbury and Khaki Campbell – are reasonably well known. As a domesticated bird, though, ducks have never been as popular as the chicken because chickens have much more white lean meat and are easier to keep confined, making duck comparatively expensive. Consequently, it's less of a mass market meat.

Ducks are not farmed for their meat alone. Their eggs and down are important too. But trying to domesticate a duck like the Common Eider, the down from the nests of which is collected to make the warmest duvets (see Chapter 4), would be impossible because they need access to shallow seawater and feed on mussels and other molluscs. The females of most breeds of domestic duck are very unreliable at sitting on their eggs and raising their young, and it has been the custom on farms for centuries to put duck eggs under a broody hen chicken for hatching. These days incubators are usually used where ducks are reared on more of a factory scale.

Other domestic ducks have been derived from the tree-nesting Muscovy Duck, a large black duck with white wing patches found wild in Mexico and parts of South America. Muscovy Ducks had been domesticated by various Native American cultures when Columbus arrived there and the first few were brought back to Europe by explorers in the 1500s. Most domesticated forms, rather oddly considering the dark colour of wild Muscovys, are white.

Muscovy breeds are popular because they have stronger-tasting meat – sometimes compared with roast beef – than the domesticated varieties derived from the mallard. The meat is lean when compared with the fatty meat of mallard-derived ducks, its leanness and tenderness often being compared with veal. Muscovy ducks are also less noisy, and sometimes marketed as 'quackless' ducks, even though they are not completely silent. So they are easier to keep.

There is one food derived from ducks or geese that is particularly controversial. It's foie gras, a rich, buttery – and pricey – delicacy made from specially fattened duck or goose livers. The controversial bit is that in France, where the bulk of it is produced, the birds are force-fed with corn pushed down a tube inserted into their oesophagus. Not surprisingly, many people believe it's a cruel practice. It could hardly be described as kind!

The French didn't dream up force feeding to produce foie gras. That was done by the ancient Egyptians, never slow when it came to new ideas. So the technique dates back to about 2500 BC. The Romans had a liking for foie gras too, though according to Maguelonne Toussaint-Samat in her *History of Food* (Blackwell Publishing Professional, 1994), the decadent Roman emperor Marcus Aurelius Antoninus fed his dogs on foie gras during the four years of his chaotic reign.

France produces about 18,000 tonnes of foie gras a year, three-quarters of the world's total, of which 96 per cent is duck liver and the rest goose liver. And most of it is eaten in France. Approximately 30,000 farmers are members of the French foie gras industry. Hungary is the world's second-largest foie gras producer and the largest exporter, with perhaps 30,000 Hungarian goose farmers dependent on the foie gras industry there too.

Toulouse geese and Moulard ducks are the breeds most commonly used for foie gras. Moulards are a cross-breed between a male Muscovy Duck and a female Pekin Duck. The force feeding results in a distended liver which can be up to six times its normal size. As a result of animal welfare concerns some countries have banned foie gras production and/or consumption.

The turkey – which first appeared on the Christmas menu in England in 1585 – was originally domesticated in Mexico when Europe was in the Neolithic age! Sometime between 1525 and 1532 domesticated birds were first brought to Britain, probably by William Strickland of Boynton-on-the-Wold in Yorkshire, an English landowner who was known to have sailed to the Americas at the time. As a result, he was allowed to take as his family crest 'a turkey-cock in his pride proper', and the official record of his crest in the archives of the College of Arms is said to be the oldest surviving European drawing of a turkey.

Turkeys still exist in their natural habitat. The Wild Turkey (see Chapter 1) is now doing well in the US but the more colourful Ocellated Turkey in parts of Central America is declining because of hunting. The smaller, dark-coloured guineafowl, of which there are six species, all native to different parts of Africa, seem to be holding their own.

When guineafowl were first domesticated is anyone's guess but the Romans, who obtained vast numbers of all sorts of wild animals from Africa, kept them for food. More recently, Portuguese explorers in the 15th and 16th centuries brought them to Europe.

Ostriches have been domesticated for their meat and in the second half of the 19th century they were certainly being bred in large numbers for their feathers (think feather dusters as well as ornamental), in the Cape Province of South Africa especially.

By about 1915 ostrich feather use was at its peak and maybe three-quarters of a million of these huge flightless birds were being 'farmed' in South Africa where they live in the wild. Some were reared as domestic birds in other countries too, in North Africa, the US and Australia for instance, but the industry collapsed after World War I and has never revived except on a small scale in a few countries for meat, a few decorative feathers and for their skin which is used for leather.

Ostrich meat is red; it looks and tastes like beef but is low in fat (even less than chicken and turkey) so it's promoted as a healthier meat option. And in case you're wondering how much meat there is on an ostrich breast compared with, say, a turkey, the answer is none! According to the British Domesticated Ostrich Association, all of the meat comes from an ostrich's legs and back.

Emus, even taller than ostriches, are also farmed in Australia where they occur naturally – as well as in Gujarat, India where they don't – again for their low fat meat, their skins to make a soft leather and for their oil.

But who first thought of domesticating cormorants? Not that anyone eats cormorants! Presumably they are edible, if rather fishy tasting and tough! But to eat them isn't the reason these fish-eating birds have been domesticated. It's to make use of their amazing fish-catching skills. And people love to eat fish.

Historically, cormorants have been used to catch fish for their keepers in Japan, in China possibly since the 4th century BC, in Macedonia and in 16th and 17th century England and France. It involves their keepers tying a band around the base of the bird's throat which allows them to dive in rivers to catch fish but stops them swallowing them. They can still swallow small fish but the keeper brings the bird back to his boat once it has a decent-sized catch and takes the fish for himself.

Both James I (1603–1625) and Charles I (1625–1649) of England employed a Master of the Cormorants who, on their monarch's instructions, travelled far and wide to display the fishing skills of their charges. No one knows for certain when the practice died out, presumably rendered useless as nets became commonplace.

In Japan, cormorant fishing still takes place in or near several cities with rivers, though today for tourists rather than for culinary necessity! On the Nagara River at Gifu, it has taken place for 1,300 years. Here the cormorant fishing masters – they use the Japanese Cormorant which has a black body with a white throat and a yellow beak – are nominally employed by the emperor and are called Imperial Fishermen of the Royal Household Agency. They take the birds out by boat on the river to fish.

As you might imagine, training the birds so that they are used to human contact can be a long and laborious business. First they have to be captured, often by luring them using decoy birds already domesticated and getting them to land on sticks smeared with sticky bird-lime.

Kept in cages, the birds are frequently massaged on their heads and bellies so that they get used to their keepers. They are fed with fish as the keepers gradually introduce the neck restraints. The whole process takes about three years. With cormorants possessing a pretty formidable beak to snatch and hold slippery fish, it doesn't sound like the kind of pursuit for the nervous.

On Lake Lashihai, Chinese fishermen have an equally close relationship with cormorants they have partly domesticated. It's one of the few surviving examples of a practice that is known to date from the Sung dynasty (960–1279).

The fishermen fit rings, rather than ties, around the necks of the birds so they can't swallow the fish they catch. Then they row their boats out into the lake, with the cormorants lined up meekly along the sides, and release them to swim and dive. When a cormorant catches a fish it's trained to return to the boat to disgorge its trophy, then dive again.

When the fishermen call it a day, they remove the rings, allowing the birds to swallow any more fish they catch. Both return to shore well fed, the cormorants standing in the boats holding their wings out to dry like crucifixes drifting across the water. It's an enigmatic sight, especially as darkness looms over the waters.

These days, in Britain especially, fishermen see nothing useful in a cormorant. Quite the opposite! Most fishermen see them as public enemy number one because of the competition they provide for fish. Conservationists sometimes pose a question about which of them was first on a river!

In some parts of the world, though, domestication has advanced far, far less than it has in western developed countries. In the central highlands of Papua New Guinea, cassowaries (there are three different species) – large dark ground birds over a metre tall with colourful necks – are hunted by Huli Wigmen and other tribes. The Wigmen, as their name suggests, are famed for their great, flower-decked wigs of human hair worn by the adult men.

If the Huli kill a hen cassowary, her young are often taken alive and reared by tribespeople. An orphaned chick becomes imprinted on its new 'parent' and doesn't leave them. The bonding works both ways and the adoptive parent cares for the growing bird, finding large amounts of fruit and small animals to feed it. It's pretty much a full-time job. Cassowaries get through a lot of food!

But cassowaries are aggressive birds. Full grown, they are large and very sturdy. And they are equipped with a formidably big and strong claw on the central toe of each foot. With it they disembowel small animals to eat! And a grown cassowary regards any human other than its 'parent' as a threat. The bird has to be penned most of the time and the day will come when it's ceremoniously killed and eaten.

Similar imprinting on humans is the basis of a parallel relationship between ducks – very much less frightening than a full-grown cassowary – and people on a scatter of Indonesian islands. From an early age, ducklings are fed next to something very visible like a stick with a white flag on it. Soon, they go en masse wherever the white flag is taken, to feed on spilt grain in a paddyfield maybe. It's called 'imprinting'. When they are sufficiently well fed the growing ducks can be killed for food.

Ducks are driven in flocks to the rice paddies where they feed on all sorts of small water animals. Their guardian is a boy or an old man who leads them with the little banner of white cloth on its stick. This he plants in the ground and he can then go away for the rest of the day, confident that his ducks will not wander off.

At sundown the trained ducks gather around the flag waiting to be taken home. When the duck-guardian arrives, the flock is all together, and at a signal from the flag, they march home, straight as penguins and in perfect military formation.

These are examples of a simpler relationship between domesticated forms of what were wild birds and the people who ultimately exploit them for food. It's a kinder life for the birds in which they are allowed to show their normal behaviours and it must suggest that this was an earlier form of domestication that we in the west have long surrendered to the expediency of fast food and cheapness.

Ironically, in western societies, we have for a long time lavished enormous amounts of care, attention and expense on our domesticated pets, a level of regard that would astonish most people in the developing world. Yet only in recent years have we begun to pay more than scant regard to how the domesticated animals that supply us with food, which are sometimes treated more akin to machines than living creatures, are cared for. Perhaps in striving for less intensive forms of bird (and other animal) rearing – and much more free range and organically raised birds – we are turning the clock back at least a little. Many would claim that it's for the better.

Domesticating wild birds to breed varieties capable of providing large amounts of meat, eggs and sometimes other products has benefitted mankind enormously by producing guaranteed year-round supplies of plentiful, healthy, nutritious and often cheap food.

But it runs enormous risks. And those risks have really hit home in the last few years as the fear of bird flu has spread amongst domesticated flocks and – on thankfully rare occasions – infected (and sometimes even killed) people in close contact with them. If this or a similar virus was to become more commonplace in human hosts, the consequences could be horrendous.

In the ramshackle Romanian village of Ceamurlia de Jos, a community of more than 1,200 people just inland from the western shore of the Black Sea and part of the delta of the majestic River

Danube, every other household has always kept a few hens for their eggs and meat. A lot of people keep a few ducks too. It has been this way in the village since time immemorial.

A few farmers around the village have much more intensive poultry rearing units holding thousands of chickens, some for eggs and others for meat. It has become a profitable business in a desperately poor part of Europe.

Then, on 7 October 2005, bird flu arrived in Ceamurlia de Jos, apparently carried by wild birds migrating from the tundra of northern Asia (where they nested) via western China and the Black Sea coast on their way south to Africa for some winter warmth.

In the Danube delta, a European birdwatching hotspot, hundreds of thousands of migrating ducks, geese, swans, herons, egrets and a plethora of smaller birds hunker down for a few days or weeks of frenzied feeding amongst its huge areas of marsh, reedbeds and damp meadows. They're doing it to get their strength and energy back for the next leg of their exhausting flight.

But some of them, wild swans or ducks perhaps, might have noticed a readily available food supply too good to miss after a long, energy-sapping flight: grain scattered around farmsteads for outdoor-reared, domesticated hens and ducks.

And if one or two of these hungry wild birds were infected with the H5N1 strain of the influenza virus – bird flu – might they have contaminated the feed and passed the deadly disease on to the nearby poultry? No one is really sure.

However it arrived, Ceamurlia de Jos was suddenly transformed. Any vehicle on every road to the village had to drive through a disinfectant bath. Men clad in protective suits with breathing masks sprayed disinfectant in every poultry house and barn while others had the gruesome task of killing and incinerating thousands of chickens. Nearly 19,000 domesticated poultry were killed in the village.

The villagers were in a state of despair. Local poultry farmers saw their livelihood dying before their very eyes. Kate Connolly, reporting locally for the Australian newspaper *The Age*, wrote on 17 October:

> The policemen given the task of culling the village's entire poultry population ... looked drained as firemen hosed them down following the morning shift. Eighty men had managed to round up 6,000 birds which they placed in green wheelie-bins into which a gas pipe was inserted.
>
> As carbon monoxide was pumped in, the birds were heard flapping and squawking inside. After five minutes they were still. The operation was watched over by police who stood guard with assault rifles and stun grenades lest any locals tried to sabotage the cull.
>
> At first many villagers tried to prevent their birds being seized. Some hid them in wardrobes or fireplaces. Others killed their stock and as most of Ceamurlia's residents do not own refrigerators, placed them in buckets of salted water in the hope that they could preserve them into the winter. But by yesterday they were fully aware of the dangers. Villagers, many of whom initially insisted that their homemade plum brandy was enough to keep the virus at bay, have since received flu jabs.

Little more than a month later the quarantine restrictions were lifted and the poultry-keepers have since been compensated. So far, their newly introduced poultry are disease-free. And, happily, no one died of bird flu in Ceamurlia de Jos.

Bird flu isn't new. It was first recorded in Italy around 1878 and was at that time known as fowl plague. There have been several outbreaks over the years and in many countries worldwide. When a few chickens were kept as a bit of an add-on extra in a mixed farm, its impact was not that great.

Today, though, with millions of chickens and other poultry often kept closely confined – heaven-sent conditions for a contagious disease like flu to spread – its impact can be devastating.

In 2003, more than 28 million poultry were slaughtered in Belgium, the Netherlands and Germany because of an outbreak, a strategy that, combined with putting a protective cordon around the disease area, is designed to prevent its further spread.

Infected birds usually have a lack of appetite, respiratory symptoms and diarrhoea although some may show few symptoms. Only some of them are killed by the virus.

The outbreak in which the particularly virulent bird flu strain H5N1 was identified started in Southeast Asia in 2003, and more than 200 million poultry have been killed to try to bring it under control. From there it spread west through much of Europe and Africa. In all, according to the United Nation's Food and Agriculture Organization (FAO), 62 countries have experienced outbreaks.

It remains most active in Bangladesh, China, Egypt, Indonesia and Vietnam, although the number of outbreaks has been declining. According to data compiled by FAO, 11 outbreaks were reported worldwide in June 2008 in five countries compared with 65 in June 2006 and 55 in June 2007, though under-reporting by some countries is likely.

Up to mid 2009, according to FAO data, worldwide a total of 262 people had died of bird flu out of 436 contracting it, a staggering 60 per cent mortality rate. The most deaths, in declining order, have been in Indonesia, Vietnam, Egypt and China.

Almost all of them were farm workers or others in close contact with the poultry but, so far at least, the disease has not swept into the general population in the pandemic that some experts predicted. The huge worry is that the virus mutates into a form that then efficiently transmits from person to person … and retains its virulence. Considering that less than half of those people contracting H5N1 survived, the impact of this could be catastrophic. Some leading experts have put the death toll into the hundreds of millions. Not surprisingly, huge amounts of money are being invested in learning more about this flu virus and in developing a vaccine to protect people against it.

Apart from other poultry, wild birds seem to be the major source of the disease in poultry. Migrating waterfowl such as ducks, geese and swans do carry the flu virus, often without becoming sick themselves. One of the most obvious places for interchange between domesticated ducks and waterfowl is at the extensive rice paddyfields of Southeast Asia where most of the H5N1 outbreaks have been (and still are). Spreading poultry manure as fertiliser, or water runoff from infected farms into wetlands and other wild bird habitat, can all help this extremely nasty virus to get around.

And it seems that a wide variety of other birds can get infected too, opening up the spectre that the international trade in wild birds, both legal and illegal, could help the disease spread. For a time, international racing pigeon events were banned but tests showed that pigeons didn't carry the virus and the restrictions were lifted.

Britain hasn't been immune. H5N1 has appeared in the UK, both in wild birds and in a very few poultry farms, most notably one belonging to the Bernard Matthews company in Suffolk in 2007. In that outbreak, 160,000 turkeys were killed to contain it. According to Defra the source was likely to have been turkey meat imported from Hungary; the company had previously been warned about hygiene lapses on its premises.

Since November 2008 the UK has been declared officially free of bird flu and trade in poultry with other EU countries began again in July of that year.

It isn't the domestication of birds that's caused disease – it's just that large numbers of domesticated birds kept in close proximity can spread an infection amongst themselves so easily if they get one. Nevertheless, the enormous benefits that mankind has gained from domesticating a wide range of birds far outweigh the downsides. And it's not only food – from wild-caught or domesticated birds – we obtain. We get many other products and services from them too, and that is the subject of the next chapter.

4

A softer life

Since time immemorial, we have used birds to help keep us warm, to help us communicate with each other and to protect us from harm. Without them, too, some of our sporting activities would be impossible.

I'm sitting in an isolated, pine-clad house on tiny Hvallatur Island in Breidafjordur Bay off the west coast of Iceland watching dainty Black Guillemots as they swim on the shallow sea outside and meander between olive-green and tan-coloured mats of seaweed.

A myriad of other tiny rocky islets dominate the tranquil scene while looming in the distance are the snow-covered peaks of the mountains on the mainland that surrounds this huge bay on three sides. Altogether there are perhaps 2,500 islands and rocky islets out here, so many it's impossible to count them.

It's June, midsummer, and the light fades only a little through the night but an icy breeze still pervades the clear air. Aside from the ebony and white Black Guillemots with their persistent, high-pitched whistles, there are speckled brown wading birds with scarlet beaks and legs – Common Redshank – breeding here on the grassy island knolls. Birds' calls that persist all day seem to fill the sharp night air too. It's as if the round-the-clock northern daylight never allows them to sleep.

But it's not these birds that I've come all this way to see or listen to, nor even the huge white-tailed Eagles that sometimes hunt here for fish in these wildlife-rich coastal waters.

Scattered about in the foaming sea shallows between the kelp-clothed islets and rocks are some large white, green and black ducks, some of them making a far-carrying crooning call to their plainer, speckled brown females. Common Eider ducks. And it's these attractive ducks, abundant all around Iceland's coast, that have brought me to this idyllic spot.

For here it is that eiderdown got its name. Every year, around three to four tonnes of incredibly lightweight, brown-coloured and highly insulating feather down is taken from eider nests without harming the birds or affecting the hatching of their eggs.

More than 400 Icelanders, mainly landowners, are registered as eiderdown collectors, some with a few nests and others with more than 2,000. Even Iceland's president, Ólafur Ragnar Grímsson, has a colony at his farm home on a headland on the west coast near Reykjavik.

It's an industry that's been active since Iceland was first settled in the 9th century. And it's a rare example of sustainable exploitation from which the collectors gain financially, the birds are protected and might even be increasing in number, and those affluent consumers who can afford the incredibly expensive but highly insulating duvets that are the end product keep very much warmer at night.

Before the Russian Revolution in 1917, Imperial Russia was the main eiderdown supplier in the world. The Russian Orthodox Church owned some eider colonies near the White Sea and had monks gather and process the down and make comforters for the high clergy. In the 20th century, the USSR even used eiderdown inside astronauts' suits. Today, though, Iceland provides at least 70 per cent of eiderdown worldwide.

'It takes the down from about 65 nests to produce a kilo of finally cleaned and sterilised down', says Thorvaldur Björnsson who, with six friends and family members, owns 200–300 tiny islands out here including the home island, Hvallatur. This is their summer base where they have renovated a substantial house, the only habitation. All of them have other full-time jobs. And I'm spending a couple of days with them to see first-hand how the down is gathered from these exquisite wild ducks.

'We've been collecting eiderdown since 1992, the year after we bought the islands. We're here for about three weeks in June collecting and previous owners probably did the same every summer, right back to the 1700s or before. We have five inflatable boats so we can split into small groups to get to the different islands', comments Thorvaldur.

The small, fine down feathers that insulate a bird's body and form a layer underneath the visible outer feathers come loose on the female eider's chest at breeding time. Watching female eiders walking on some of the islets, you can see a few loose down feathers poking out slightly on their breasts. The duck takes them off with her beak and lines the nest with thousands of them. Male eiders are notorious for their lack of contribution to the whole nest-building, egg incubation and chick rearing process. They simply chill out, relaxing in the shallow waters around the islands. An easy life if you can get it!

On a sunny, early June afternoon three of us – Thorvaldur, 16-year-old Fannar Mar Andresson and me – set off from Hvallatur at low tide and walk through the shallow water across barnacle-encrusted black rocks to nearby Trésey, a much smaller mound of an island, its slopes grassy and well grown enough to hide more eider nests than I would ever have guessed could be there.

Mottled brown and sitting tight on her four greenish eggs, the first female eider we encounter suddenly flies off with a clatter of her wings when we are no more than a couple of metres from her nest, a grassy scrape between some rocks but lined with a large bunch of tiny, incredibly soft brown feathers.

'We remove the eggs carefully, take out all the down, then replace the eggs after filling the nest with dry hay. We cut and dry the hay ourselves on the island. Studies done here have shown that the hay insulates the eggs just as well and the eggs hatch normally', says Thorvaldur.

Each nest we find, the female eider comes zooming off, glides down to the sea below to meet up with others, maybe her mate included, does a lot of dipping in the cool water presumably to wash, then waddles back to the nest just a few minutes after we have left it. Even in the chilly Icelandic air, the eggs barely have time to cool a little before she is brooding them again.

In two hours of searching Trésey we take a bunch of down from each of no fewer than 97 eider nests, more than a kilogram of the precious duvet filler.

With our harvest, Thorvaldur takes me to a small, stone-built hut back at Hvallatur. Warm air circulates from a diesel generator through wire mesh shelves piled with masses of earthy brown eiderdown.

Drying slowly, it has to be heat sterilised here after being put through a small shaking machine that separates out the pieces of grass that are always mixed with it in the nests. After that, a kilogram is sold for about £500 to dealers on the Icelandic mainland. They clean it up even further before it's sold on to the duvet makers.

In my hand, it's so light – lighter than a feather! – it's hard to realise I'm holding anything at all. Compress it and it springs back to its original volume time and time again. That's why an eider duvet is so insulating and retains its shape.

On the group's islands, there are about 3,800 pairs of these attractive ducks yielding 50–60 kg of down worth up to £30,000. With an estimated 230,000 pairs of Common Eiders breeding in the whole of Iceland – one of the largest populations in the world – and probably thousands of people collecting the valuable down, including many farmers on their own land, Iceland produces up to four tonnes a year.

Fuglavernd, the Icelandic Society for the Protection of Birds, has no concerns about down collecting.

'It is evident that harvesting eider duck down is not harmful for the ducks', comments Björk Þorleifsdóttir of the Society. 'It is very beneficial for them as the people take care of the colonies and try to create new ones and thus give the ducks all kinds of protection, especially against predators.'

Predators are a huge concern to the down collectors though. Thorvaldur and Fannar were constantly on the lookout for signs that ravens or gulls had taken the eggs from an eider nest after dislodging the reluctant duck or while she has left them for a short spell to go down to the sea shallows. We found several nests they said had been destroyed by one or the other.

On the mainland, escaped mink (once reared for their fur) now living wild are a major problem for many ground-nesting birds. The Icelandic government supports their trapping and shooting. Arctic foxes – common and natural predators on Iceland – take eggs and even the adult birds, and, more controversially, landowners often shoot them too, especially if the eiderdown cash crop is threatened.

Thankfully the islands are free of mink. There are no foxes out here either. And that's the way Thorvaldur Björnsson and his fellow down collectors want it to stay!

'Mink are under control in the northeast part of Iceland but not elsewhere', comments Helga Jóhannesdóttir of the Icelandic Farmers Association. 'Eider farmers can shoot foxes at any time if they threaten breeding birds or livestock. Some use electric fences to protect colonies on the mainland and others use sticks to protect the nests from predatory birds. Others broadcast radio music 24/7 because the foxes don't like the noise but the eiders don't seem to mind.'

'A farmer tries to attract eiders to his area, makes comfortable places for nesting and protects the area 24 hours a day. The eiders are clever and even though they come to the same nesting area every year, they move to the next area if the farmer there offers them better protection', adds Jóhannesdóttir. Whatever else, Iceland's eiders are doing very well out of this deal.

Fuglavernd, though, is not as sanguine about predator control.

'Most of it benefits the huge numbers of breeding birds we have in Iceland – all of which nest on the ground and are vulnerable – but we need to make sure that rare predators, such as the White-tailed Eagle, remains fully protected and no one starts to kill them. In any case, the eagles sometimes take mink so they are working with the eider farmers', comments Björk Þorleifsdóttir.

Common Eiders start nesting in late April or early May on Iceland and their four, five or even six eggs hatch after 28 days in June. Within 24 hours of hatching the tiny grey, down-covered chicks follow mother down to the nearest bit of sea where she teaches them to feed in the shallows and

to find mussels, crabs and other crustaceans. With more females bringing chicks onto the water, crèches develop with flotillas of chicks and adults, probably a precaution to protect their charges against attacks from hungry gulls on the lookout for a nutritious chick.

At Dún & Fidur, a shop specialising in eiderdown duvets and pillows on Reykjavik's Laugavegur shopping street, I meet the owner, Oli Ben, who has been running his business here since 1959. The eider duck down is the top of his extensive duvet range. I hesitate to ask about prices!

'A single size duvet filled with eiderdown is 269,800 ISK [about £1,300] and a double, 394,150 ISK [about £1,900]', says Oli. 'We mostly sell to Japanese, German or American tourists, but some Icelanders buy them too. They are incredibly lightweight and warm. They really are the best that money can buy', comments Oli. That is, if you can afford them!

Down is warmer than feather-filled duvets because the much smaller feathers trap more insulating air. Most down-filled duvets use down from domesticated birds, mostly geese and ducks killed for meat. Far cheaper because it's available in huge quantities, none of the common – but far, far cheaper – alternatives are as insulating as the real McCoy of course. But any feathers are much better than no feathers.

If birds' feathers are so good at keeping us warm at night, why not wear clothes stuffed with them? Before modern lightweight and highly insulating materials were manufactured, many people living in and near the Arctic certainly did.

In Alaska, for instance, warm parka jackets were made from the skins of different seabirds, sewn carefully together with the insulating feathers, of course, on the inside. Crested Auklets and Parakeet Auklets were often used, two common Arctic seabirds related to puffins, though sometimes others such as cormorants or Long-tailed Ducks were used. The birds would have been caught in long-handled nets as they flew into their nesting spots, then killed, skinned and the feather-covered skins washed and dried outdoors. They were usually worn underneath an outer parka made of sealskin to provide waterproofing.

According to the British Museum, which has a late 19th century bird-skin parka from Greenland in their collection, they were lightweight, warm and waterproof but they did tear easily and the feathers started to fall off with age. Presumably they retained a fishy or oily smell, not something that most people today would endure.

The Ainu, an ethnic group nowadays few in number, living in northern Japan and in the very far north of parts of Russia where winters are severe, also used bird-skin clothes in the past. But theirs were more often made of gull or cormorant skins.

In the south of New Zealand where conditions never become as cold, kiwi feather cloaks were sometimes worn by Maoris, but apparently only from the second half of the 19th century. Chicken-sized, flightless, shy, nocturnal birds with long, shaggy brown feathers, all of them are today endangered. By the 1880s the kiwi cloaks, often with more colourful feathers from other birds interwoven, had become prestige garments, though possibly more for fashion – and certainly for festive occasions – than warmth!

Some of this feather collecting has, in the past, been extremely destructive. The island of Torishima, one of the Izu Islands south of Japan, had large numbers of Short-tailed Albatrosses, a large white seabird with black wing patches, breeding there in 1887 when a settlement was first established. The Japanese settlers set up a trade in their feathers and killed an estimated 5 million of them in 17 years. Volcanoes, and laws to ban the slaughter, eventually stopped the trade but, by 1939, only about 40 albatrosses survived.

Today the colonies are protected and there are more than 2,000 pairs. But albatrosses, though long-lived (if they are left alone!), are slow breeders. Combined with the threat of volcanoes, introduced predators, and fishing boats in the sea around taking much of the available fish, are thought to be limiting their recovery.

Not only feathers in quantity but individual feathers, too, have long been of considerable use to people. Arguably their most destructive use was as a key part of one of the most infamous and feared weapons of war – the longbow with its feather-fletched arrows – that held supreme on many a battlefield for several hundred years (see Chapter 5).

Many arrows used in sports archery today are still fletched with feathers though some now use plastic fletching instead. When natural feather fletching is used it is critical that all the feathers come from the same side of the bird so that they are similarly shaped. Goose feathers are the normal source.

The discovery of the first stone arrowheads in Africa tends to indicate that the bow and arrow was invented there for hunting, perhaps as early as 50,000 BC though no one knows whether feathers were used to fletch the arrows. No wooden or animal parts have survived! But archaeologists have evidence that between 25,000 BC and 18,000 BC feathers were glued and tied with sinew to the arrow shafts.

Exquisite rock drawings on cave walls in the Sahara certainly show hunters with bows and quivers of feather-fletched arrows. They date from about 7500 BC.

In September 1991, an incredible discovery was made of the frozen body of a man exposed by melted ice high in the Alps near the Italian/Austrian border. Tests revealed that 'Oetzi' – as he was named – was a hunter. He was 45 years old and died around 3300 BC, presumably while he was out hunting because he was carrying a bow plus a leather quiver containing 14 arrows, the quiver complete with a flap to keep the arrow feathers dry.

Hunters in some tribal societies still use bows and arrows to kill birds and other animals for food but today most feather-fletched arrows are used in sport archery.

Another sport commonly uses feathers too – badminton. It's played with racquets and a shuttlecock which is made from plastic or formed from 16 overlapping goose feathers embedded into a rounded cork base. The 'shuttle' part of the name was probably derived from its back-and-forth motion during the game, resembling the shuttle of a loom; the 'cock' part of the name probably from the resemblance of the feathers to those on a cockerel.

The cost of good quality feather shuttlecocks is similar to that of good quality plastic ones but plastics are far more durable, typically lasting many matches without any impairment to their flight. For this reason, many clubs prefer to play with plastic shuttlecocks. Most experienced and skilled players, though, greatly prefer feathers, and serious tournaments or leagues are almost always played using feather shuttlecocks. In Asia, where feather shuttlecocks are apparently more affordable than

in Europe and North America, plastic shuttlecocks are hardly ever used and all senior international tournaments use only feather shuttlecocks of the highest quality.

It might seem very dated now, but for many hundreds of years feather quill pens were the most common writing instrument in the world. After the fall of the Roman Empire, monks throughout Europe needed to produce copies of the Christian Church's religious documents. Printing had not been invented so the work had to be performed by hand. Reeds, cut carefully to form a nib at the business end, had been in use in other parts of the world but the monks took a liking to the quill of a goose feather and learnt to split and shape its hollow end. It was a better writing and drawing tool.

The hollow quill held the ink and the split end was the nib, different writing pressure giving thick and thin strokes. The writing life of the quills was extremely short and they needed constant re-trimming. A sharpening tool was soon developed … and the penknife was born! They also had to be dipped in ink after every few words because they held so little. Each bird – usually geese but sometimes swans and turkeys – supplied only 10–12 good quills from their wings. After the quills had been plucked and sorted, they were usually buried in hot sand to dry and harden them.

The word 'pen' itself is derived from the Latin 'penna' for feather, and the French 'nom-de-plume' – for pen name – has a similar origin.

There is a specific reference to a quill pen in the 7th century writings of the Spanish theologian St Isidore of Seville in Spain, but pens fabricated from bird feathers probably date from much earlier. Quill pens were the writing instrument from 600 to 1800 and were of such importance that it is said that geese were specially bred by US president Thomas Jefferson (1743–1826) to supply his own vast need for quills. At one point Russia was selling 27 million quills a year to the UK.

Writing with quill pens changed little until the mid 19th century when metal pens and pen nibs took over, although metal pens had been used in some places considerably earlier. In the 16th century wealthy people had gold- and silver-nibbed pens, often giving them as gifts, but it is uncertain if these were truly writing pens. In any case, the vast mass of people couldn't possibly afford them and relied on the cheap and cheerful quill.

By 1850 quill pen usage was fading and the quality of steel nibs had been improved by tipping them with hard metals. It wasn't long before the modern ballpoint pen, invented in the late 1930s by László Bíró, a Hungarian newspaper editor who was frustrated by the amount of time that he wasted filling up fountain pens and cleaning up smudged pages, stole the whole market until that now old-fashioned contraption called a typewriter became commonplace.

Goose quills were always cheaper and preferred by many people who found swans' quills too stiff to write with easily. However, according to the Vintners' Company (who have owned many Mute Swans on part of the River Thames in London since the Middle Ages), one swan's quill was supposed to last as long as 50 goose quills. Apparently, quills invariably had their feathers trimmed well back to make writing easier so it's a common mistake in historical dramas to see someone supposedly writing with a fully feathered quill.

At the Abbotsbury Swannery near Weymouth in Dorset, Mute Swans have been protected since Benedictine monks managed it as a ready source of meat in the 11th century. From the 16th century on, it's been in the same family ownership through 15 generations.

'The number of swans here is between six and 800 and we collect the large wing feathers when they moult in midsummer', says Dave Wheeler, known as The Swanherd, at the Swannery.

'We sell them for about 30 pence each, as many as we can collect. Some we sell to a fine art brush maker who uses them for the small shaft of his special brushes. Bee-keepers often buy them for sweeping bees off the honeycomb and clock repairers use them too. And we sell some to calligraphers for their very special writing; they cure them in hot sand and cut the nib to shape. They usually want swan quills from the left wing because most people are right handed. Lloyds of London used to buy some too because it's a tradition there to enter details of ships lost at sea in the official record using ink and a quill. But they haven't bought any for a while. Perhaps not as many ships are going down these days! That's good, but not for our business', he adds.

Quill pens have some ceremonial uses too. According to the US Supreme Court Historical Society, 20 goose-quill pens, neatly crossed, are placed at the four counsel tables each day the Supreme Court is in session. Most lawyers appear before the court only once, and gladly take the quills home as souvenirs.

But if quill pens made from feathers seem at least a little outmoded, using feathers to make an angling lure – an object attached to the end of a fishing line and designed to resemble and move like an item of fish prey, thereby attracting the fish onto the hook – is certainly not.

They can be made out of a huge range of different materials but birds' feathers – often those of pheasants because they are colourful – are frequently employed to make the more specialised artificial fly lures designed for use in fly fishing.

The idea in fly fishing, an art form in itself, is that the artificial fly imitates a particular form of fish prey when cast onto the water surface or into the water. As aquatic insects such as mayflies, caddisflies and stoneflies were the primary prey being imitated during the early developmental years of fly fishing, there were always differing schools of thought on how closely a fly needed to imitate the fish's prey. Today, a huge range of artificial fly patterns are produced commercially though many fly fishermen still make their own.

Particular feathers, from particular birds, have been put to some even more unusual tasks. The so-called 'pin feather', a short, very pointed feather found near the main flight feathers on the wing of a woodcock (now called the Eurasian Woodcock) – a snipe relative found, not surprisingly, in woods – has been used to paint accurate fine lines. The gold line down the side of a Rolls-Royce car, details on small model soldiers, and lines along bicycle frames are a few examples.

Other parts of birds have long been exploited too – like their fat for instance! Anyone who's cooked a chicken, turkey, duck or, most fatty of all, a goose will notice that a fair amount of fat comes out of them as they cook. Goose grease used to be popular, often mixed with other ingredients, as a skin treatment, a sandwich filler and, especially, for rubbing into the chest of a child with respiratory infections – not that many would perhaps tolerate it today! Goose grease used to be applied to leather to soften it, just as it softens blistered skin too.

Seabirds also contain quantities of fat stored in their bodies – it helps keep them warm – a fact not lost on seamen and anyone stranded on islands. When the birds were cooked for food their oil was often collected and used to run lamps for lighting or to fuel fires for cooking and heating. Many different species were harvested, particularly at huge nesting colonies on islands, and the slaughter was often on a massive scale.

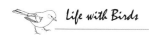

Penguins were important sources. In the Falkland Islands in the South Atlantic, hundreds of thousands of them were harvested each year into the 19th century for their oil alone. The fat of 11 birds apparently provided about one gallon of oil, and each schooner or gang of men would return, after a month or six weeks of killing, with 25,000–30,000 gallons of oil. Much of it went by ship to London, used mainly for treating leather. And many species of penguin went into obvious decline.

Oil wasn't only obtained from seabirds. The nestlings of the nocturnal reddish-brown Oilbird, related to nightjars and found mainly in parts of South America where they eat only fruit and sleep the day in caves, have a particularly high oil content and used to be harvested to make torches.

Native American Indians used to preserve the oil or fat from Passenger Pigeons they had killed which they used instead of butter. Supposedly there was formerly scarcely any Indian village in the interior where a hundred gallons of this oil might not at any time be purchased. The squabs, or young pigeons, when taken in quantity, were also melted down by white settlers as a substitute for butter or lard, a trade that ceased when these abundant birds were driven to extinction because such vast numbers were killed for food (see Chapter 1).

A P.L. Simmonds writing in *The American Journal of Pharmacy* in 1871 comments on some unexpected sources:

> Ostrich fat has much local repute. The first care of the sportsman after securing his bird, is to remove the skin, so as to preserve the feathers uninjured; the next is to melt down the fat and pour it into bags formed out of the skin of the thigh and leg, strongly tied at the lower end. The grease of an ostrich in good condition fills both its legs, and as it brings three times the price of common butter, it is considered no despicable part of the game. It is not only eaten with bread and used in the preparation of couscous and other articles of food, but the Arabs reckon it a valuable remedy in various maladies. In rheumatic attacks, for instance, they rub it on the part affected till it penetrates thoroughly; then lay the patient in the burning sand, with his head carefully protected. A profuse perspiration comes on, and the cure is complete. In bilious disorders, the grease is slightly warmed, mixed with salt and administered as a potion.
>
> The grease of the emu is held in great esteem by both colonists and natives as a cure of bruises and rheumatism. The skin of the bird produces six or seven quarts of a clear, beautiful, bright yellow inodorous oil. The method of obtaining the oil is to pluck the feathers, cut the skin into pieces and boil it.

Every time we tuck into a whole chicken, turkey or other large bird, at Christmas or Thanksgiving for instance, most of us throw its bones away! In supposedly less well-developed societies, such a throwaway mentality is largely unknown. New Guinea tribes, for instance, when they eat a cassowary they have killed or raised from a chick, use its feathers, keep its sharp claws for making arrows and carve daggers and other tools out of its leg bones!

Most birds' nests have never been much use to us, except the edible nests of swiftlets found in Southeast Asia (see Chapter 1). After all, a rather random, and presumably uncomfortable, collection of sticks typical of most crows is not something anyone can make much use of. But the softer mix of expertly woven grasses, moss and horsehair constructed by some small birds is a better bet. Indeed, such nests built by tiny Penduline Tits in central Europe (named as such because their nests hang from a tree branch) were once used as slippers for small children!

Then there's pigeon post. Not some wisecrack about the speed, or otherwise, of mail delivery but a message written on thin, light paper such as cigarette paper and rolled into a small tube attached to the bird's leg. And because homing pigeons (a variety of domesticated rock doves) have been bred over centuries to enhance their innate ability to find their way home, and rapidly because they are fast fliers, they were used until very recently to send messages – usually at times of war – over long distances.

As a method of communication, pigeon post is likely to be as old as the ancient Persians (around 500 BC) from whom the art of training the birds probably came. The Romans used pigeon messengers to aid their military more than 2,000 years ago; Frontinus, one of the most distinguished Roman aristocrats of the late 1st century AD, said that Julius Caesar used pigeons as messengers in his conquest of Gaul (modern-day France and Belgium).

Flights as long as 1,800 km have been recorded by birds in competition pigeon racing (see Chapter 2). Their average flying speed over moderate distances is around 48 km/hour (30 mph), but they can achieve bursts of speed up to about 95 km/hour (59 mph). So in the days before telephones and even the telegraph, when a horse and rider could average maybe 6 km/hour after allowing for rests and obstacles like rivers, a pigeon could transport news extremely quickly.

Reputedly, Noah's dove flew over the horizon away from the biblical ark to find land and returned after it had found an olive tree. Pliny the Younger, writing in the 1st century AD, recorded that Brutus, besieged by Mark Antony in the city of Modena in northern Italy during 44–43 BC, still managed to communicate with his allies by tying his dispatches to the feet of pigeons. What use to Mark Antony, Pliny wryly noted, were his rampart and watchful besieging force, and even the barriers of nets that he stretched in the river, when the message went by air?

Athletes at the first Olympics in 776 BC carried with them pigeons from their home villages to the Games. If they won, they would tie a strand of the finish line to the bird's foot, its arrival home signifying the local athlete's victory. Even today, the release of pigeons or doves (doves are generally small pigeons but otherwise there's no distinction) is still a part of the opening Olympic ceremony, though it isn't these days as spectacular as much of the other showbiz hype that accompanies the formal Games' openings.

In 1860, Paul Reuter, who later founded the Reuters press agency, used a fleet of more than 45 pigeons to deliver news and stock prices between Brussels and Aachen before the two then financial centres were connected by telegraph.

Pigeons were often used on a grand scale to sneak messages out of battlefields or from cities during sieges. They were used as messengers throughout World War I and to a much lesser extent in World War II as well (see Chapter 5).

After pigeon post between military fortresses had been thoroughly tested, attention was turned to using the birds for sending messages to ships in nearby waters. It was also used by news agencies and private individuals at various times, while governments in several countries established pigeon lofts of their own.

Laws were passed making the destruction of such pigeons a serious offence; payments were made to private pigeon societies, and rewards given for the destruction of birds of prey. Before the advent of radio, pigeons were used by newspapers to report yacht races, and some yachts were actually fitted with their own pigeon lofts.

Possibly the first regular airmail service in the world, begun in 1896, was Mr Howie's Pigeon-Post Service from the Auckland, New Zealand suburb of Newton to Great Barrier Island, a distance

of about 100 km. Certainly the world's first 'airmail' stamps were issued for the Great Barrier Pigeon-Gram Service from 1898 to 1908.

Homing pigeons were still employed until recently by certain remote police departments; for example, India's Police Pigeon Service in Orissa State in eastern India provided emergency communication services following natural disasters. The birds were finally 'retired' in 2002 because of the internet.

Not that modern communication is always better than pigeon post! In 2009, a South Africa IT company pitted an 11-month-old pigeon armed with a 4 GB memory stick against the ADSL service from the country's biggest web firm, Telkom. Winston the pigeon took two hours to carry the data 97 km (60 miles); in the same time the ADSL had sent 4 per cent of the data.

The idea for the race came when a member of staff at Durban-based Unlimited IT complained about the speed of data transmission on ADSL. He said it would be faster by carrier pigeon. 'We renown ourselves for being innovative, so we decided to test that statement', Unlimited's Kevin Rolfe told South Africa's *Beeld* newspaper.

With training, pigeons can carry up to 75 g on their backs. In 1977 a carrier pigeon service was set up for the transport of blood samples from outlying hospitals to a central NHS laboratory in Plymouth in southwest England. Carrier pouches made of soft leather were specially designed for the job. Trials began and the service proved faster and cheaper than hiring taxis. So a loft was built and a stock of carrier pigeons installed. In its first year it saved about £26,000. The service was stopped in the early 1980s when several of the hospitals were closed. With the need to cut energy consumption and lead more sustainable lifestyles, perhaps the NHS could investigate pigeon post again!

Rather more bizarrely, Canada's *Globe and Mail* ran a story in March 2009 about pigeons flying in and out of a prison in Marilia, Brazil of which the guards took no notice until they spotted some of them struggling a little as they flew. Guards caught a few of the stragglers and discovered what was slowing them down. The birds were drug runners – smuggling narcotics and cell phones in little pouches!

But it isn't only pigeons which have been used to carry – or convey – messages. The huge, narrow-winged, mainly black-coloured Great Frigate Bird, a sea-going giant, was used in the past to carry messages between Pacific Islands. Swallows too were used to carry messages. Pliny the Elder, who was an author and naturalist as well as a military commander, wrote at some point in his life:

> One Roman gentleman who was particularly fond of chariot racing would catch swallows from a nest at his country home and take them to the races in Rome. To give his friends advance results, he would paint the birds with the colour of the winning team and release them to fly back to their nest. Swallows were excellent carriers as their speed meant they were rarely caught by predators.

Birds like ravens – presumably because they breed inland – have in the past been used by mariners to sight shore. They were released when land was thought to be near but couldn't be seen; if the bird flew off, it confirmed its existence. And its direction too!

Birds have also, very occasionally, been used to warn of the presence of intruders – or to see them off! An aggressive male goose – a gander – can apparently be more fearsome than many a guard dog. The Crested Roman Goose, a domesticated variety of great antiquity, reputedly saved Rome from invasion by the Gauls in 390 BC by cackling and alerting the city's inhabitants. Today, many farms keep a few geese, including an aggressive gander, to warn intruders off … or at least to alert the owners to their presence.

Message-carrying by birds has most certainly saved lives. But there is one bird in particular that has been used in a very different way as a lifesaver. And that bird occurs naturally on just a few islands in the world.

With a warm breeze blowing gently across the sun-drenched, sparsely vegetated, arid landscape of Lanzarote, one of the Canary Islands off the northwest coast of Africa, I'm listening to a delightful twittering song that's ringing out from some telegraph wires on a quiet roadside. It's the song of a canary.

Birds native only in the Azores, here in the Canary Islands, and on Madeira, wild canaries – now called Island Canaries – are small finches, mostly yellow-green, with brownish streaking on the back. And it's because of that tinkling song that canaries have long been bred in captivity well away from their native islands and are popular cage birds the world over.

Much more importantly, however, that tinkling song has been a lifesaver. Deep underground in coalmines – an environment about as far removed from their wild island habitat as being on the moon – when the caged canary stopped moving around, miners knew that they were being warned that death might lurk close by.

The canary in the coalmine is arguably the first biological indicator used to monitor whether something's wrong with our environment – or, in their case, the potentially poisonous conditions of a coalmine where odourless carbon monoxide could be a killer. Canaries, like all small birds, are very sensitive to poisonous gas because they have a much faster heart rate than humans and they take about 200 breaths a minute. Any small bird would have done, but canaries were already common and easily bred cage birds.

It wasn't until 1986 that more than 200 canaries were out of a job in Britain's coalmines, replaced by more accurate electronic carbon monoxide detectors, as they have been around the world. It ended an era dating from 1911 since which date two lovingly looked-after caged canaries had been kept in each pit in case they were required in a rescue deep underground. Many of the miners treated them as pets. They weren't routinely taken down the mines but were kept for rescues where the risk of toxic gases was often a life-or-death issue.

'The Mines Rescue Service used to use them during rescues. Each rescue station would have between 10 and 20 canaries in addition to the two kept at each mine', says Mark Tibbott, Operations Manager (Wales) for the Mines Rescue Service Ltd who bred mine canaries in his back garden in the Rhondda Valley. 'The birds were well looked after and were only taken to what is called a fresh air base – this is the part of the mine from where the rescue officer and mine official would direct operations below ground. The rescue team would travel further into the mine using breathing apparatus.'

'They would detect carbon monoxide or oxygen deficiency faster than a human because of their small bodies and would scrape their beaks or sit on the floor of the cage. So the rescue officer would watch for that sort of behaviour indicating that the mine atmosphere was not safe for the rescuers to stay. The bird would then be put into a special cage fitted with an oxygen cylinder to supply fresh oxygen it. These birds would always be changed when a rescue team was changed over', adds Tibbott.

And although the miner's canary might be out of a job, a plethora of other birds are being used as modern-day indicators – not to indicate poisonous gases but to monitor the state of our natural environment much more comprehensively.

For instance, the UK government, with advice from its conservation agencies, has defined 18 biological indicators that are monitored regularly to see what's happening to our natural environment. They include a set of breeding farmland, woodland, water and wetland birds and seabirds (in total just over a hundred different species), data on which is amassed by a huge number of amateur volunteers coordinated by the highly professional British Trust for Ornithology.

From the 1970s up until 2007 (the most recent data), both farmland and woodland birds have been in decline in the UK. Numbers of farmland birds reached a low in the 1970s and 1980s as a result of EU and UK government funded intensive agriculture, when hedgerows were grubbed out, wetlands drained and crops lavishly sprayed with insecticides to increase production. Since then they have started to make only small gains as farming has become a little more environmentally friendly. Continuing to monitor their numbers will give us an indication of the health of a large part of our countryside.

So using birds as environmental monitors is not entirely new. Using birds in times of war, though, has a very much older provenance. Some battles would most certainly not have been won without them … and birds have been used in conflicts much more recently than you might guess, as the next chapter reveals.

5

Off to war

It might seem unlikely but birds have played a vital role in battles, sieges and all-out war.
Wars have even been fought because of them. And many battles would not have been
won without the crucial role played by their feathers.

Standing on an expanse of ploughed brown earth on a late October morning, elegant poplars lining the edges of the huge fields surrounding me, it's impossible to imagine now that tens of thousands of soldiers once lay where I stand, many dead, the others writhing in agony, their screams dulled only by the shouts of the oncoming enemy.

Where I stand in the Pas de Calais in northern France there were so many French dead, along with huge numbers of their horses, that they piled up in great mounds, so high it was almost impossible for those still alive to clamber over them.

To my left are the little scattered woodlands fringing tiny Tramecourt village. To my right is the village of Azincourt, itself fringed with trees. Today it's warm and sunny, the ground dry, very different from that late October morning in 1415 when the very same ploughed earth was sodden with rain and the day broke drizzly damp and dull.

But what has this, the horrendous medieval battle we know as Agincourt, to do with birds? Surprisingly, maybe, the answer is everything. For without them the English army led personally into battle by King Henry V could not have annihilated the elite of the French army that stood where I stand now.

For the English army consisted largely of English and Welsh archers. They carried the longbow, at that time a war weapon virtually confined to Britain. And the arrows that caused such mayhem in the French ranks, and won the day for King Henry, could not fly through the air unless they were fletched with feathers to stabilise their flight. Without feathers, arrows simply tumble out of the air uselessly.

On the morning of 25 October 1415 the bedraggled remnant of the English army, many of its men exhausted and suffering from dysentery, lined up a few hundred metres away from the French army on this very soil. About 6,000 English fighting men faced at least four times that number of Frenchmen, maybe six times as many. The accounts vary.

The French army was rested, well trained and well armed. Its commanders had chosen the site of battle. Everything was on their side to win the horrific exchange to come. But they had no longbow archers. Most of their fighting men were armoured, the knights of the day, the supposed elite of any medieval army.

Feathers, goose feathers the much preferred choice, were carefully cut and fixed onto wooden arrow shafts by highly skilled 'fletchers' who made the arrows. It was the fletchers, a surname still extremely common today, who were as important as the longbowmen and were paid the same.

Juliet Barker in her compelling account of the battle and the lead-up to it, *Agincourt* (Abacus, 2005), summarises the outcome:

> Some four hours later, in defiance of all logic and the received military wisdom of the time, the English were victorious and the fields of Agincourt were covered with what one observer graphically described as 'the masses, the mounds, and the heaps of the slain'. Perhaps most astonishing of all was the fact that virtually all the dead were French. Almost the whole nobility among the soldiery of France had been killed. The English had lost only two noblemen, a handful of men-at-arms [the armour-clad knights] and perhaps a hundred archers.

Barker, in her book, makes clear how vital the arrows and their fletchings were:

> Arrows were produced in sheaves of twenty four. Each archer was normally armed with between sixty and seventy two arrows, carrying two sheaves in his canvas quiver and the rest stuck in his belt, ready for immediate action. Additional supplies were carried on wagons and boys were employed to act as runners to bring more to the archers on demand … An archer who could not fire ten aimed arrows per minute was not considered fit for military service.
>
> Military arrows used flights made out of goose feathers which were fixed to the shaft with glue and bound in place with thread. At times of crisis the king would send an order out to the shires to provide goose feathers and, though no such order is extant for the Agincourt campaign, in December 1418 Henry V commanded his sheriffs to find him 1,190,000 by Michaelmas.

A military longbow needed enormous strength to draw its bowstring which was made of hemp or gut. Archery practice was compulsory for all able-bodied men between the ages of 16 and 60, leaving many bowmen with twisted spines and increased bone density in their over-developed shoulders, upper arms and elbows because of the physical effort involved. They probably endured awful pain if they lived as long as middle age!

According to an analysis by Gareth Rees in *Physics Review* in 1995, the 60 g arrow they used, fired from what were extremely powerful bows, would have an initial speed of about 216 km/hour (130 mph). Aimed high in the air to follow an arc rather than directly at any specific target, such an arrow would have a maximum range of 240 metres and it would rain down on its target with a speed of up to 162 km/hour (just over 100 mph).

Being on the receiving end must have been a terrifying experience! The English army's 5,000 archers were firing a fusillade every six seconds (contemporary accounts suggest that the arrows darkened the sky as they flew in an arc through the air). So in just one minute of continuous firing, these archers released volleys totalling about 50,000 arrows.

So what damage might such an arrow cause? Most of the French soldiers at whom these heavy war arrows were directed would have been wearing armour. At the time of Agincourt, a typical suit of armour was made of wrought iron which is rather soft. It is certainly a lot softer than steel. Its thickness varied according to the part of the body being protected, from 1 mm up to 4 mm. The armour couldn't be too thick because the weight would prevent the knight from moving. It already was – and would prove further to be – a bad enough impediment.

The arrows with their specially shaped and hardened iron heads would easily penetrate 1 mm of armour but the vital areas of the body would have been very unlikely to be hit. The effect of a massive hail of fast-moving heavy arrows, such as the French encountered at Agincourt, would probably have been to cause huge numbers of disabling injuries, but perhaps only one arrow in a hundred would have killed outright the man it struck. Injured, concussed by the impact and maybe fallen, these poor souls would probably have been trampled to death by their own men pushing forward or finished off with a blow from an English mallet or sword!

Henry's 5,000 archers at Agincourt had a stock of about 400,000 arrows. Each archer could shoot about ten arrows a minute so the army had enough ammunition for only about eight minutes of shooting at maximum firepower. But what devastation they caused.

'It was the equivalent of a Second World War machine gunner, so in modern terms we can imagine Agincourt as a battle between old-fashioned cavalry, supported by a few snipers [crossbowmen] on the French side, against a much smaller English army equipped with machine guns. Perhaps from this point of view the most remarkable fact about the battle is that the French ignored the very great military advantages of the longbow', writes Rees.

Agincourt was most definitely not the first military battle, nor the last, to be largely decided by the devastating impact of feather-fletched arrows. Graeme Jeffrey of the Centenary Archers Club in Ipswich, Queensland, Australia has compiled a comprehensive timeline of the use of bows and arrows through history.

While hunting bows have probably been employed as weapons of attack and defence between the hunters themselves since the bow and arrow was first invented (probably in Africa around 50,000 BC), one of the earliest recorded uses as a weapon of war that Jeffrey lists is in 5000 BC when the Egyptians used bows and arrows against the Persians.

The bow and arrow wasn't always a weapon used by soldiers on foot either. Many civilisations trained their archers to fire on horseback – some standing, others sitting – or from fast-moving, horse-pulled chariots. And today's archers think shooting at a fixed target while standing still is difficult!

Not that the archers always won. Jeffrey mentions the Battle of Marathon (near present-day Athens) in 490 BC when the Athenian infantry of 11,000 men with long spears, swords and armour defeated Persian archers after a rapid charge to avoid the shower of arrows. The Persian army of 15,000 men lost more than 6,000 of them while the Athenians reputedly lost only 192 men.

One of the most infamous uses of the bow and arrow in battle was in 1066 at the Battle of Hastings close to the south coast of England. Here King Harold II, the last Anglo-Saxon king of England, was defeated by the Norman invaders led by William the Conqueror.

Harold's army was lined up along a ridge to form a shield wall, a common battle tactic of its day, while he waited for more of his troops to arrive from an earlier battle against Vikings further north in England.

William's army had the disadvantage of attacking uphill. His archers tried shooting at the shield wall, but their arrows were stopped by the troops' shields or flew over their heads. So William changed tactics and ordered his archers to aim high and thus lob their arrows in an arc onto Harold's troops rather like the archers would do at Agincourt hundreds of years later. This rain of arrows decimated the English army and allowed the Norman foot soldiers to break through the shield wall.

Near the end of the exhausting nine-hour battle, legend – and some evidence – suggests that King Harold was killed by an arrow through the eye which resulted in victory for William. Other historians believe he was felled by a blow from a sword or by a sword following an arrow injury! Whichever, he had only been King of England from 5 January to that fateful day, 14 October.

According to Graeme Jeffrey, it was in 1333 at the Battle of Halidon Hill by Berwick-upon-Tweed on the English/Scottish border where the Scottish army was defeated by Edward III of England that the full potential of the English longbow in battle was first thoroughly demonstrated. Some 22,000 Scottish heavy cavalry were defeated by 2,000 English archers and 500 knights.

And just 13 years later at the Battle of Crécy south of Calais in northern France, Edward III led his army against the French in a battle that had the hallmarks of what was to come nearly 70 years later at Agincourt. Some accounts of the battle say the English archers had kept their flax bowstrings dry by putting them under their helmets because it had been raining the day before.

The French force of crossbowmen attacked from the front but, perhaps due to the rain, many misfired or their bowstrings snapped. The English archers showered them with arrows before they could reload. Most of the crossbowmen fled. The French cavalry then charged, but were decimated by the English archers. More than 1,500 French knights were killed that day but with only 50 English deaths.

Devotees of American Western films will be more than familiar with the bow and arrow used by many American Indian tribes, particularly those who hunted on the open plains where they fired from horseback, killing huge animals such as bison and elk for food.

Bows played an incredibly important role in the lives of Native Americans. Made entirely of wood, of wood and bone or of wood wrapped in sinew, they were protected and kept unstrung in a carrying case when they weren't being used.

Although hunting was the main purpose for the weapons they were also used in times of war. Indians were taught to use the bow at a young age and, because of this, Native Americans were extremely skilful. Ancient stories say that in war an Indian could shoot four or five arrows one after another before a man could reload his gun.

The fletching for the arrows was often made from the feathers of eagles, crows, geese and hawks, though it could also be from other birds found locally. But turkey feathers were the preferred choice. The feathers were sewn to, or inserted into, the arrow shaft and animal sinew was generally tied around them, tightening as it dried.

So birds' feathers, as an essential part of the structure of each and every arrow fired, have played an incredibly vital role in warfare for many thousands of years, reaching their zenith perhaps in the Middle Ages. As a weapon, frightening fusillades of longbow arrows were every bit as lethal as machine guns used in more recent wars.

On medieval battlefields such as Crécy, Agincourt and many other battle sites before, the piles of dead human bodies would have undoubtedly attracted numbers of crows and magpies, as well as other large birds such as Common Buzzards and Red Kites. Contemporary accounts of the Battle of Agincourt state that by the following day the dead bodies had all been stripped of every piece of armour and clothing by poor local people, so it was impossible to compile an accurate list of the dead. Most simply couldn't be identified!

It's about as gruesome as you can get but to the local carrion-eating birds, of course, this was like the promised land. So many dead bodies that there was far more 'carrion' than they could possibly eat. And this is almost certainly one of the reasons why many such birds, crows especially, are often considered an augury of death by the superstitious (see Chapter 12).

In warmer parts of the world wherever vultures occur, such quantities of human bodies left after battles would undoubtedly have attracted plenty of them too.

Not surprisingly, there are very few accounts of birds on battlefields while the actual fighting is taking place. It's easy to assume that most of them would be frightened well away by all the noise, explosions and activity. On the mud-churned, shellhole-pocked landscape of the World War I front lines, this must surely have been the case. But no.

Saki, the pen name of Hector Hugh Munro (1870–1916), the British writer whose witty and sometimes macabre stories satirised Edwardian society and culture, wrote an account from that Western Front where he had joined the Royal Fusiliers in spite of being overage. His account is published in *The Complete Saki* (Penguin, 1982):

> Considering the enormous economic dislocation which the war operations have caused in the regions where the campaign is raging, there seems to be very little corresponding disturbance in the bird life of the same districts.

He goes on to comment on the numbers of owls, especially Barn Owls, making 'laudable efforts to thin out' the huge numbers of mice and rats that proliferated in and around the trenches. The owls were seemingly nesting in damaged buildings and farms. Rooks, usually easily spooked by a few little bangs, apparently tolerated shell blasts nearby as they fed on village refuse heaps.

He spotted occasional partridges feeding on undamaged areas of croplands. Crows and magpies nested in what trees still stood or even in the shell-splintered trunks of poplars blasted away in the fighting, and he records watching a Sparrowhawk and crows having a squabble while four biplanes were engaged in battle not far above them. Although Common Buzzards seemed to have made a sharp exit, Common Kestrels were frequently hovering above the battlefield on the lookout for mice, even as shells landed!

> The skylark … has stuck tenaciously to the meadows and croplands that have been seamed and bisected with trenches and honeycombed with shell-holes. In the chill, misty hour of gloom that precedes a rainy dawn, when nothing seemed alive except a few wary waterlogged sentries and many scuttling rats, the lark would suddenly dash skyward and pour forth a song of ecstatic jubilation that sounded horribly forced and insincere. Once, having occasion to throw myself down with some abruptness on my face, I found myself nearly on the top of a brood of young larks.
>
> [...]
>
> At the corner of a stricken wood … at a moment when lyddite [a high explosive] and shrapnel and machine-gun fire swept and raked and bespattered that devoted spot … a wee hen chaffinch flitted wistfully to and fro, amid splintered and falling branches that had never a green bough left on them. The wounded lying there, if any of them noticed the small bird, may well have wondered why anything having wings and no pressing reason for remaining should have chosen to stay in such a place … There was sorry enough in that wood.

Saki was killed at Beaumont-Hamel, France in November 1916 by a German sniper as he took cover in a shell crater.

While birds' feathers have played a key role in killing very many thousands, probably millions, of people through the ages, one particular bird has played a completely peaceful, but absolutely vital, role at times of war. It's the humble pigeon. It has long been employed as a message carrier, exploiting the homing instinct that these instantly recognisable birds have by the bucketful.

One of the earliest accounts of their use is in AD 1150 when the Sultan of Baghdad strapped capsules filled with little papyrus sheets to the leg or back feathers of pigeons, and used them as messengers. Carrier pigeons were also used more than 3,000 years ago by the Egyptians, Persians and Romans.

The birds normally carried messages only one way, to their home. But, by placing their food at one location and their home at another, pigeons have been trained to fly back and forth up to twice a day, allowing them to cover 160 km in a round trip.

The outcome of the Battle of Waterloo in 1815 was first delivered by a pigeon to England, but arguably the most famous use of carrier pigeons in a war was during the Franco-Prussian War in 1870/71 when they were used to carry mail out of and into the French capital, Paris, during its four and a half month siege by the Prussian army.

As had been expected, the normal channels of postal and telegraph communication in and out of the city were interrupted during the siege. The city was encircled on 18 September 1870 and the last overhead telegraph wires cut the next morning; the secret telegraph cable in the bed of the Seine was located and cut on 27 September.

Although in the earliest days of the siege a number of postmen got through the Prussian lines, others were captured and shot, and there is no proof of any post reaching Paris from the outside, certainly after October, apart from private letters smuggled in. To be sure of getting messages into Paris, the only successful method was the time-honoured carrier pigeon. Reputedly about 150,000 official and 1 million private messages were taken into the besieged city this way, in spite of the Prussians deploying hawks to try to kill the pigeons in flight.

The French eventually surrendered, but not before they had been forced by near starvation to extend their well-known broad culinary interests to include dishes such as 'Epaules et filets de Chien braisés' (dog), 'Salamis de Rats, sauce Robert' (rats) and 'Plum-pudding au rhum et à la Moelle de Cheval' (horse). But there are no records of pigeon on restaurant menus of the time!

What homing pigeons achieved in Paris revived interest in the training of pigeons for military purposes. Numerous societies were established for keeping pigeons in several European countries and, in time, various governments established systems of communication by pigeon post for military purposes.

After pigeon post between military fortresses had been thoroughly tested, attention was turned to using the birds for sending messages to naval ships in nearby waters. Governments in several countries established lofts of their own and laws were passed making the destruction of such pigeons a serious offence; payments were made to private pigeon societies, and rewards given for the destruction of birds of prey.

Homing pigeons were used extensively during World War I, and by the end of the war France had mobilised 30,000 pigeons and declared that anyone impeding their flight could be sentenced to death. Carrier pigeons often flew in spite of clouds of poisonous gas and heavy shelling from the opposition.

One of their number, named Cher Ami, was awarded the French *Croix de Guerre* for his heroic service in delivering important messages despite injury and for saving the lives of the US 77th Infantry Division's 'lost battalion' at Verdun.

On 3 October 1918, US Major Whittlesey and more than 500 men of his battalion were trapped in a small depression on the side of a hill. They were surrounded by enemy soldiers, and on the first day many were killed and wounded. By the second day few more than 200 men were still alive or not wounded. The major sent out several pigeons to tell his commanders exactly where he was, and how bad the trap was. Seemingly, none got through.

During that afternoon the Americans tried to send some protection by firing hundreds of big artillery rounds into the ravine where the Germans surrounded Major Whittlesey and his men. Unfortunately, the American commanders didn't know exactly where the American soldiers were and started dropping the big shells right on top of them.

Major Whittlesey called for his last pigeon, Cher Ami. He wrote a quick and simple note, telling the men who directed the artillery guns where his soldiers were located and asking them to stop. The note that was put in the canister on Cher Ami's left leg simply said:

We are along the road parallel to 276.4.
Our own artillery is dropping a barrage directly on us.
For heaven's sake, stop it.

Accounts vary somewhat but it seems that, as Cher Ami tried to fly back home, the Germans saw him taking off into the air and opened fire. For several minutes, bullets zipped all around him and it looked like the pigeon was going to fall, that he wasn't going to make it. The doomed American infantrymen were crushed; their last hope was plummeting to earth against a very heavy attack from German bullets.

But somehow the pigeon managed to fly on and he started gaining height, higher and higher beyond the range of the enemy guns. He flew 40 km in only 25 minutes to deliver his message even though he was badly wounded. When he finally reached his coop, he could fly no longer and the soldier who answered the sound of the bell which was automatically triggered as he entered it found him on his back covered in blood. He had been blinded in one eye and a bullet had hit his breastbone. A leg was all but severed but attached to it was the silver canister with the all-important message.

The shelling was stopped, and more than 200 American lives were saved.

The pigeon recovered, though his leg was amputated and he was repatriated back to the US. He was seen off personally by the senior US commander, General John Pershing.

If you wish, you can still see Cher Ami! He was stuffed and is on display at the National Museum of American History in Washington, DC, preserved alongside the French *Croix de Guerre* with Palm that was awarded to him by the French government for his bravery.

On the opposite side in World War I, the Germans knew a thing or two about pigeons as well. They even had photographer-pigeons with cameras strapped to their bellies, a system that was abandoned only when aerial reconnaissance planes were introduced later in the war.

Carrier pigeons, though, were only used when telegraph and telephone communications failed, in emergencies especially, and their use was soon overtaken by the development of radio communication. All the same, at the end of World War I there were more than 22,000 pigeons, 150 mobile lofts and 400 personnel looking after pigeons on the British side alone. More than 100,000 pigeons in total had served Britain during those harrowing four years but despite this, the Royal Navy, Royal Air Force, and Army all demobbed their pigeon services promptly at the end of the war.

It proved a bit premature. Surprisingly, considering that telegraph and radio were widely used by then, 200,000 pigeons were supplied in World War II by private breeders to the British army alone. Many airmen owed their lives to the SOS messages carried by pigeons released when their aircraft crash-landed at sea. These birds would be kept in a box and would ride alongside the air crew. If the aircraft was shot down, the pigeons would, hopefully, go into action. The navigator would place the crash position on a piece of paper which he attached to the pigeon and the bird's job was to wing it back home to inform authorities of the loss in case they could organise a rescue.

One such pigeon, Sam, based at RAF Linton-on-Ouse, had a narrow escape. During a raid over Berlin, Sam's bomber was hit and a piece of shrapnel flew into the cockpit and straight through his tin flying box, taking his beak with it. Luckily, he survived the ordeal. So did the aircraft during the bombing raid. Sam came back to base and was retired from RAF use! Harold Wood, from Copmanthorpe in York, was just a lad when his father supplied RAF Linton with pigeons for the nightly raids. One of his jobs was to water the pigeons before they were collected by the RAF. He gave Sam his last drink on the day of his accident.

Not very James Bond-like but homing pigeons were useful for espionage purposes too. Nearly 17,000 of them were parachuted to the Resistance in German-occupied Europe during World War II and 2,000 returned safely back to Britain with their messages.

But using pigeons was certainly not a guarantee of getting your message to where it needed to go, even if enemy gunfire didn't end their days. Bad weather and exhaustion could divert a pigeon or cause its death. So could a bird of prey like a Peregrine on the lookout for a meal. No satisfactory method of protecting the birds seems to have been developed, though the Chinese many years before had provided their pigeons with whistles and bells in an attempt to scare away birds of prey (there's no evidence to show that it worked). To reduce the risks to carrier pigeons during World War II, virtually every Peregrine in Britain was shot. They took decades to recover their pre-war population.

During that war, 32 pigeons including an Irish pigeon called Paddy and an American named G.I. Joe (pigeon names are not terribly adventurous!) received the Dickin Medal, Britain's highest award for animal bravery which saved human lives. G.I. Joe had flown 32 km in 20 minutes with a message that stopped US planes from bombing an Italian town that was occupied by British forces.

During the D-Day invasion, many soldiers were sent with a pigeon beneath their coats. This was a period of radio silence, so the use of pigeons for relaying messages was vital. The pigeons were able to send back information on German gun positions on the Normandy beaches for Allied bombardment.

During World War II, 82 homing pigeons were dropped into Holland with Britain's First Airborne Division as part of Operation Market Garden, the attempt in 1944 by the British to capture key bridges over the Rhine at Nijmegen and Arnhem. The pigeons' loft was located in London which would have required them to fly 390 km to deliver their progress notes.

The Australian army made extensive use of more than 13,000 pigeons – donated by pigeon-keepers – in World War II in New Guinea and the islands around. With the rugged terrain and unusual atmospherics, wireless communications often failed but the pigeons didn't. They were looked after by soldiers who had had experience of pigeon-keeping before the war.

Australian birds won two Dickin medals for bravery in World War II. The first flew more than 60 km to Madang on the Papuan New Guinea coast in a thunderstorm after its boat foundered during the Australian action to re-take the area after the Japanese had invaded in 1942. The second covered nearly 50 km, part of it under heavy fire, to bring news of a US company trapped by the Japanese on nearby Manus Island.

Australia's lifesaving carrier pigeons, though, didn't have a glorious welcome back home. Owing to quarantine regulations, all of them were destroyed at the end of the war. So much for valour.

In case you're assuming that pigeons are now never used to carry messages during conflicts, they were in fact employed as recently as 1990 by the Iraqi army during the first Gulf War when an international coalition force sanctioned by the UN expelled the Iraqis from Kuwait.

And drug traffickers today continue to escape technological advances in surveillance by sending flocks of pigeons, each carrying 10 g of heroin, between Afghanistan and Pakistan.

So birds, pigeons anyway, have been heroes in several wars, probably over thousands of years. Unfortunately, however, other birds – or more accurately a bird product – have actually been the reason for some nations going to war and for international disputes which linger between governments even today.

Unlikely as it might seem, that product is guano, the polite word used to describe the excreta of birds. Less politely, bird shit. And this is a story about bird shit in very, very large quantities indeed.

Where huge colonies of perhaps millions of seabirds like gannets, penguins and cormorants breed cheek by jowl with one another – often on islands – guano can build up year after year, eventually becoming many tens of metres deep. Some of these birds, because they are quite large, can deposit a kilogram of odoriferous, mainly white-coloured shit a month! When it's dry, though, it's apparently odourless. And when it dries it sets to a crusty, rock-like or powdery consistency.

Guano is valuable because it's a good fertiliser rich in phosphorus and a gunpowder ingredient due to its high levels of phosphorus and nitrogen. And therein lies the trouble!

The word 'guano' originates from the Quichua language of the Incas. The Incas collected it by hand for centuries from the coast of Peru for use as a soil enricher. They valued it hugely, restricting access to it and punishing any disturbance to the birds with death.

Guano can be harvested without harming the birds because they spend most of their time at sea and only come ashore to breed (and defecate) for a few months.

Guano has been harvested for centuries along the coast of Peru on islands and rocky shores. The Guanay Cormorant, a large, black and white cormorant, has historically been the most important producer; its guano is richer in nitrogen than that from other seabirds though other important guano-producing species off that coast include the equally large, dark-coloured Peruvian Pelican and the black and white Peruvian Booby, a long-winged seabird. The cormorants nest close together, about three pairs to a square metre, the others a little less so. And some of their breeding colonies might consist of a million birds, sometimes a few million!

The era between the 1840s and the 1890s was marked by a guano harvesting frenzy similar to that of America's gold rush. To Peruvians, guano was tantamount to gold, and for good reason. One tonne of guano is the equivalent of 33 tonnes of farmyard manure.

Guano islands were discovered, scraped clean, and abandoned. Not all were off the South American coast. In March 1843, for example, an expedition chartered by a Liverpool businessman found guano (mostly from gannets and African penguins) to a depth of eight metres on Ichaboe Island off the coast of present-day Namibia. By early 1844 no fewer than 100 ships were carrying it away. The ensuing year saw an insurrection by the workers and several violent struggles for control. In January 1845 the islet was host to 450 ships and 6,000 men. By May it was deserted, cleaned out!

In Peru, unscrupulous speculators brought in Chinese labourers to dig the guano and worked many to death. A typical worker moved up to four tonnes of guano a day. So appalling were the conditions that 60 Chinese labourers shovelling Peruvian guano between 1852 and 1854 committed suicide. But the ruthless exploitation continued and exports skyrocketed to nearly 1 million tonnes in the 1860s. People were making money, lots of it, and a war-hungry Europe guaranteed an ever-increasing market.

Between 1848 and 1875 more than 20 million tonnes of the stuff was shipped from Valparaiso in Chile to Europe and the US, and in 1909 the Peruvian government started protecting these breeding seabird colonies and setting aside rocky coastal headlands as potential new breeding grounds to try to conserve some of the squandered resource.

Fortunes could be made, and were. William and George Gibbs from Somerset built up a substantial trade in guano from former Spanish colonies in South America. The firm's profits were such that William Gibbs became one of the richest men in England; in 1843 he bought Tyntes Place in Somerset which he then enlarged and modified to create the highly picturesque mansion of Tyntesfield, bristling with turrets, as a country home for his family. Since 2002 it's been a National Trust property.

The United States got into the game in 1856 with the Guano Islands Act which allowed American citizens, in line with early American tradition, to claim uninhabited guano-bearing islands as sovereign US territory! More than 50 were eventually annexed. The act was a reaction to the near-monopoly enjoyed by Peru, which had the world's best guano thanks to dry conditions along its coast that yielded a particularly concentrated product.

On the Chincha islands (three small islands off the Peruvian coast) guano had built up over centuries to leave a thick crust containing perhaps 11 million tonnes, and by the 1840s a brisk trade had developed. Income from guano accounted for a whopping 80 per cent of Peru's revenue. So valuable was it for agriculture and weapons production that more powerful countries manoeuvred to cash in. Spain occupied the islands in 1866, ending the Peruvian windfall.

Other disputes between countries also resulted. The so-called War of the Pacific, from 1879 to 1883, was a conflict between Chile and the joint forces of Bolivia and Peru. It arose from disputes over the control of territory that contained substantial mineral-rich deposits, much of it guano. It ultimately led to the Chilean annexation of much Peruvian territory and left Bolivia landlocked.

Today, proud Bolivia still retains a navy from the days when it had sea access. But its days of sea-going are over. It's forced to confine itself to proudly patrolling its half of Lake Titicaca and a few large rivers! It can sail nowhere else. It is, in fact, the largest navy in the world maintained by a landlocked country, having several thousand personnel.

The War of the Pacific left traumatic scars on all societies involved in the conflict. For Bolivians, the loss of their coastal territory remains a deeply emotional as well as a practical issue. Popular belief attributes many of Bolivia's problems to its landlocked condition; accordingly, recovering the sea coast is seen as the solution to most of these difficulties. Consequently, all Bolivian presidents have made it their policy to pressure Chile for sovereign access to the sea. Diplomatic relations with Chile have been severed since 1978 in spite of considerable commercial ties. And Bolivians annually celebrate a patriotic 'Dia del Mar' (Day of the Sea) to remember their crippling loss.

Chile fared better, gaining a lucrative territory with major sources of income from guano and minerals. The national treasury grew by 900 per cent between 1879 and 1902 due to taxes coming from the newly acquired Bolivian and Peruvian lands and the bounty they held.

By the early 20th century most of the deposits had been exploited, so that by World War I most large deposits of guano had been stripped and chemical manufacturers had started switching to inorganic sources of nitrate. Today guano fertiliser retains a niche market for organic farmers and gardeners. It's back in fashion, but on a much smaller scale. And many of the guano islands are protected to conserve their breeding seabirds.

The story of the exploitation of birds' droppings is one of terrible greed and exploitation. Happily, apart from wild birds being exploited as a source of food, and the killing of birds for sport which often has some rather surprising results, most other purposes for which birds have been used have been considerably more positive. And in a few, albeit rare, instances that use has benefitted people and birds at the same time, as the next chapter shows.

6
Helping each other

We exploit birds. They exploit us. But, the world over, there are exceedingly few
examples of birds and people both gaining advantage
from making use of one another.

It wasn't long before the metronome-like rhythm of the prayer chanting, led by the two white-robed priests in their tall hats, became soporific in the leaden heat of the late afternoon. A Nass-esalar – a corpse bearer – also dressed in a white cotton tunic, trousers and cap, sat reverently at the side of the dead man on the cool stone floor.

The sacred dog, a small tan and white mongrel, was led in, sniffed around the body to check that there was no life remaining, and was led out again in a ritual as important to the Parsis – the followers of Zoroastrianism, one of the world's oldest religions – as what would follow later.

Outside the low, whitewashed building occupied by the family and close friends of the old man who had died in Mumbai the previous night, gardeners in their mud brown uniforms went about their everyday business, watering exotic shrubs and scarlet-flowering climbers while the heady aroma of cypress trees hung heavy in the air. To me, hardly used to such events, it all seemed rather surreal.

Black Kites swirled high above, wheeling and soaring on the hot upcurrents of air. And the raucous, grating calls of scraggy black House Crows were interrupted by the occasional shriek of a parakeet in the lush gardens here on Malabar Hill, the largest green lung in this overcrowded, noisy, sprawling and – too often – squalid city.

Then, after perhaps half an hour, the prayers were over. The priests came out into the scorching sun, removed their hats and chatted to the deceased man's family. It was the cue for the mourners to file slowly past his body, the last time for the family to see him.

When they had finished, the body, covered entirely now by a white sheet and raised on a metal bier, was carried at shoulder height by the four Nassesalars – one at each corner – down the steps and out into the blaze of the late afternoon sunshine.

Immediately behind them, leading the procession to the top of Malabar Hill to a low, stone tower where the body will be placed, come the two priests, ritually joined by a white cloth held between them. Next are the close family, then more distant relatives and friends, all in pairs joined by a small white cloth, a token of sympathetic grief and a contact believed by Parsis to strengthen them against the demon of contamination associated with dead bodies.

As I watch, I'm struck by how dignified this all is. No pomp and circumstance. No elaborate dress code. No music. And never any different whether the dead person comes from a rich background or a poor one.

Only Parsis can join the procession to the open-topped towers. And when they reach the tower allocated for their particular loved one, they can go no further. Only the Nassesalars can enter inside to lay the body, face upward and naked, on the exposed stone surface of the tower's top. The only time when these Parsis will ever enter the tower, they will already be dead.

Noshir Mulla, bursting with energy in his Mumbai draper's shop not far from Malabar Hill where he makes traditional Parsi clothes, is keen to describe for me what happens next. Or, rather, what for millennia always used to happen. He remembers his grandmother's funeral as if it had just taken place, he says. Tears well up in his deep, dark eyes as he recalls the occasion.

'I was 14 then and asking lots of questions', he says. 'When the Nassesalars carried her body on the bier and we walked behind in procession, there were many vultures in the air. They seemed to follow us to the tower, landing on the stone parapet around its edge. There must have been 70 or more.'

'Once the Nassesalars had left her body on the tower, they clapped their hands. It was the sign for the vultures to descend to gorge themselves. They took less than an hour. They had done their work perfectly according to our Parsi tradition', he adds.

The year was 1957. But exactly the same funeral ritual has taken place at Mumbai's Towers of Silence, sometimes as many as three or four times a day, almost every day since. It is a rare example of the interdependence of birds and people; the Parsis dependent on the vultures to quickly, and hygienically, dispose of their dead and the vultures reliant on an easy – and regular – meal. Both the vultures and the Parsis gain. The world over, there are very few such examples of mutual benefit between birds and people. This is one.

But now there is a problem. A major problem. For well over a decade there has not been a single vulture at Malabar Hill to consume the Parsi dead. They have disappeared, too, from their nesting colonies some miles outside Mumbai from where they used to fly in every morning.

And it isn't only Mumbai's vultures that have died out. They are now on the cusp of extinction throughout India as well as in Pakistan, Bangladesh and Nepal. Across this vast subcontinent larger than Europe they used to be so commonplace, no one gave them a second thought. They do now.

A decade ago, India alone had perhaps 40 million of the most common species, the Oriental White-backed Vulture. A dark, grey-brown bird with a characteristic featherless head, it has partially white underwings and its namesake white patch. It's about 80 cm long. It was the most abundant large bird of prey in the world. Today it is almost impossible to find one. For every 1,000 Oriental White-backs recorded in India in 1992, only one remains today.

White-backed Vultures nest in trees, sometimes in solitary pairs, sometimes in colonies. The same nest is often used year upon year, 'renovated' with a few green branches each spring. When they were abundant, as they had been for millennia, it was possible to find breeding colonies of up to a thousand or more breeding pairs.

Long-billed Vultures used to be almost as common in India as white-backs. Much lighter brown in colour, long-bills have a darker neck and a contrasting yellow beak. They frequently accompanied white-backs wherever there was any habitation but unlike their cousins, long-bills nest in small colonies on cliff ledges.

Similar in size to its long-billed cousin, the other vulture known to be decimated in number, the Slender-billed Vulture, has – as you might imagine – a thinner beak than the long-bill and an almost black neck. However, unlike the other two, it's found only in northern India around the

foothills of the Himalayas. So it was never present at the Towers of Silence. Now there are fewer than a thousand left in India.

In little over a decade, vast numbers of these vultures have died. According to experts at Britain's Royal Society for the Protection of Birds (RSPB), it's the fastest decline ever recorded in any animal species worldwide. Faster, even, than the decline of the Dodo.

What's been causing this cataclysmic fall in vulture numbers across the Indian subcontinent is a simple painkiller closely related to ibuprofen. It is called diclofenac. For years it was readily available and very cheap, and farmers used to buy it to help reduce painful lameness or mastitis in their cattle and water buffalo. Diclofenac is used as a human medicine too, especially for rheumatic-type pain, often marketed as Voltarol.

Across this huge subcontinent, millions of farmers rely on cows and water buffalo for milk and muscle-power. Without them they can't easily farm at all. And when a cow or water buffalo eventually died, the farmer would rely on the local vultures to spot it and devour the whole corpse. He only had to dispose of the bones.

What no one knew – and could not have predicted – was that these vultures were incredibly susceptible to a side effect of the painkiller, one that paralysed them with acute gout from feeding on the corpses of any animals treated with the drug before they died. For the vultures, very unusually, it was lethal.

Mumbai's nearly 46,000 Parsis – their largest single community in the world – carry on the Zoroastrian tradition of laying out their dead for the sun to dry their bodies and for vultures, or other carrion eaters, to devour them naturally. It's always been fundamental to their belief that their dead must not pollute land, air or water.

Mark Twain visited Mumbai in 1896 on his round-the-world trip. After visiting the Towers of Silence he wrote in his *Following the Equator* (Samuel L. Clemens, Hartford, Connecticut, 1897):

> On lofty ground, in the midst of a paradise of tropical foliage and flowers, remote from the world and its turmoil and noise, they stood. The vultures were there. They stood close together in a great circle all around the rim of a massive low tower – waiting; stood as motionless as sculptured ornaments, and indeed almost deceived one into the belief that that was what they were.

In ancient Persia where the religion was founded, pre-Islam, by Zarathustra who lived from about 630 to 550 BC, it was almost certainly the custom to leave dead bodies untended where they would be eaten rapidly by wolves, jackals and vultures. The alternatives were impractical anyway. Presumably, wood for funeral pyres would have been scarce. Rivers would have been seasonal. And the often arid, rocky ground would not have lent itself to easy burial.

Relationships between humans and vultures are doubtless very ancient. Early man probably tracked these scavenging birds to locate dead animals to see if they could get a feed too. Eight thousand years ago, the inhabitants of the Neolithic city of Catal Huyuk in Anatolia, one of the world's first towns and now part of modern-day Turkey, appear to have exposed human corpses to vultures as part of their preparation for burial. Some archaeologists believe that the Parsi practice of vulture use started there. Catal Huyuk is close to the modern border between southern Turkey and Iran, the former Persia.

In India, where most Parsis settled in the 8th century AD having been ousted from Persia, the process became ritualised at stone towers built specially for the purpose of encouraging vultures to consume their dead quickly. After all, vultures were then incredibly abundant, perfect for the form of body disposal central to their faith.

Nor would the vultures have needed much encouragement to stay around. In Mumbai, the Parsi community is slowly depleting as its population ages and because it never accepts converts to the faith. You have to be born a Parsi. And not enough are being born. Up to 900 of them die annually in the city.

When vultures were abundant at the Towers of Silence, after each laying of a body its flesh would have been consumed within an hour, leaving the skeleton to desiccate in the hot sun. After a few weeks the corpse bearers would return to sweep the brittle, powdering bones into the tower's central pit where they would join those of thousands of other Parsis. The process was rapid, hygienic and non-polluting.

In the words of a former Parsi High Priest, Dastur Khurshed S. Dabu who died in 1977, the process was speedy; it was hygienic because the earth, fire, water and air are not defiled; it offered natural food to nature's scavengers; it produced no false sentimentality, no fuss, no monuments, no epitaphs, no urns … and it was cost-free.

Sir Monier Monier-Williams, then the city's Surveyor-General under British colonial rule, wrote a vivid account of the role of the vultures at the Towers of Silence after a visit he paid there in 1870:

> The parapet of each tower possesses an extraordinary coping. It is a coping formed, not of dead stone, but of living vultures. These birds had settled themselves side by side in perfect order, and in a complete circle around the parapets of the towers with their heads pointed inwards. And so lazily did they sit there and so motionless was their whole mien that, except for their colour, they might have been carved out of the stone-work.
>
> The first funeral I witnessed was that of a child. A sudden stir among the vultures made us raise our heads. At least a hundred birds, collected round one of the towers, began to show symptoms of excitement, while others swooped down from neighbouring trees. A funeral procession was seen to be approaching.
>
> The Nassesalars speedily unlocked the door [to the tower], reverently conveyed the body of the child into the interior, and, unseen by any one, laid it uncovered in one of the open stone receptacles. In two minutes they reappeared with the empty bier and white cloth.
>
> But scarcely had they closed the door when a dozen vultures swooped down upon the body, and were rapidly followed by flights of others. In five minutes more we saw the satiated birds fly back and lazily settle down again upon the parapet. They had left nothing behind but a skeleton.
>
> I could not help thinking that however much such a system may shock our European feelings and ideas, yet our own method of interment, if regarded from a Parsi point of view, may possibly be equally revolting to Parsi sensibilities.

But now there are no vultures at the Towers of Silence to perform the function that they have carried out continuously for hundreds of years. Only crows and Black Kites remain and they, even in substantial numbers, take days or longer to devour a human body. The absence of the vultures is causing strains in the Parsi faith.

'When the vultures disappeared, I suggested that we should construct a large netted aviary around one or more of the towers', says Khojeste Mistree, a leading Parsi authority based in the sprawling, noisy city. 'With the necessary licences to capture a few remaining birds we would have bred vultures there and kept them on site so that our traditional practices could continue. We had advice from vulture breeding experts. They advised us that it was feasible.'

'But the Bombay Parsi Punchayet [their ruling body] eventually turned down the idea because of concerns that diclofenac residues in human bodies might kill the vultures. It's very disappointing', he adds.

Most experts agree that although diclofenac breaks down within days in any animal, further breakdown stops at death. So livestock or humans given the drug shortly before death to relieve pain might retain enough in their vital organs to kill vultures.

Instead, the Punchayet has gone for a novel – and controversial – solution. Solar reflectors have been installed on three of the four towers to concentrate the sun on the bodies in order to desiccate them more rapidly so that there is no smell of slow decomposition.

'I contend that the bodies must burn, contrary to our beliefs', argues Khojeste Mistree. 'They get heated to 125°C. It's like a grill. It's heretical. It's so hot that the crows and kites can't even land there until sundown. Then in the monsoon months, of course, the reflectors don't work at all. Allowing kites and crows to eat the bodies, albeit much more slowly than vultures, would be acceptable. Most of the priests agree with me but their views have been marginalised. It is so wrong.'

Other Parsis I interviewed who declined to be named shrug their shoulders, seemingly resigned to using the reflectors as a necessary alternative. Needs must, they suggested.

'Most Parsis are concerned that using the reflectors isn't appropriate but they feel it's inevitable', comments Dr Viraf Kapadia, a Parsi and homeopath in Mumbai. 'They want the bodies to dry rapidly to eliminate any decomposition odours that they fear if slow consumption by kites and crows is the only alternative.'

But there is hope, at least in the long term. In 2006, the Indian government banned diclofenac manufacture for veterinary use, and conservation organisations like the RSPB, BirdLife International and the Bombay Natural History Society (BNHS) have pressed successfully for a ban in Nepal and Pakistan too. In Nepal efforts are underway to protect wild populations through the provision of safe food and to replace stocks of diclofenac with meloxicam, an equally effective, safe – it's been tested on vultures – and cheap drug which sells for the same price as diclofenac.

Since the ban, though, some unlicensed drug companies have been making and selling diclofenac illegally or selling to farmers the products made for human treatment as a painkiller. The Indian government has ordered a crackdown on these companies. Diclofenac imports aren't yet banned either. And many Indian farmers have stockpiles of the drug. So getting it out of the environment so that vultures can be reintroduced safely back into the wild is going to be a long job.

Vultures aren't the prettiest of birds! Most people would agree that they are seriously ugly – the bare head and neck; the powerful hooked beak; their usually sombre colour; and those drooping, cloak-like wings. Combine all that with their reliance for food on dead animals – or, in this case, people – and it perhaps isn't surprising that they have rarely been regarded other than with disdain. Except, that is, by Parsis.

But vultures are in fact some of the most useful birds in the world. By eating up all manner of dead animals – farmed and wild – across most of Africa, Southeast Asia, the Americas and even the very south of Europe, they are a major factor in stopping the spread of diseases.

'When vultures were abundant in India, they kept everything else at bay when they were feeding on a dead cow', says Dr Andrew Cunningham, Head of Wildlife Epidemiology at London's Institute of Zoology. 'Now, these corpses hang on for days and feral dogs hold sway with rats, jackals, feral pigs, crows and black kites feeding on them.'

'Why diclofenac kills vultures but doesn't seem to affect other carrion feeders we simply don't know', he continues. 'But there are no reports of dogs dying and I've seen plenty of puppies around the corpses. Feral dogs are on the increase. Most of them carry rabies.'

The World Health Organization records 30,000 rabies deaths annually in India based on Indian government estimates. With little medical care outside cities, and precious little recording of causes of death, Cunningham reckons the true total is a lot higher and that the burgeoning feral dog population will send it up still further.

'Bubonic plague, spread by rat fleas, is endemic and dogs might carry it too', he says. 'Typhus could spread. Cows sometimes die of anthrax but when vultures ate the corpses the bacteria were killed in the vultures' gut. Now, with corpses lingering, there's every chance of the lethal spores spreading. Flies also spread a plethora of diseases and in the monsoon, rain will wash all manner of harmful bacteria into water supplies', he adds. Cunningham is convinced that the public health implications are grave.

Three breeding centres to save the last of the three vulture species threatened with extinction have been set up so far in India: in Haryana in northern India, in West Bengal, and in Assam. Two other centres are operational in Nepal and Pakistan. All of them are housing the three vulture species, in total more than 200 birds. But they need more. And each breeding centre, according to the RSPB, costs about £100,000 to build plus running and staffing costs. Supplying each one with uncontaminated meat accounts for much of the cost.

Genetics experts advise the RSPB that they need around 300 vultures of each species in order to breed a population with a good range of genes, thereby giving them a better chance of surviving some untold catastrophe again in the future when they get back into the wild.

India's captive ultures have started breeding. Two White-backed chicks were successfully reared in 2008 and several other females laid eggs. And in 2009, two young Slender-billed Vultures – now more threatened in the wild in India than the tiger – were reared successfully in captivity, plus three more white-backs.

'This news is hugely exciting. It is clear we are refining our expertise, but with extinction in the wild likely in the next ten years, we don't have a moment to waste. The more vultures that we can bring into captivity means a better chance of survival. Birds can only be saved from extinction through banning all retail sale of diclofenac, including preventing the use of human formulations for veterinary use, promotion of meloxicam, and the capture of more birds for the breeding programme', says Chris Bowden, the RSPB's Vulture Programme Manager.

'But, even with diclofenac banned', comments Dr Debbie Pain, former Head of International Research at the RSPB and a leading expert on the Indian vulture problem, 'vultures breed very slowly so it will be decades before even a reasonable number are back in the wild. I'm not sure that we shall ever see the huge numbers that there were in the past.'

This successful captive breeding combined with the diclofenac ban has given Khojeste Mistree a little more hope too. He is now a member of the board of the Bombay Parsi Punchayet so he has returned to his argument of wanting to build an aviary around two of the towers and to house vultures there. With the drug banned, he believes, there should be no reason for Mumbai's Parsis not to construct a large aviary over one or more of the towers and to breed captive White-backed Vultures on site. For obvious reasons, their food supply would be guaranteed.

'If the Indian government builds another vulture breeding station on the outskirts of Mumbai as it's suggesting, then some of the vultures there could be brought by road to the Towers on a rotational basis. So they would again serve our religious needs and we would be helping their conservation and re-establishment', he says.

Without captive breeding of vultures on Malabar Hill, it's unlikely that this highly unusual practice benefitting both humans and birds – enshrined in Parsi tradition for millennia – will take place again in Mumbai for many years. Maybe it will be longer still.

Finding other examples of practices or traditions in which birds and people both benefit – called mutualism by biologists – is difficult. It's easier to find examples of one benefitting and the other remaining unaffected, known as a commensal relationship. Eiderdown collecting fits that bill; the human collectors benefit while the ducks are unaffected. Flocks of Black-headed Gulls following a tractor ploughing a field also represent such a relationship. The birds get a plethora of invertebrates to eat that are churned up in the soil and the farmer isn't disadvantaged.

Some might suggest that oxpeckers (olive-green and yellow, starling-sized birds) taking parasitic insects off the backs of livestock in Africa – or drongos (slightly larger, all black, forked-tailed birds) doing the same in Southeast Asia (see Chapter 8) – are examples of mutualism. It certainly provides food for the birds. The cattle, or other livestock, might gain healthwise. And the cattle owner gains indirectly because his livestock are fitter. But it isn't a direct benefit for the farmer … and it's pretty marginal anyway.

Could shooting Red Grouse (see Chapter 2) be an example of birds and people both gaining? Maybe. The grouse shooters certainly gain pleasure and benefit because they acquire the birds to eat, or to sell. And some conservationists argue that without grouse shooting as a land use, many of the moorlands that support these and many other birds, in Scotland and the north of England particularly, would have been planted up with crops of conifer trees years ago. That would have meant bye bye grouse.

So, it could be argued that Red Grouse gain too. But only in the sense that their population is greater than it might have otherwise been. Grouse shooting is not exactly of any advantage to the hapless individuals which get shot!

There is, though, another bird/human relationship in which both parties gain directly that has been suggested but isn't proven. It's a link-up between people and the largest bird of the intelligent crow family, the Northern Raven, that's widespread across Europe, much of Asia, North America and from the extremes of the Arctic to the desert edges of North Africa. It's a very versatile bird, existing largely on the bodies of any sort of animal that's died naturally or been killed.

Ravens have one of the largest brains – for the size of the bird – in any bird species. Hence their intelligence. And they have long been known to follow wolf packs so that they can scavenge carcasses at wolf kills once the animals have had their fill. Even with their large beaks, they can't penetrate the tough skin of a dead moose or bear so they make their raucous calls until a wolf comes along to see what's happening, opens up the carcass and feeds. Then the ravens can feed too.

In the Arctic, ravens follow polar bears hoping for a kill. They will frequently follow people too, at campsites for instance, knowing that where humans have been there's a chance that something edible might have been left behind when the campsite is vacated. I've seen it happen with brown-necked ravens in the Sahara, where there is precious little food unless they find a dead animal.

A pair of these birds would almost always arrive in the evening when we set up camp and perch on nearby rocks from where they had a good view of what we were doing. At dawn they would still be there and, once we had broken camp and moved off a kilometre or so, they'd be down on the ground hopping around to see if there were any scraps left behind.

So it doesn't take a huge leap of imagination to understand that ravens will follow hunters knowing that a kill might result which could just give them a bite to eat. They sometimes follow deer hunters in the Scottish Highlands for this very reason. They do the same with moose hunters in the northern US and Canada because they know that they might be able to feed on moose offal cut out of the carcasses.

Bernd Heinrich, a biologist at the University of Vermont in the US, in his *Mind of the Raven* (Harper Perennial, 2006), suggests that ravens and hunters in the Arctic might have developed a closer working relationship still. He suggests that there is evidence that ravens signal to the hunters – by tucking in one wing momentarily as they fly or making a certain call – to indicate that prey such as caribou are nearby. If the signalling raven then flies off in a certain direction, the hunters might rightly presume that the animals are that way.

Heinrich's idea is based on anecdotes from Inuit hunters on ice-bound Baffin Island in the Arctic between Greenland and the very north of Canada. He doesn't have objective proof for it but, if he is right, then both the ravens and the hunters gain.

Heinrich writes:

Abe Okpik, an elderly man who was no longer a hunter … later had told me that when out on the land hunting caribou, or out on the ice hunting polar bear, a hunter seeing a raven fly over used to look up and call its name loudly three times: 'Tulugaq, tulugaq, tulugaq'. Having the bird's attention, he would then yell to it, telling it to tumble out of the sky in the direction of the prey. If the raven gave its gong-like call three times in succession, then the hunters went in that direction and killed it. 'They believed in the raven strongly, and followed it', said Okpik. 'And after they killed the caribou or the bear, they always left the raven the choicest tidbits of meat as a reward.' It seemed absurd to me that a hunter could signal to a bird, and the bird would in turn provide information asked of it. Yet I wanted to keep an open mind to the possibility of communication.

Whether or not the raven/hunter relationship really does exist, there is one very similar relationship between a much smaller bird and certain tribesmen that most certainly does. It involves a very tasty food – honey. And it takes place across parts of southern Africa where grassy savanna plains, forests and scattered trees dominate the landscape.

Here, in the partly forested hill country a few hundred kilometres north of Nairobi, Kenya's capital, the Ndorobo people have retained much of their hunting and hunter-gatherer culture. Moved out of their traditional forest environment in the 1970s in a bid to force them to settle and become cattle farmers like their Samburu neighbours, many have clung to living closely with the wildlife they have always exploited sustainably.

Robert Lentaaya, a Ndorobo in his forties with a family to support, lives in the Karissia Hills forest about 300 km north of Nairobi. And like many of his Ndorobo people, he frequently makes use of honeyguides – rather drab, thrush-sized, olive-green and brown birds – who guide him to bee nests. Once these incredible birds have shown them where the nest is, the Ndorobo smoke it out to subdue the bees, then break in to extract the honeycomb to take back to their homes, always leaving a piece for the waiting honeyguide to eat.

It's a relationship that has probably been in existence for thousands of years, though its origins are a mystery. And there is an awful lot about honeyguides that isn't at all well known. Seventeen species exist, all but two of them in Africa south of the Sahara. The other two are to be found in southern Asia south of the Himalayas. Some of the African honeyguides that live only in forests are so rarely seen, even though they might not be uncommon, that very little is known about them. And two of the species were discovered only during the last 50 years.

The best known is the Greater Honeyguide, smaller than a thrush and differing from the mainly olive-green others in that it looks rather like a very large sparrow – it's a brown, black and dirty cream-coloured bird, the male possessing a slightly chubby pink beak. Most experts believe this is the only honeyguide known to guide people to a bees' nest. Lentaaya's day-to-day experience, though, is very different.

In conversation with Luca Borghesio, an Italian ornithologist working for BirdLife International in northern Kenya, Lentaaya makes clear that the Ndorobo use other honeyguides to find bees' nests too.

'While every Samburu knows about the Lodokotuk [Greater Honeyguide] and its guiding behaviour, only the Ndorobo can also use other honeyguides, the Silasili [Scaly-throated Honeyguide] and Airiguti [Lesser Honeyguide]', he says. Lentaaya uses the Samburu language because the Ndorobo lost theirs gradually as they assimilated with the Samburu over many decades.

'When we meet a Giochoroi [the general Samburu name for all honeyguides] the Ndorobo start singing a particular song to invite the bird to show them the way to the nearest bee nest. We have a different song for each species. The song for the Lodokotuk is a joke that asks the bird to lead the Ndorobo to the bees and requests it not to show the way to other Ndorobos. The song for the Silasili and the Airiguti refers to them as a girl because their voices are softer than that of the Lodokotuk', says Lentaaya.

'The Lodokotuk is the best guide. The other two we use but they are not as accurate because they don't go up to the bees' nest entrance and because they are less reliable at guiding. I collect about 10 litres of honey in a year and sell it for about 2,000 Kenyan shillings (£17) so I can pay for school fees for my children.'

It's an amazing and, seemingly, unique relationship. Honeyguides are always attracted by human sounds whether it's talking, chopping wood, cooking or anything else. At a campsite they will often come very close, inspecting the tents and other equipment. But when a honeyguide wants a tribesman to open up a bees' nest, it acts rather differently.

The bird perches in a bush or tree close to the person it wants to attract and makes a persistent, double call to attract attention, a harsh, rattling chatter of a noise. It's the sort of noise, close-by, that's hard to ignore! Most of the Greater Honeyguides that do so are females or immature birds … though no one knows why. The tribesman responds with his particular call, having first checked to see which it is, Lodokotuk, Silasili or Airiguti. But if the person it's trying to attract doesn't respond, honeyguides can be very patient. They'll wait up to an hour, sometimes longer, to get a response!

Then the fun and games begins. Having secured human interest, the honeyguide flies away to another tree but using a strange undulating flight and flashing the white feathers on the side of its tail so that it can be seen. The tribesman follows. Each tries to keep the other in sight as the honeyguide leads the tribesman towards the bees' nest it has identified. It might be a kilometre or two away.

But the bird won't allow the tribesman to lose it in spite of the often dense scrub and trees that make it hard to follow. It flies back to show itself to the tribesman, the two keeping in contact by calling to each other.

Eventually, this partnership reaches the bees' nest. The bird signals that it's the end of the journey by staying in the same area and by making a softer, less persistent call to the man. Once he has found the nest – usually in a cleft in a tree or rock with a narrow entrance – the tribesman smokes the bees to calm them using some hand-held vegetation he has set fire to. Bee stings can be nasty and the last thing the tribesman wants is a swarm of aggravated bees.

So the smoking-out process, followed by breaking into the nest, can take some time. The honeyguide waits; its reward is coming. The tribesman gathers the honeycomb to take back to his family but always leaves a piece of the comb for the bird to eat.

Opening up the nest often attracts other honeyguides too. Peculiarly, though, it's immature honeyguides that are dominant when it comes to eating the wax. Older birds take a back seat, with males further away than females. Even older immatures, should they come along for a feed, take second place behind the younger ones.

But why does the honeyguide need people to get into the nest? The answer is simply because they don't have large, strong beaks to break in and because, in spite of having thickened skin, presumably to give them some protection, they are still vulnerable to being stung.

Honeyguides have been seen in the cool early morning scraping bits of honeycomb at a nest they can partly access, presumably at which time the bees are still rather cool and dopey! But honeyguides have sometimes been found dead, too, and always close to a bees' nest, killed by an overwhelming bout of bee stings. It's a dangerous business.

So why eat bee honeycomb in the first place? For some unknown reason, honeyguides are particularly keen on wax and are some of the few birds anywhere that can digest it. They do eat other things, mainly spiders and a wide range of insects, including scale insects which have a waxy covering, as well as some fruits like figs. And when they gorge on honeycomb they are, of course, also eating quite a lot of bee eggs and grubs at the same time.

According to Lester Short and Jennifer Horne's account of the honeyguide family in the *Handbook of the Birds of the World, Volume 7* (Lynx Edicions, 2002), these unusual birds almost certainly have a very good knowledge of wild bee nests in their home areas. Their eyesight and hearing are both excellent and they might well be able to track individual honeybees to a nest.

Dr Hussein Isack, an ornithologist at the National Museum of Kenya in Nairobi, is a honeyguide expert. His three-year research project in northern Kenya in the mid 1980s found that 96 per cent of wild honeybee nests were accessible to the birds only after people had opened them up. So the birds have a lot to gain from their human relationship.

He also found that tribesmen took an average of nearly nine hours to find a bees' nest without any help from the birds but just over three hours when guided – and that was a conservative estimate of the time difference because it didn't include days on which no nest was found, something that was rare indeed when the birds were doing the guiding.

This close interrelationship between birds and people has probably been in existence for thousands of years. There are written accounts of it in the 17th century and early religious missionaries in Africa were surprised by birds that came to their altars and took pieces of wax from their beeswax candles. In Asia, 3rd century Chinese scribes wrote of 'little birds of the wax combs' based on reports about the Yellow-rumped Honeyguide of the Himalayas, though they are not known to guide.

There have been suggestions that the honeyguide/human link-up derived from a similar relationship between honeyguides and ratels (honey badgers), attractive grey and black badgers up to a metre in length. Very fierce, ratels can easily kill snakes, even venomous ones, as well as a variety of small and larger animals. But they also have a liking for beehives and wild bee nests. Many experts doubt that honeyguides direct the badgers to a bees' nest to open it up because there are no confirmed sightings. Robert Lentaaya, though, is quite sure on this point. He has seen a Greater Honeyguide leading a ratel on several occasions.

Unfortunately, however, this amazing relationship between honeyguides and people is not likely to last very much longer. Few people, even among the Ndorobos, now bother to follow the birds and collect wild bee honeycombs because many people now raise bees themselves in hives. The birds themselves, too, might well decline as more and more woodland is felled for fuelwood and not enough is planted to replace it, although the best guider, the Greater Honeyguide, is a bird more of open ground with scattered trees than of forest.

But trees are doubly essential for honeyguides. They are often the location for bees' nests. And older trees with rot holes and other cavities are the breeding places for barbets (colourful, stout-bodied birds with stubby beaks), bee-eaters, starlings and woodpeckers in whose nests honeyguides lay their eggs, cuckoo-like, and let these foster families do all the hard work of raising their young. No parental responsibilities, yet maybe several sons and daughters, helpers to get their food, and honey into the bargain. It's not a bad life being a honeyguide.

A perfect partnership between a bird and a person like this can only develop among people whose lives are still entwined with the natural world. As people the world over become more and more distanced from a way of life in which nature is part of their everyday existence, such close relationships will become rarer still. Most will die out.

Our increasingly large, noisy, bustling and often brightly lit cities are as far removed from that natural world as it's possible to be. Yet, they are often surprisingly attractive places for birds, and many are thriving in them. These city dwellers, then, are the subject of the next chapter.

If it moves, shoot it. A male Wild Turkey displaying in the woods of Virginia in the eastern US.
(*Courtesy of Department of Game and Inland Fisheries, Virginia State.*)

Lunda veisla – Icelandic puffin feast

Ferskt salat með reyktum og gröfnum lunda
Fresh salad with smoked and cured puffin

Marineraðar steiktar lundabringur með maltsósu
Marinated fried breast of puffin with malt sauce

Macarponefrauð með bláberjahlaupi og bláberja krapís
Mascarpone mousse with blueberry jelly and blueberry sorbet

3 réttir 6.980
3 courses 6.980

Left: Food for thought. Two courses of Atlantic Puffin, smoked or fried, on the menu at the popular Lækjarbrekka restaurant in Reykjavik, Iceland.

Right: They couldn't last. Passenger Pigeons (juvenile, male, female from left) were killed in massive numbers in the US for cheap food. They were extinct by 1900. From a painting by Louis Fuertes (1874–1927).

Below: An acquired taste. Nests of Edible-nest Swiftlets from Southeast Asia for sale in Chicago's Chinatown. (*Courtesy of Bobby Maisnam.*)

A free lunch

Above: The Glorious Twelfth. Robbie Douglas Miller shooting Red Grouse
from a butt on his moor in Scotland's Lammermuir Hills.

Below: Coming home. Racing pigeons are trained to return to their home lofts, hopefully
as fast as possible. This one waits in its Manchester home to be entered for a race.

Left: When killing comes naturally. Khalfan Butti Alqubaisi, a falconer in the United Arab Emirates, with his Gyrfalcon and Houbara Bustards it has killed. (*Courtesy of Khalfan Butti Alqubaisi.*)

Below: A quick clean-up. Cockfights are commonplace in much of Southeast Asia. In Indonesia, this proud owner of several fighting cocks gives his prize fighter a clean before his next contest.

A sporting chance

Above: Christmas is coming. Week-old goslings reared free range on Karol Bailey's farm in Cheshire. After eight months they are ready for Christmas.

Right: Pigeon food. An 18th century, brick-built, octagonal dovecote on the Erddig Estate in North Wales, now a National Trust property.

Domestic bliss

Left: Not quite oven ready. Selling pigeon squabs (young birds) and eggs at Luxor market in Egypt.

Below: Ready plucked. Chickens for sale in public market, Mazatlan, Sinaloa, Mexico. (*Courtesy of Tomás Castelazo.*)

Domestic bliss

Above: Keeping warm. Thorvaldur Björnsson on Trésey island off Iceland's west coast temporarily removing eider duck eggs to gather their precious down.

Far right: Catwalk for birds. Feathers, in this case black-dyed cockerel plumes, are still used to adorn clothes. (*Courtesy of Giles Deacon.*)

Right: Sense of smell. Cage-reared canaries like these were used in coalmine rescues to detect poisonous gases.

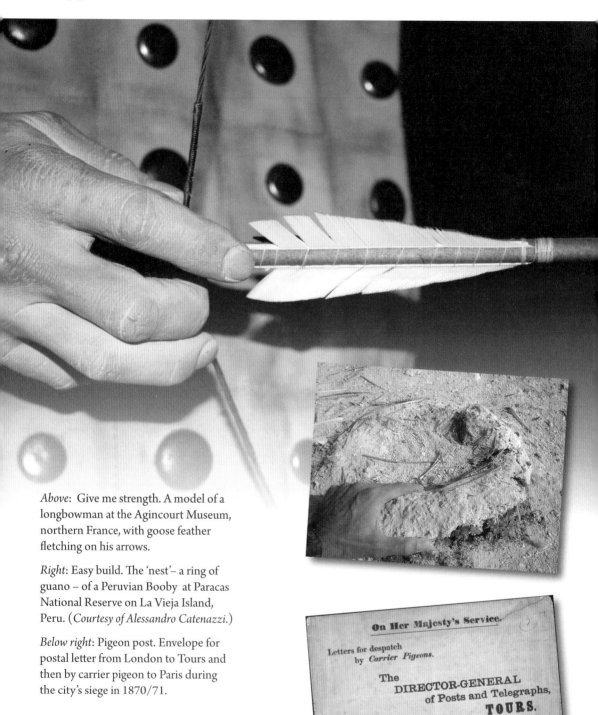

Above: Give me strength. A model of a longbowman at the Agincourt Museum, northern France, with goose feather fletching on his arrows.

Right: Easy build. The 'nest'– a ring of guano – of a Peruvian Booby at Paracas National Reserve on La Vieja Island, Peru. (*Courtesy of Alessandro Catenazzi.*)

Below right: Pigeon post. Envelope for postal letter from London to Tours and then by carrier pigeon to Paris during the city's siege in 1870/71.

On Her Majesty's Service.

Letters for despatch
by *Carrier Pigeons.*

The
DIRECTOR-GENERAL
of Posts and Telegraphs,
TOURS.

Weight of Letters ———— ozs.
credited to France under
Art. 1, Table 2 of the Letter Bill.
GENERAL
Post Office.
LONDON.

Left: Guiding light. Robert Lentaaya in northern Kenya, having been guided to the nest by a honeyguide, smokes the bees to extract their honeycomb. (*Courtesy of Luca Borghesio/ BirdLife International.*)

Below: Hunter's accomplice? Northern Raven at Bryce Canyon National Park, Utah, US.

Bottom of page: Every little helps. Common Mynas taking insect parasites off cattle in India. (*Courtesy of Ami Vitale.*)

On their last legs. White-backed Vultures in a breeding centre in Haryana Province, northern India, some of the last survivors. (*Courtesy of Ami Vitale.*)

Helping each other

Top to bottom: Home from home. Nanette Mickle cleans out her Purple Martin nesting boxes ready for the birds' eagerly awaited springtime arrival in Washington, DC.

View from the top. A Peregrine perched near its nest high on skyscrapers in Manhattan, New York City. (*Courtesy of Barbara Allen Loucks.*)

Cheeky chappie. House Sparrows (this one a male in Australia) live with us almost worldwide in villages, cities and countryside. (*Courtesy of Flagstaffotos.*)

Jetstream. A posse of Common Swifts zooms between the buildings of a Spanish town. (*Courtesy of Gabriel Sierra.*)

Above: In a paddy. Cattle Egrets and Little Egrets (plain white) feed in an Indonesian rice paddy. (*Courtesy of Eric Bajart.*)

Below: Food handouts. Fishermen on a Norwegian boat throw lumpfish discards to a flotilla of Northern Fulmars.

Getting into a paddy

Above: Fateful crowd. A flock of thousands of Red-billed Queleas in Namibia on the lookout for crops to devour. (*Courtesy of Alastair Rae.*)

Right: Plastic killer. A Eurasian Oystercatcher, a common seashore wading bird starved to death because of plastic debris at Killard Nature Reserve, Co Down, Northern Ireland. (*Courtesy of Craig Nash.*)

A load of garbage

Above: Share and share alike. City pigeons join in with workers taking a lunchtime break in the centre of Bristol, UK.

Left: Who dares wins. An aggressive seaside Herring Gull dives to steal some food in Ostende, Belgium.

Right: Litter pickers. A noisy group of House Crows in Oman work their way through the contents of a skip to find anything edible.

A load of garbage

Above: A good start. Primitive rock drawings, 10,000 years old, including images of ostriches, in the Akakus Mountains in the Libyan Sahara.

Left: Masterful. Painting of a Greater Flamingo by John James Audubon, arguably the greatest bird artist ever. (*Courtesy of The Natural History Museum, London*)

Far left: Drink up. Playing card toucan image, advertising the well-known Guinness stout. (*Courtesy of the Guinness Collectors Club.*)

The art of using birds

Right: Killer looks. One of the few surviving Bali Mynas in the world. This one is at San Diego Zoo. (*Courtesy of Mike McDonough.*)

Below: Caught out. Two Black-naped Orioles and a Hill Myna captured from the wild for sale illegally at Chatuchak Market, Bangkok.

The beauty stakes

Above and left: Beauty parade. Lesser Bird of Paradise displaying and showing off its fabulous tail plumes that are used as dance decorations in New Guinea. (*Courtesy of Robert Lancione.*)

Below: RSPB original. 'The Croft' in Fletcher Moss Gardens, Manchester where in 1889 the Plumage League, a forerunner of the Royal Society for the Protection of Birds, was formed.

Flying off? A statue of a
Kinnon, a mythological half
man, half cockerel, finished
in gold leaf at the Wat Phra
Kaew, part of Bangkok's
Grand Palace, Thailand.

Left: Baby carrier. White Storks settle in on a Spanish roof ready to breed. (*Courtesy of Gabriel Sierra.*)

Right: The chief. Fast Thunder of the Oglala Sioux photographed with a full war bonnet of eagle feathers. (*Courtesy of Paul Burke/First People.*)

Below: Slippery slopes. The high mountains with their precipitous slopes on Madeira where shepherds still attribute the ghostly night wailing sounds of the rare Zino's Petrel to dead shepherds who lost their footing.

7
City slickers

More and more birds have adapted to life in our towns and cities … and often do very
much better as a result. A few have adapted so well that they
have even given up their natural homes.

It's an early spring evening in Woodbridge, a modern suburb of Washington, DC, and a group of us are having dinner al fresco on the wooden deck outside Nanette Mickle's home. A cool breeze still bites and the daylight is beginning to fade as the sky glows burnt red where the sun set half an hour ago.

There's a great deal of chatter going on. But it's not from us, Nanette's dinner guests. We are purposely keeping rather quiet. The chatter is coming from a set of homes 20 yards away and it's reasonable to admit that we are all enraptured by it. The occupants' incessant chattering – and, at times, their chaotic coming and going – is the very reason we are gathered outdoors to watch and listen.

These are not next door neighbours but Nanette's breeding colony of Purple Martins, 20 cm long birds, larger than their swallow relatives, the males a lovely iridescent purple-black, the females greyer. And they are settling in for the night in the purpose-built set of 50 nestboxes she has provided them with in her garden, boxes she regularly tends to make sure their occupants are doing just fine.

So many householders along the eastern side of the US provide Purple Martins with nestboxes that the birds no longer seek out their natural nesting sites of tiny cavities in trees and cliffs. They don't need to. For this species of bird, nestboxes are no longer a supplement to their natural nest sites as they are for many birds. They have become their sole nesting places.

The Purple Martin has taken its dependence on human buildings and structures to the extreme but a plethora of other birds, too, make use of our bricks and mortar for breeding, though not usually as exclusively as these martins. Some, though, have done so ever since we first started constructing buildings to shelter ourselves from the elements thousands of years ago.

'I've gotten 11 boxes within a wooden nesting house plus about 50 gourds [large, hollow, dried fruit shells], each one with a small entrance hole for the birds', says Nanette. 'On average I get over 50 breeding pairs and they feed all round the area, often bringing back large dragonflies they've caught to feed their chicks. I bought some of the boxes ready-made [they cost about $18 each] but most I've made myself. They have to be waterproof but each one has an air vent. It gets pretty hot here in summer.'

In the east and Midwest US, Purple Martins breed exclusively in these nestboxes. A different subspecies, much less common, that breeds in the western US still nests in tree cavities.

'At least a million people in the States put up housing for martins', comments Louise Chambers, a Director of the Purple Martin Conservation Association, a charity with around 5,000 members. 'Some have one, 12-room house; some offer homes for 600 pairs. In total they possibly accommodate tens of millions of pairs.'

'They eat only flying insects which they catch in flight. Their diet is diverse, including dragon-flies, damselflies, flies, tiny gnats, midges, mayflies, leafhoppers, butterflies, moths, grasshoppers, cicadas, bees, wasps, flying ants, and ballooning spiders. They don't specialise in any type or size of insect, and from one food collecting trip, a martin parent may return with one or two flies, bees and damselflies all at once. Or up to 80 or so smaller insects like leafhoppers. But martins aren't prodigious consumers of mosquitoes as is so often claimed by companies that manufacture martin housing!' adds Louise.

'I have problems with some other birds getting into the boxes and stopping the martins using them. House Sparrows, introduced here from the UK, are a pest but if bluebirds or Tree Swallows get in, I leave them alone. They deserve nesting holes too', says Nanette.

'I started putting up boxes years back when we lived in Louisiana. I bought one advertising 2,000 mosquitoes a day eaten by a pair of Purple Martins! And, boy, there are a lot of mosquitoes in Louisiana. They didn't touch mosquitoes but they were so interesting to watch. It's a real community. Snakes can climb up the pole supporting the nestbox gantry so we have to put a barrier on the pole. Owls and hawks, even crows, sometimes try and get at them too', she adds.

So when did all this nestbox provision for Purple Martins begin?

'Native Indian tribes were the first martin landlords – mainly the Cherokee, Choctaw and Chickasaw – who put up dried, hollowed out gourds for them to nest in', comments Louise Chambers. 'Martin houses came later, when Europeans arrived and saw them nesting in gourds. We don't know how or why the Indian tribes learned that martins would use gourds or what decided them to put up gourds for their use but Cherokee mythology includes a story of how the martin got its gourd.'

'We imagine the Cherokee valued the martins for the same reasons we do today: fun to watch, nice to listen to, and insect control. Plus they may have chased off hawks or vultures that tried to eat meat or fish the Indians were drying for winter food stores. The martins can be surprisingly noisy and harass a bird of prey if it comes near!' she says.

In Europe, the first nestboxes were clay flasks used in medieval times in the Netherlands to house Common Starlings and House Sparrows whose young were then eaten. The first provided simply to encourage birds for pleasure or observation – not food – were perhaps those put up by Charles Waterton (1782–1865), a slightly eccentric country gentleman, in Yorkshire during the early 19th century, by which time most were constructed of wood. They were built for owls, Sand Martins, Western Jackdaws and starlings.

Scientific researchers began to make use of nestboxes early in the 20th century, for example in a study of the house wren in the US. As the exact needs of the birds became better known, the modern types of boxes evolved, and materials other than wood began to be used such as cement, hardboard, plastic and more recently non-rotting woodcrete, a mixture of sawdust, clay and con-crete.

Another trend during the last few decades has been the extension in the range of birds catered for, from the original nesters in holes and cavities such as tits and robins to species like Common

House Martins, Common Kestrels and Tawny Owls. Boxes are even designed for bats, hedgehogs and some insects!

According to the US Department of the Interior Fish and Wildlife Service, more than two dozen North American birds will nest in bird boxes, or bird houses as Americans call them. They include bluebirds, wrens, flycatchers, woodpeckers and owls depending on box design, size and location. Nestboxes are now a common sight in many European countries and the US, as well as in some other countries. And not only in gardens but in the grounds of schools and other institutions, and increasingly on industrial and commercial premises too. In fact, nestbox manufacture is big business.

The Nestbox Company based in Solihull, Birmingham, is the UK's largest nestbox manufacturer.

'There are no figures for the total number of nestboxes sold in the UK annually', says its owner, Peter Bubb. 'We produce around 10,000 a year, all out of high quality plywood, but that includes some made for small mammals too. A lot of others are imported. The market for them is pretty steady but the market for more specialised boxes, with cameras included in them, is actually increasing.'

Ordinary nestboxes are certainly in widespread use in people's gardens in Britain. In 1997, John Tully, a Bristol ornithologist, and colleagues counted 546 boxes in the gardens of just over 1,700 houses (of a wide mix from small terraced to large detached) in a northern suburb of his home city. Seemingly, 134 were occupied by nesting birds, 72 per cent of them by Blue Tits.

But lots of city birds certainly don't require nestboxes to encourage them to breed. In the deep urban 'canyons' of New York with their huge, vertical 'cliffs', the fastest-flying bird on earth has set up shop. Many Peregrines – steel-grey coloured falcons – are now thoroughly urbanised, attracted by safe building ledges for nesting and an abundant supply of birds like city pigeons to eat.

Each year, the New York State's Endangered Species Unit (ESU) compiles information on its breeding Peregrines. In 2008, the state had 67 pairs, of which 60 bred and raised a total of 129 young falcons. The state, though, includes very large areas of countryside including mountain ranges and extensive forests. So the largest number of Peregrine pairs (30) were still breeding on cliff ledges, their natural breeding sites. But 17 pairs nested on bridges in and around New York City, eight on buildings and five on other structures such as artificial nest towers put up specially to encourage them.

But what's interesting is that the Peregrines breeding in the city on bridges, buildings and other man-made structures always produce more young birds per pair than the Peregrines breeding at natural sites on cliffs. In 2008, nests on buildings produced, on average, 3.5 young birds per pair; cliff nest sites only half that. Quite why this should be, no one is sure. It would seem a bit odd to argue that city Peregrines get disturbed less than they do in the country. Instead, it might be that the city slickers have a better guaranteed food supply … city pigeons fed on good quality New York City food scraps!

'One of their favourite nest sites is nearly 700 feet up on one of the huge towers of the Verrazano-Narrows Bridge, a double-decked suspension bridge that connects Staten Island and Brooklyn across the Hudson River', says Barbara Allen Loucks who coordinates the Peregrine programme state-wide for the ESU.

'And on buildings their nest sites vary enormously in height from the lowest at just four stories – a bank in Utica [a small city in upper New York State] – to the 58-floor MetLife building, 800 feet up over Manhattan. We've had a pair at MetLife since 1989.'

Usually seven pairs of Peregrines nest – and generally stay year-round – in Manhattan itself, New York's major commercial, financial and cultural centre and one of the mostly densely populated urban areas in the world. Before the mid 1990s there were none so their colonisation is pretty recent.

And New York's urban Peregrines have clearly cottoned on to the notion that they're in the 'city that never sleeps'! Robert Decandido and Deborah Allen, two New York-based ornithologists, watched them on 77 dark evenings at the Empire State Building from August to November 2004 and saw them hunting migrating birds during 25 of those nights.

It used to be assumed that urban Peregrines lived off a diet of city pigeons and almost nothing else. But Decandido and Allen found that they captured 37 different birds including migrants flying past at night such as Yellow-billed Cuckoos and Baltimore Orioles. They catch bats too! The lights associated with skyscrapers are thought to disorientate migrating birds, probably making them more vulnerable to attacks from the fast-flying Peregrines. And the skyscrapers supply hunting perches at altitudes often flown by night-time migrants.

In Britain, ornithologists Ed Drewitt and Nick Dixon spent ten years collecting more than 5,000 food items from Peregrine breeding sites in Bristol, Bath and Exeter. As in the New York study, they found that the birds' diets were much more varied than anyone had thought. City pigeons made up over half of their meals by weight but Drewitt and Dixon found the bones of no fewer than 98 different species of birds ranging in size from tiny Goldcrests (Europe's smallest) to Mallard ducks! After pigeons, the most abundant prey were Common Starlings – many of them young birds – Eurasian Collared Doves, Redwings (thrushes that winter in the UK) and Greenfinches.

But some of the birds the Peregrines were killing are known to be shy and secretive, hard enough even for keen birdwatchers to see and presumably extremely difficult for a bird of prey to attack in its own habitat. They included Common Quail, small ground birds brilliantly camouflaged in the meadows they inhabit. And Water Rail, a skulking bird of wetlands and heavily vegetated pond edges that rarely ventures out into the open! So the assumption is that the Peregrines caught them in flight at night (because these birds rarely move anywhere by day), maybe when they were migrating or moving to a different piece of habitat.

Waterbirds' camouflage may work very well when the birds are in their normal habitats, flying very low. But it clearly wasn't designed for flying over well-lit cities at night! Most waterbirds are pale coloured underneath but dark on top, camouflaging them as they search for fish or other prey in the water below while making them more difficult to see swimming on the water's surface from above.

Flying at night over cities makes their light undersides very conspicuous against dark skies when viewed from below. And Peregrines perched high up on buildings will look down on dark silhouettes as they fly past against the illuminated buildings. Many night-migrating birds also get badly disorientated by illuminated cities and can easily end up crashing into buildings so it's little wonder that these adaptable birds of prey do well in lit-up cities. After all, disorientated birds are an easy meal for hunters like Peregrines. Around the world, these birds of prey have woken up to the advantages of a bit of night-time insomnia. French, German, Dutch, Hong Kong, Taiwanese and Australian city Peregrines all seem to do the same.

Most UK cities and large towns, probably more than 60 – London, Cardiff, Belfast and Edinburgh included – have established breeding Peregrines nesting on the top of tall buildings, ranging from cathedrals to bridges, ex-power stations to civic clock towers. London has several pairs. And they attract lots of human admirers, something the RSPB has been quick to capitalise on by installing video filming, temporary information centres and telescopes to encourage their appreciation.

It isn't only Peregrines that often hunt by night in cities. Nightjars and nighthawks – both long-winged, dark brown and cream-coloured birds – are attracted to street lights in towns. The lights attract flying insects, the staple diet of these hunters. Common Nighthawks will nest on city roofs while the Savanna Nightjar hunts above the streets in Jakarta and other Indonesian cities. Standing on dusty roadsides at night in Bamako, Mali's capital, I've seen nightjars snatch insects under street lights, giving me such surprisingly short glimpses of the birds that I couldn't be sure which species it was.

In São Paulo and other Brazilian cities, Black Vultures have likewise taken up residence on apartment blocks and high-rise offices. No one gives them a second glance. Every day they feed on the garbage dumps on the edge of the city and drift back in among the high-rise buildings on warm breezes to roost.

In fact, many birds of prey seem to have taken to our cities rather well, killing other urban-dwelling, small birds in tree-lined parks and city pigeons perched nonchalantly on building ledges. But why? The noise, the pollution, the 24-hour lighting and the vast numbers of humans milling up and down streets doesn't seem to put them off their stride at all.

Northern Goshawks, larger versions of fast-flying Eurasian Sparrowhawks, have established themselves in several German cities including Hamburg, Cologne and Berlin. They breed in Moscow too.

In Hamburg, where they have been particularly studied, they nest in trees in public parks, cemeteries, hospital grounds and private gardens but they hunt for birds in forests and parks on the city edge as well as in built-up areas in the city centre. Blackbirds, magpies and city pigeons are high on their most wanted lists. The researchers there were surprised by the birds' tolerance of people as they plucked the feathers off their catch while sitting on TV aerials, roofs and chimneys. In the countryside, Northern Goshawks are pretty shy birds.

And in warmer countries wherever there is the chance of food, at a garbage dump or an abattoir perhaps, vultures are never far away in spite of often continual disturbance by people, machinery and vehicles.

At the city abattoir in formidably hot Addis Ababa, Ethiopia, not one of the city's tourist attractions, it's quite common to see a couple of hundred vultures – often Hooded (a dark brown, fairly small vulture), African White-backed (a pale brown and white bird) and Ruppell's Vultures (spotty black and white) – right in the middle of the hot and dusty city. There'll probably be other scavenging birds too – Marabou Storks the height of a small person, pretty scruffy grey storks with ugly, hanging throat pouches that seem to delight in human refuse.

So why have so many different birds of prey found our cities to their liking? Firstly, most have a year-round food supply in the form of smaller birds or plenty of food scraps. And secondly, they can usually nest safely on high-rise buildings where they attract little attention from the hordes of city dwellers and workers down below intent on going about their business.

But for most birds in cities, smaller birds in particular, life isn't quite as rosy as it might seem. Research by the British Trust for Ornithology (BTO) in Britain found that most urban-nesters laid their eggs earlier, laid fewer of them and raised fewer, lighter weight chicks than the same species in the countryside. It suggests that their food supply is more limited than we imagined and, as Mike Toms, Head of the BTO's Garden Ecology Team explains, garden 'bird table' food like seeds, grain and suet isn't appropriate for feeding young chicks. It's aimed at adult birds. In their first weeks chicks often need tiny insects, not something usually in good supply in towns and cities.

On the other hand, birds might live longer in urban areas because they don't have to endure winter temperatures as low as in the countryside and because snow and ice melts more quickly, covering the ground for less time and allowing birds to feed more frequently. And although urban cats might be killers, there are far more predators to avoid in the countryside.

Birds have had a long time to adapt to our increasingly urban ways of living as towns and cities have expanded. But they've had far less time to adapt to some of our other engineering marvels. Cars and lorries have hardly been around in any numbers for a century. Little wonder, perhaps, that vast numbers of birds get killed by them on roads, frequently caught out by the speed of vehicles which travel much faster than they can.

But many birds are incredibly adaptable and a few very intelligent birds have even adapted to our car culture. Many snatch a meal from road-killed corpses (see Chapter 9). Carrion Crows – arguably the world's most intelligent birds – in Japanese cities drop hard-shelled nuts they can't open themselves onto busy roads so that passing vehicles break them apart. Some of them have even stationed themselves on pelican crossings so that they can more safely retrieve the kernels when the traffic stops to allow pedestrians across!

Far from tolerating, or even admiring, their cleverness, most Japanese city dwellers seem to want to bump off their crows. Much of the trouble they cause is the result of the birds nesting on electricity poles and sometimes blacking out sections of cities. Crows have carried away baby prairie dogs and ducklings from Tokyo zoo, say city officials, and snatch food from children, even though such misdemeanours don't seem to be commonplace in other countries.

While no one knows the precise number of crows in Japan, bird experts and government officials in cities across the nation say populations have increased enormously since the 1990s due, apparently, to the growing abundance of garbage, a product of Japan's embrace of more wasteful western lifestyles. There is, then, an obvious answer!

'The crows are trying to outfox us', said Kazuhide Kyutoku, deputy chief of Kyushu Electric's facilities safety group in Kagoshima. Mr Kyutoku said that, despite the twice-weekly patrols which have removed 600 nests since they began three years ago, the number of nests keeps increasing, as have electricity blackouts. In Tokyo, utility companies have reported crows cutting fibre optic cables, apparently to use as materials for nests. Blackouts have become common nationwide, including one in 2007 in the northern prefecture of Akita that briefly shut down the high-speed bullet train service.

Tokyo was one of the first to take lethal measures. In 2001, the city began setting traps in parks and nature reserves, using raw meat as a lure. In the following seven years, the city captured and killed more than 90,000 crows and the number of crow-related complaints from residents has dropped as a result.

Ever since man started to build large structures, birds have shared them with us. The first large buildings, the Egyptian pyramids, are still home to feral pigeons descended from their original wild inhabitants. Many wild pigeons around the world have since taken a liking to our houses, farms, villages and towns, not always for nesting but certainly to live in close proximity to.

Eurasian Collared Doves, slim and pale pink-brown in colour, are a good example. Originally inhabitants of Asia, they've spread over much of Europe since the 1890s. They reached Britain in 1953 where there are now over 200,000 pairs. They don't breed on or in our buildings – they nest in trees – but they are extremely common perching on buildings and in gardens and parks as well as at outdoor cafes. And they have become commonplace at bird feeders in gardens.

Laughing Doves, also quite small pigeons but rusty-brown and blue-grey in colour, are common in the countryside, towns and villages across much of Africa south of the Sahara, the Middle East and southern Asia east to India. They also usually nest in trees but often on buildings and they scavenge for spilt seeds, grain and small insects along many a dusty, hot African village roadside and, especially, around farm buildings.

The larger, long-tailed, light grey and pinkish-brown Mourning Dove of the US and Central America has become as common in town suburbs and around farms as they are in the countryside, exploiting seeds that they can scrounge in almost any habitat. There are hundreds of millions of them and while most nest in trees, some use building ledges rather like city pigeons do.

There are some birds whose engineering expertise is so great that they have become expert at building their nests clinging to the outside of our buildings, in all probability allowing them to become much more abundant than they would be if they still relied on cliff-faces and caves. Perhaps the most obvious example is the House Martin, now called the Common House Martin and a relative of the nesting box-breeding Purple Martin of the United States.

Common it most certainly is. Associated with homes across Europe and Russia, this bird of the swallow family looks black and white but is really a very dark blue and white. It still uses some cliff and cave nesting sites but it now largely uses human structures such as bridges and houses where it builds an architecturally amazing mud cup with an opening only at the top, usually under the eaves, every bit of mud carried by the birds in their beaks and carried time after thousands of times from nearby ponds, streams or puddles. It's an incredibly arduous task.

House Sparrows frequently attempt to take over the nest during construction, with the House Martins having to rebuild elsewhere if they are successful. Unlike the Woodbridge Purple Martins, they don't have a Nanette Mickle to look after their interests! By the time the House Martins get close to finishing their mud home, the entrance at the top of the cup is so small that the chunkier sparrows cannot then make a takeover bid.

With three or four growing youngsters shoe-horned into the cup, they have virtually no space for a bit of wing testing. So young House Martins get one chance, and one only, to get their maiden flight reasonably alright when they take their first plunge into the air maybe ten metres above ground. It's a hazardous start in life!

There are thought to be between 20 and 50 million Common House Martins, although the bird is declining in some parts of its breeding area, especially in the UK and some other parts of western Europe. This might be due to a decline in small, airborne insects or to deaths on their annual migrations north–south to the middle of Africa across the massive Sahara.

While new housing has created more nest sites, and less air pollution has enabled breeding in the centre of major cities like London, poor weather and poisoning by agricultural pesticides (both of which can reduce the abundance of the flying insects they eat), lack of mud for nest building and competition with House Sparrows can all reduce their numbers.

Without doubt, the droppings from their nests can make a pretty awful mess around doorways and windows and, as a result, some nests get destroyed. But most people tolerate, even welcome, their martins, associating them with warm summer weather, and admire their incredible building skills.

If House Martins are frequently welcomed over much of the northern world as the harbingers of spring, there is one bird – a very large one – that has even more deeply established credentials as a town dweller. It is said to bring good luck when it nests high on the very tops of our buildings. It is thought to be a sign of a good farming harvest. But it is arguably best known as the bringer of babies! No pressure then for the White Stork.

Standing well over a metre tall, white with black wings, red legs and a large red beak, White Storks are an impressive sight. Even more impressive is a pair of them standing on top of their huge stick nest perched maybe 50 metres up on the top of a church spire! They breed across much of Europe, North Africa and Southwest Asia though unfortunately not in Britain. Poland has the largest number of breeding white storks with over 50,000 pairs. Spain comes second followed by Portugal.

Some White Storks nest in trees but most prefer the roofs of buildings, churches, castles and large manor houses, the tops of telephone poles and tall chimneys and even the big metal pylons that carry high-voltage electricity cables. Some householders even add artificial platforms such as wooden wagon wheels to old chimneys to encourage them to build a nest, so popular are these huge birds.

Sitting in the fabulous medieval Plaza Mayor of the old Extremaduran town of Trujillo in western Spain on a warm spring day, the clattering noise from the White Stork nests high on the church roof and on the roofs of the old mansions that line this beautiful square is nothing unusual. This is bill clattering, done by both the male and female storks on their nests, apparently to enhance their attachment to each other.

It's a wonderful display, both birds simultaneously arching their heads way back, then clattering their beaks as they bring their heads forward again, almost touching. At the same time they sometimes get into a bobbing-up-and-down display. It's all calculated to take your concentration away from your café cortado at one of the little cafes around Trujillo's lovely square!

Though White Storks are protected by popular opinion over most of their range, they are persecuted in other areas. Large migrating flocks circling the eastern end of the Mediterranean are vulnerable to shooting in Syria and Lebanon, and several thousand are killed each year. They are also subject to hunting pressure in many parts of Africa, where their large size and tendency to flock in large numbers make them attractive targets.

Between the years 1970 and 1990 there was a sharp decline in the White Stork population in Europe; the census count was at its lowest in 1984. At least a good part of the decline was due to loss of the damp habitat they need to feed where they take frogs, snakes, fish, rodents and other creatures, the result of pesticides, pollution and wetland drainage.

But good news! White Storks are on the up again, particularly in the western part of the continent, although their numbers have not yet reached those before the decline. Some of the increase is due to warmer winters where the storks spend their coldest months, usually in North Africa though some of them have found it warm enough to go no further than southern Spain.

The birds have changed their feeding too, now picking up prey on irrigated fields and at garbage dumps some of the time where they get an even more varied diet.

But while the White Stork is a classic example of a bird that builds its nest on the outside – the highest part in its case – of a building, exposed to wind, rain and sun, there are several birds that get tucked up inside the structure of our homes and outbuildings to breed.

The Jackdaw, these days called the Western Jackdaw, a smallish member of the crow family, black in colour with a grey back to its head, is one such bird. They are noisy and frequently to be found perched on house chimney pots; it's often these chimneys – disused ones – that they breed in! But they also breed in large cavities in old trees (presumably their natural breeding spots before they took to buildings), in holes in cliffs and in ruined buildings.

They are famous for using church steeples for nesting in, a fact reported in verse by 18th century English poet William Cowper. Their nests are usually built by a pair of the birds blocking up a hole by dropping sticks into it; the nest of hair, rags, bark, soil and many other materials is then built on top of the platform. This building technique has led to blocked chimneys and even to nests, with the Jackdaw – or a family of young birds – crashing down into fireplaces inside a home, startling the residents and causing fits of screaming as the disorientated birds flutter around the room scattering chimney soot as they go!

Some Jackdaw nests, added to year after year, can reach surprising dimensions. Edward Jesse in his *Scenes and Occupations of Country Life* (John Murray, 1853) describes one built in the bell tower of Eton College in 17 days in 1842. It measured ten feet in height and formed a solid stack of sticks.

In common with other members of the crow family, magpies especially, these birds have another close link with people – to be more accurate with women. They steal jewellery! Any shiny object attracts them, from a discarded milk bottle top to a fine necklace, and these objects are often stashed away in their nests.

Common across Europe, northwest Africa and into western Asia, there are millions of Western Jackdaws in towns, villages and around farms, maybe as many as 30 million.

But perhaps the best-known bird that regularly comes inside our buildings to nest is the aptly named Barn Swallow, known in Britain simply as 'the swallow'. It's the most widespread species of swallow in the world. With its dark blue upperparts and long, deeply forked tail it's found in Europe, Asia, Africa and across America.

Its typical nesting spot is on a ledge or a wooden beam in an old building, a farm shed maybe, an old garage or a barn – or even under a bridge, a good spot for the flying insects it feeds on if the bridge is over a river. Before man-made sites became common, the Barn Swallow nested on cliff-faces or in caves but their use of natural sites is now rare.

Barn Swallows build a rather rough and ready mud cup of a nest lined with a bit of straw or grass. More a bird of farms and country buildings than towns and cities – where House Martins take their place – its arrival in spring in North America and Europe is frequently welcomed by very many people in the hope that summer will shortly follow! It probably isn't only the chances of good nest sites in barns and other outbuildings that attract swallows to farms. It's a good place to be based if insects are your sole diet; there are usually plenty of them around livestock farms in particular.

Many people also spot their line-ups on telephone wires in late summer and early autumn as a sign that they will soon be setting off on their long distance flight all the way to southern Africa from Europe or to South America from the US and Canada. Barn Swallows live for around four years on average, not bad if you consider that it means eight enormous, energy-sapping journeys, almost from one end of the earth to the other!

There are thought to be around 190 million Barn Swallows in the world, their numbers doubtless much higher than they would be without humans or, more accurately, without the buildings we have constructed and the forest clearance we've done to create farmland.

Strange though it might seem at first, in North America at least, Barn Swallows frequently breed close to Ospreys, those huge fish-eating birds of prey. Swallows will build their nest below an Osprey nest, receiving protection from any marauding bird of prey, which is repelled by the Ospreys. The Ospreys, in turn, are often alerted to the presence of these predators by the alarm calls of the swallows. It's a good deal for them both.

Chimney Swifts, appropriately dark sooty brown, fast-flying birds with long scimitar-shaped wings, are common across the central and eastern United States. Originally they presumably nested in large hollow trees but now they mainly nest in man-made structures such as large open chimneys, a bigger version of a hollow tree as far as a Chimney Swift is concerned! The nest is made of little twigs glued together with saliva and placed in a shaded spot fixed to the inside vertical chimney wall.

There they will lay three to seven white eggs that have to be incubated for about 20 days. When the young swifts are maturing they exercise their long wings furiously and when D-Day arrives, they clamber up the chimney wall using their very sharp claws and launch themselves into the air. There is no second chance if they crash to the ground; their long wings don't allow them to take flight from a horizontal surface!

Like swifts the world over, Chimney Swifts actually live on the wing, catching insects as they fly and, sometimes, sleeping in flight high up in the air as if on autopilot, though usually they sleep by clinging on to tiny ledges in empty chimneys and abandoned buildings. They usually feed in groups, often zooming in screaming, jet-like parties between buildings just like the very similar Common Swift does in European towns.

There are an estimated 15 million Chimney Swifts in the US, and their numbers have almost certainly increased historically with the introduction of large chimneys as nesting locations. In more recent times, though, with many chimneys having been dismantled and the decrease in domestic fires that require them, their numbers are declining quite considerably, prompting conservation groups like the Driftwood Wildlife Association in Austin, Texas to give out advice on the building of artificial towers resembling small chimneys in large gardens and similar spots to attract these unusual birds.

Of the roughly 95 different species of swift in the world, most nest in crevices in cliffs, a few in tree crevices while just a few have adapted to making the most of cracks and crevices in our buildings. Along with the Chimney Swift, the dark brown Common Swift in Europe is almost totally reliant on buildings, constructing their primitive nests in crevices high on walls, under eaves, under windowsills, in the corner rafters of wooden buildings, in chimneys and in smokestacks. Their evening screaming calls are familiar in many a town and village as they fly in small groups between the buildings, weaving this way and that, like a squadron of fighter jets showing off their skills.

There is another bird, too, that sets up home in ours and which seems to have been our housemate since time immemorial. It's the House Sparrow. They probably evolved about 10,000 years ago in the Middle East and in other parts of the world when people slowly became crop-growers rather than hunters. The sparrows took a liking to crop seeds to vary their diet of grass and other wild plant seed. And they took a liking to the buildings that these now more sedentary farmers constructed too. Their nooks and crannies were good places to nest in. Well fed and well endowed for breeding, House Sparrows took quite a shine to people. They have been with us ever since!

As people and their habitation expanded across the globe, House Sparrows tagged along. Sometimes, according to the world's leading sparrow expert, Denis Summers-Smith, in his *On Sparrows and Man* (The Thersby Group, 2005), they've hitched a ride to get to new territory:

> Incidents of sparrows hitching lifts on ships are not uncommon. The Falkland Islands were colonised in this way in 1919 by about twenty House Sparrows that travelled there on four whaling vessels from Montevideo, a journey lasting nine days, and there is little doubt that much of the recent expansion of the Tree Sparrow [a very similar but tidier-looking, brown-capped sparrow] in Indonesia and the Philippines has been through ship-assisted passage. The longest known voyage is of a group of sparrows that boarded a ship in Bremerhaven, Germany and did not disembark until they reached Melbourne in Australia.

Not surprisingly, you can find these chirping little birds almost everywhere in the world; either they got there themselves or they got taken along by people – to the US for instance where they have since become a crop pest (see Chapter 8). They are one of the commonest, and most successful, birds in the world.

Sparrows will find nesting sites in a huge range of buildings. Summers-Smith reckons that no fewer than 16 different species of sparrows, worldwide, have been found nesting in our buildings. They'll breed amongst the branches and thatch of the roof of a Zulu rondavel in South Africa. Or in amongst the stems of a lakeside reed hut in Peru. And in a gap in the block work of a Canadian house or amongst the dense ivy clothing the high walls of a German castle.

Almost unbelievably, House Sparrows have even been known to live without any natural light in coalmines! In the 1970s, a few birds lived for several years in Frinkley Colliery in South Yorkshire, even breeding there 2,000 feet down, relying on miners providing them with scraps to eat.

A shortage of breeding cavities – as building standards improve, houses are better maintained and dilapidated buildings are converted to homes – has been suggested as one reason why the familiar House Sparrow has been declining severely in Britain. But John Tully has found that, on the contrary, there doesn't seem to be a shortage of nesting places for them.

In 2007 he and colleagues carried out a survey in a northern suburb of Bristol of 1,700 houses including a very wide range of building types (from detached to terraced) and house ages. They identified at least 270 nesting pairs of House Sparrows, a probable underestimate because it wasn't possible for them to see all aspects of every house.

So there are probably other reasons why their numbers in Britain have fallen from around 12 million pairs in the 1970s to between 6 and 7 million pairs today. What is clear, though, is that their numbers were probably artificially high for a very long time, maintained by plenty of wasted food, grain around farms especially, and by even more nesting sites in poorly maintained buildings.

Summers-Smith mentions the steady changeover from the horse and cart in towns to petrol-powered vehicles that started in the 1920s. The disappearance of spilt grain fed to the horses, and also perhaps the then steady increase in pollution killing off insects which nestling sparrows are fed by their parents, might be why town House Sparrow numbers fell around this time. He refers to surveys in London's Kensington Gardens which produced 2,603 house sparrows in 1925, down to 885 in 1948 and 544 by 1975. Today there are hardly any there.

Increasingly intensive agriculture using pesticides, and destroying hedges and other habitats through the 1960s and 1970s, caused a further drop, hitting hard an array of countryside birds including sparrows which were common around farms too. More effective storage of grain and animal feeds has undoubtedly reduced the food available to the adults.

House Sparrows have become scarcer across much of western Europe too, though, inexplicably, their populations are holding up in Berlin and Paris while they have virtually disappeared from Hamburg, Amsterdam and Brussels. So there is still much to be learnt about the decline in this, one of our most familiar birds. Denis Summers-Smith argues that the decline of House Sparrows in many cities ought to make us ask questions about the quality of life for human city dwellers. Yet there are many contradictions.

Walk around Bangkok's crowded streets in what is one of the most densely packed human urban centres in the world and neat-looking Tree Sparrows are frequently close by picking up crumbs off pavements and seeds from plants on scraps of waste ground and perching in the roadside trees alongside some of the worst, pollution-belching traffic in the world, so bad that many people wear face protection.

Sparrows like these have become relatively tame because of their long association with people. It's not unusual to sit at a pavement cafe and be joined by a House Sparrow on the lookout for crumbs. Other birds have become remarkably tame too.

House Buntings (small, rusty-brown finches) in North Africa do exactly the same but with the added habit of going inside people's homes to scrounge what they can. In Britain, gardeners are used to having European Robins follow them about, especially if they are digging over soil, when the birds will perch on a rested spade. Surprisingly, then, it's a habit never seen in robins across mainland Europe. There they are shy forest birds!

Habit accounts for a lot. Wood Pigeons in Britain became much more wary during World War II when large numbers were shot to stop them eating crops (and for food). In the years after the war, they relaxed and returned to being quite tame, especially in parks and gardens, though they remained much more wary in the countryside where they are far more likely to be shot.

European Starlings, too, have long had an affinity with our towns. Until about 20 years ago, tens of thousands of them flew into the West End of London every night, eventually settling among much purring and chattering on building ledges in 'Theatreland', the area of Britain's capital around Leicester Square, and on other London landmarks like St Paul's Cathedral and Marble Arch.

On winter's evenings they huddled up close, like lines of miniature black penguins, seemingly unaware of the traffic and human throngs on the streets below. They stood there apparently gossiping and grumbling, murmuring loudly, clacking and chattering, wonderfully oblivious to whatever took place on the streets below them including first-night appearances by film stars at prestigious London cinemas. It was warmer to roost on the capital's ledges than out in the bare winter trees on the cold Essex flatlands where many of them had fed during the day.

An account of a survey in 1932/33 reported locating 285 night-time roosts in Britain with about 20 in London. In 1949 the birds apparently stopped Big Ben because of the weight of so many of them on the clock hands! The weigh-in led to questions in Parliament and a whole episode of the then popular radio comedy, *The Goon Show*, was devoted to the perceived 'starling menace'.

Some estimates of single roosts in the past suggest that the largest contained a million birds. The former Leicester Square flock was reckoned to be about 100,000 strong. The sight of huge numbers of starlings swirling in pulsating, seemingly choreographed flight, before settling on buildings – or the reedbeds and woodlands they often roost on in the countryside – has to rank as one of the visual wonders of the natural world.

But the numbers of Britain's starlings, as in most of Europe, have plummeted by about 50 per cent since those days, and many of the great urban flocks seem to be no more. The Leicester Square roost disappeared in the late 1970s, seemingly because of more intensive farming on the lands outside the city, in Essex for instance, making them much less attractive as feeding places. While many Londoners regretted their demise, the capital's street cleaners had no regrets; the birds' droppings were nightly fouling seats and pavements as well as building up in unsightly masses on the ledges the birds occupied.

It's unlikely that starlings will ever return in those numbers; many of the building ledges they once used now have anti-pigeon spikes or wires fixed to them, making it impossible for them to land.

'Although we only have anecdotal evidence for the demise of the large winter roosts, it's likely that there really has been a decline in both the number of roosts and in the number of birds attending individual roosts', says Mike Toms, Head of the Garden Ecology Team at the BTO. 'There are three factors which, to my mind, might contribute to the change. Their overall decline in numbers; fewer starlings from the near continent moving here in winter as they used to because winters are milder there; and maybe the return of the Sparrowhawk to cities as their numbers have recovered and their increased attacks on the gathering starlings. So the starlings are dispersing to a larger number of smaller roosts instead.'

All the same, today's starling roosts can be a most impressive sight, as tens of thousands of the birds wheel and pulse in huge sky-filled flocks, one time diving low towards the seaside pier, wood or reedbed they'll eventually settle in for the night, then zooming up into the darkening sky again. The RSPB even sets up annual winter watching points for people to admire these aerial displays, for example at Brighton Pier where tens of thousands of these birds roost.

They are, as the naturalist and author Richard Mabey has put it so elegantly, 'a single plasmic organism, folding and pulsing in the dusk sky like a dark aurora. It's like a vision of mass consciousness or of the deep geometry of the universe'.

The overall starling decline is attributed to a decrease in the invertebrates in the soils of pastures they feed in during the day, probing the turf with their strong yellow beaks, and the conversion of a lot of that pasture to crop-growing. As with the House Sparrow, their fortunes are closely linked to our activities, for better or for worse. At the moment, certainly, it's for the worst.

But European Starlings remain common birds. According to the BTO, there are thought to be up to 50 million pairs Europe-wide (800,000 pairs breeding in Britain), twice that if Russia is included.

But don't get too mesmerised by the undoubted beauty and impressiveness of a European Starling flock that you might see. Like all animals, these birds aren't very PC. Adult male birds occupy the central, most sheltered and safest part of any roost while young birds, young females especially, are forced to the colder edges where they are more vulnerable to being picked off by birds of prey.

As human society has become gradually more urbanised, different birds have long adapted to city life and to sharing our buildings with us, whether in villages, towns or around farms. And more seem to be doing so, birds of prey included. Part of the reason is a more guaranteed all-year-round food supply because there is usually more choice available. In the countryside, where much – sometimes most – of our land is put over to growing crops or raising livestock for us to eat, vast numbers of birds have long exploited what we have available here too, and that is the subject of the next chapter.

8
Getting into a paddy

The crops that we grow – from rice and millet to grapes and wheat – are irresistible to birds looking for an easy feed. Stopping this pillage has always been difficult. Sometimes it's impossible.

Walking through the streets of Tarragona, a stylish town established by the Romans on a hilltop overlooking Spain's east coast, I can't say that it's easy to find a restaurant not serving paella on its tempting menu. Sometimes described as Spain's 'signature dish', its variable blend of vegetables, some chicken or rabbit, and – hereabouts especially – prawns, langoustines and maybe some cuttlefish, is hard to resist.

But a paella is not a paella without its main and characteristic ingredient. Rice. Round-grained, pearled in the centre and unbroken. The most appropriate variety – called 'bomba' – absorbs all the flavours and aromas of the more showy ingredients as the dish is attentively cooked.

Most non-Spanish paella eaters will assume, wrongly, that the rice on menus hereabouts comes from Southeast Asia where the lion's share of the world's staple food is grown. In fact, the rice you'll eat in your paella in Tarragona is as local as the langoustines.

Around 100,000 tonnes of rice is produced annually from over 20,000 hectares of rice paddies in the delta of the Ebro where this great Spanish river flows into the Mediterranean southwest of the city. The paddies occupy two-thirds of the land, mixed in with wildlife-rich marshes and pools.

Spain's rice growing isn't much compared with Southeast Asia's annual production of 550 million tonnes but the local rice paddies are increasingly valued as much for their wildlife as they are for their edible crop.

As I walk quietly behind some reeds fringing a ditch in the middle of the delta, wrapped up against the still sharp springtime breeze, the birds I can see in the paddy shallows soon take my mind off numb fingers.

Tall, Black-winged Stilts, black and white with their extra-long red legs, wade delicately in deeper water; a couple of darkly coloured Purple Herons stand motionless near one of their commoner Grey Heron cousins; and a single Pied Avocet with its curiously upturned beak is sifting through some mud on the water's edge. At another water-filled paddy nearby there's a flotilla of ducks, Common Pochard, the males with their burnt red heads plus a few of their larger Red-crested Pochard cousins with more gaudy red beaks.

A decade back, when the EU was considering reducing the support it provides for Europe's mainly Spanish, French and Italian rice growers, it was, surprisingly, the UK's RSPB that leapt to their defence. It argued that the supports were invaluable because the paddies are essential for wildlife.

'Rice is still the best conservation option in those areas where natural wetlands have long been drained and converted to farmland. The paddyfields are a major source of food for a huge range of birds, some of them of concern because they are declining', said an RSPB spokesperson at the time.

Without subsidies, Europe's rice farmers can't compete with Southeast Asian producers with their economies of scale and cheap labour. In 2003, when the new EU 'rice regime' was announced, supports were reduced but not removed and rice growing here is still a major land use.

In the last few years, rice growing in several parts of southern Europe has become more environmentally friendly and even better for wildlife.

The paddyfields in the Ebro delta near the little village of Els Muntells, where RietVell SA (a company set up by the RSPB's Spanish equivalent, the Sociedad Española de Ornitologia) manages 50 hectares of paddies organically, are a good example. RietVell use chicken manure not chemical fertilisers. Insecticides are banned. Weeds that compete with the rice crop are reduced by control-ling water levels to drown them as well as by hand weeding rather than spraying weedkillers.

'We get large numbers of Little Egrets and Grey Herons feeding in the paddies', says Ignasi Ripoll, RietVell's manager. 'A lot of Black-winged Stilts and Purple Swamphens [chicken-sized, iridescent blue waterbirds like giant moorhens] and sometimes Greater Flamingos feed here. They eat the crayfish, frogs and small fish in the warm water.' It's this artificial wetland habitat, full of life, that attracts most birds, not the rice itself.

The paddies impose an artificial rectangular pattern across the delta, each separated by a low earth bank of dried mud, grasses and reeds sprouting an occasional willow or tamarisk tree. Water channels supply the fresh water the rice requires, extracted from the Ebro upstream and carried to the paddies via a system of sluices so that the water depth can be controlled.

A similar system operates in the Camargue, the equally vast area of wetland, parts of it still natural marsh, reedbed and lakes, in the delta of the Rhône in southern France where nearly 20,000 hectares of rice is cultivated.

At Domaine de Paulon farm near the tiny hamlet of Le Sambuc in the centre of the Camargue, I'm sitting in the summer heat with Monsieur and Madame Blanc, one of around a hundred rice farmers hereabouts, outside their cream roughcast farmhouse with its powder blue shutters. Their three dogs are fast asleep in the sun.

The Blancs grow 40 hectares of rice as well as wheat and lucerne, a grass-like forage crop for the bulls that have long been an integral part of Camarguese culture (as are the famed white horses). But they are not optimistic about the future of rice growing.

'We grow some of our rice organically without pesticides and artificial fertilisers', says Mme Blanc. 'We only produce organic rice one year in three on the same field to stop pests building up. For the rest of the crop we try not to use too much insecticide. It's expensive and it's not good for the environment. But most farmers here use a lot', she says. 'It's difficult to make any profit even with the EU subsidies. If these are reduced any more, we'd have to look at growing other crops, maybe lentils or peas, or whatever the market wants.'

Giving up on rice would be a disaster for wildlife. Deltas like the Camargue and the Ebro have long been drastically modified. Their giant rivers have been embanked to stop them flooding as they would have done historically. And most of their marshes, reedbeds and shallow pools have been drained so that their rich soils could be ploughed and farmed.

Rice paddies are the best of a bad job. They are not as rich for wildlife as the natural marshes they have replaced, but because they are filled with shallow water for much of the year they become breeding places for a plethora of invertebrates and amphibians like frogs. So they attract a wealth of both breeding and migrating birds.

Nicolas Sadoul, an ornithologist I arrange to meet at the Station Biologique de la Tour du Valat near Le Sambuc, has considerable experience of the value of Camargue rice growing for birds.

'The paddies are seeded in late spring, and then flooded with water', he comments. 'That attracts Mediterranean and Black-headed Gulls because the water brings worms to the surface. We get migrating wading birds like Common Redshank and Black-tailed Godwit in the paddies then too.'

'As the rice grows, but before it's too tall [the crop reaches a metre high], Grey Herons, Squacco Herons and Little Egrets feed in them. The herons and egrets breed communally in groups of trees scattered about the delta but they rely on the paddies for feeding. In winter a lot of farmers keep their paddies flooded to attract duck and other birds because hunting is so central to the Camarguese culture', adds Sadoul.

In the Ebro delta, almost all of the rice farmers have entered an agri-environment scheme devised by the Catalan government. It provides them with payments in addition to their EU subsidies for farming more sensitively.

'It's a good scheme', comments Ignasi Ripoll. 'The farmers have to keep the paddies flooded in winter for birds to feed and they can't burn the rice stubble after harvesting the crop. They have to plough it back into the soil.'

'Now dragonflies, and other insects, are abundant again here. There are clouds of them in summer. And counts we have done show that our organic paddyfields are even more wildlife-rich. They attract twice the number of feeding birds that the conventional paddies have', he adds.

The world over, a plethora of wetland birds are attracted to rice paddies for an easy meal. None of the wading birds eating up invertebrates, fish, frogs and the like pose a huge problem for the rice farmers – sometimes they bring benefits – so the two live together in relative harmony. However, different birds attracted to the crop as it matures (rice seed is, of course, good eating for seed-eating birds) are a somewhat different matter.

In Thailand, where 22 per cent of the country's land area is rice paddy (compared with under 8 per cent which is natural wetland), Dr Sansanee Choowaew, Programme Director for Natural Resource Management at Mahidol University in northern Bangkok, is clear that overall birds bring benefits for rice farmers.

And that's even though rice cultivation has intensified (Thailand is the world's biggest exporter of rice). Water levels are now closely controlled in many paddies because they are irrigated and instead of one crop of rice a year in traditional rainwater-fed paddies, there are often three crops a year. All the same, paddies remain a rich community of water-living plants, insects, frogs, snakes and fish because they substitute, in part, for natural wetlands.

'Several of the larger wading birds help control populations of rice pests such as the golden-apple snail and crabs which eat young rice shoots. These can destroy large parts of a crop within days if they aren't controlled', she says. 'Birds add free fertiliser from their faeces too and, because their faeces have a high calcium content, that helps reduce soil acidity which is a big problem in some rice-growing areas. Over a hundred different bird species have been recorded from our paddies.'

'Since the 1980s, there's been a shift in Thailand from rice growing using chemicals to organic production. Organic rice fetches a higher price for the farmer and attracts more wildlife although it might not ever be more than perhaps 10 per cent of the total rice area', she adds.

'Asian Openbills [black and white storks] commonly feed in our rice paddies along with several species of egrets and other wading birds. We also have globally threatened birds such as the Greater Adjutant [a huge dark-coloured stork in severe decline] and the Spot-billed Pelican and several of Thailand's endangered birds like Painted Stork and the Oriental Darter [a rare, cormorant lookalike that swims almost submerged]', comments Philip Round, Assistant Professor at the Department of Biology at Mahidol University and a leading ornithologist in Southeast Asia.

'Buntings and other seed-eating birds like some of our finches, as well as some insect-eaters like shrikes, have declined though. Birds of prey, too, have declined and it might well be because more herbicides and insecticides are being used in the intensive irrigated rice paddies to get bigger crop yields. The trouble with these intensive paddies, unlike the traditional rain-fed paddies, is that there's no dry period when the land lies fallow for birds to get seeds from grasses and other weeds before the paddy is ploughed again. In the irrigated paddies, once a crop is harvested, they're ploughed and re-planted again straight away', says Professor Round.

It's when the rice is getting mature, though, that birds can be a problem for the farmers because seed-eating species are attracted by the ripe grain. Watch a flock of sparrows and munias (small, mainly brown finches) descend from nearby perches in trees or a telephone wire into a paddyfield full of ripening rice plants, and it's easy to imagine that farmers eking out a living from their crops would rather be rid of them. That's why illegal trapping of such birds sometimes goes on.

The Nutmeg Mannikin, a native of Asia, was introduced to Hawaii in the late 19th century and almost single-handedly destroyed rice farming there by consuming the ripening grain. It's now something of an agricultural pest in eastern Australia, though not of rice! In South America, particularly in Brazil and Argentina, the Chestnut-capped Blackbird, a bird whose name very adequately describes it, nests in and near rice crops and can be a substantial pest when the crop is ripening. It's a very common bird so trapping and spraying with poisonous chemicals, not usually a clever idea wherever there are edible crops and water, are both done to try to reduce its numbers.

But research at the Faculty of Biology at the University of Havana in Cuba, where rice is the second most important crop after sugarcane, found that many of the small birds feeding in the ripening rice are actually taking a lot of insect pests and weed seed and don't take as much of the rice crop as local farmers believed. As a result, many Cuban rice farmers are now more tolerant of birds in and around their paddies. Whether this tolerance spreads worldwide, only time will tell.

But not all news is good news. Hard though it is to imagine, a sinister human health threat might well lurk in the paddies because of their attractiveness to birds.

In 2008, the UN Food and Agriculture Organization announced that concentrations of ducks and people at rice paddies, where they are in close contact, are primarily responsible for outbreaks of potentially deadly bird flu across Asia (see Chapter 3). Many rice farmers keep domesticated ducks for their meat and eggs. In the day they wander into the rice paddies to feed and there it is that they mix with wild birds, sometimes including wild ducks, some of which just might be carrying bird flu. The domestic ducks could pass the disease to farmers who close their birds up at night to protect them from predators. So far, though, the predicted bird flu pandemic has not materialised.

Recently, the importance of traditionally managed rice paddies for wildlife has begun to be officially recognised. In 2005, the Kabukuri-numa ('numa' means 'marsh' in Japanese) and the surrounding rice paddies in Osaki City, Japan were added to the list of wetlands of international importance under the RAMSAR Convention, set up to protect wetlands worldwide. With other paddies in the area they are vital for thousands of migratory Thick-billed Bean Geese and White-fronted Geese which fly in from Russia every winter and feed in them while they lie fallow without a crop. More such places might get official protection in future.

Birds and rice farmers coexist pretty well. But there are many other farmers worldwide whose life can be completely ruined by the depredations of birds.

In the south of sun-scorched Mali, I talked to Amadou Coulibaly, a local millet farmer, about the crop he had recently harvested. Mali, in West Africa, is one of the top ten millet producers worldwide. A tall cereal crop, millet is incredibly tolerant of arid conditions and is easy to spot with its upright spikes of seed heads left out in the scorching sun to dry after harvesting. In Mali it's a staple, made into a thick porridge and bread, essential to feed Amadou's family, and very many others.

What he says he most fears when the small area of millet he depends on is growing is an invasion by queleas. Red-billed Queleas are the world's most abundant bird. Sparrow-sized, all 1.5 billion of them live in Africa south of the Sahara. And they are seed-eaters. Living in huge flocks, they can descend on fields like a massive swarm of locusts, darkening the sky and clearing the place of crop and wild plant seeds within minutes.

Not for nothing are they often called 'locust birds'. Amadou explains that his crop is most vulnerable from November through to March but much depends on whether there's a good amount of wild plant seed about. Queleas prefer that, if they can get it, he says. So far, he's been lucky.

Even extreme control measures such as dynamiting their nesting colonies and spraying crops with poisons, often killing up to 180 million birds each year during recent decades, has had no discernible effect on their total numbers. In fact, queleas are probably increasing, ironically because the crop area continues to expand.

What's more, these sorts of controls are notoriously indiscriminate, killing many insects and other birds that happen to be in the way; in addition, large numbers of quelea corpses can be eaten by scavenging birds and mammals that, in turn, are poisoned too. Apart from using smaller doses of poison and greater care, nothing that's more effective in reducing quelea numbers has yet been found.

Wherever crops are grown in the world, birds have muscled in for a free feed. And the larger the growing area of any crop they can feed off or amongst, the more crop-feeding birds there are likely to be. With a trend, especially in Europe and the US, away from mixed farming with its wide variety of crops to maybe just one or two types of crop per farm, we have ended up with less variety of farmland birds and a super-abundance of a few … the pests.

In Japan, Dr Kazuo Nakamura of Okinawa University lists Carrion Crows and Jungle Crows as the most problematic, especially the damage they do to watermelons and fruiting vegetables like tomatoes.

Only a tad prettier, Brown-eared Bulbuls, called *hiyodori* in Japan, come in at number two because they make a beeline for citrus fruits and vegetables, especially in winter. Tree Sparrows come next on his offenders' list because they eat crop seeds, rice especially. Pigeons and doves damage legumes like pea crops, and grey sparrows have a particular liking for pears.

Across Europe and western Asia wherever they are common – and they frequently are – Wood Pigeons are the bane of a vegetable grower's life! They love brassicas like cabbages and Brussels sprouts, causing as much damage as rabbits, but they also go for peas, cherries and other soft fruit, pecking at leaves, ripping the plants up in the process, stripping buds and gobbling up fruit.

The British Trust for Ornithology estimates that Wood Pigeons, by far the most common pigeon in Britain, now number more than 8 million breeding birds, that their numbers have trebled since the 1960s, and that they are still increasing!

Wood Pigeons cause most damage by feeding on recently planted crops in the spring and on overwintered crops when food is scarce. Brassicas, therefore, need to be protected from December through to May. During the winter months, overwintered cabbage and cauliflower is particularly vulnerable as the birds are threatened with starvation and will often risk being shot in order to feed. When available, Wood Pigeons prefer young, tender plants to more mature crops (who wouldn't!). Red cabbage, though, they usually avoid if other brassicas are available.

According to *Factsheet 04/05: Brassicas*, produced by the Horticultural Development Council in 2005 and written by Nigel MacDonald, growers are encouraged to provide the best growing conditions for their crop to reduce plant stress, use fleece or polythene crop covers, use a range of different scarers that are moved about, and consider growing a sacrificial crop such as oilseed rape, particularly when the main crop is most at risk, to attract the birds away and onto that instead!

All of this is, of course, time consuming and expensive. And for one of the most damaging bird pests in Britain, you might assume that someone has made an economic assessment of the damage they cause. Oddly, there doesn't seem to be one.

Some birds can be very ingenious when it comes to exploiting a source of food. Suddenly, in 1920s Britain, Blue Tits – those familiar little blue and yellow garden birds – started pecking through the tops of milk bottles left on doorsteps in the early morning (the tops were then made of a kind of waxed cardboard). They were after the creamy portion of the milk at the top of the bottle! Foil caps were soon the norm and the tits pecked through these too. The habit was first spotted in southern England but by 1950 it was common throughout Britain as others learnt the trick. Different birds joined in but Blue Tits dominated the milk bottle scene. Some even drowned because they leaned in too far!

Today, a pecked-open milk bottle top is an unusual sight. The habit petered out in the 1980s. The reason? Because people have become more health conscious and skimmed milk is now de rigueur! The Blue Tits gave up, probably because they can't digest milk, only the cream which is mostly fat.

In the recent past, Bullfinches (known now as Eurasian Bullfinches), the males strikingly beautiful with their pink and grey body plumage and jet black heads, have been a major scourge of British fruit orchards where they have a particular interest in eating the flower buds on fruit trees in winter and spring. No buds mean no fruit the following season!

Although Bullfinches are a protected species in Britain, their fruit-eating in Kent was so great that it was legal in that one county for growers to trap and kill them. That was stopped in 1998.

Research had shown that removal of scrub in the area around the orchard – where Bullfinches breed and also feed – was more effective than trapping them in reducing damage to fruit trees. And in recent years the issue has almost totally disappeared because growers have been doing just that.

While trapping probably depleted their numbers in Kent, it doesn't explain their decline elsewhere, particularly between 1960 and 2000. That's probably down to the removal of farmland trees and hedgerows, and a reduction in the quality of hedges generally because they are now trimmed more frequently. So their habitat and the wild buds, seeds and fruits they eat have all declined.

John Cannon has around 200 acres of apples, plums, cobnuts and pears at Roughway Farm near Tonbridge in the Kent Weald. As we walk around his farm on a sunny spring day, many of the fruit trees look splendid in blossom. Our talk turns to birds.

'Up until the early 1970s we used to shoot or trap Bullfinches', he recalls. 'It wasn't unusual to get a flock of 30 or 40 at a time and they'd strip the flower buds off the pear and plum trees, sometimes apples too. They could strip the pear orchard in a few days. It depended a bit on how much seed there was on ash trees around here; if the trees had plenty, the finches seemed to keep clear of our fruit trees.'

'We just don't see them here now so we don't have a problem with them. Wood Pigeons, though, have increased and they sometimes go for the early plums. And rooks take some of the cobnuts, flying off with them', he adds.

A number of other birds can be crop pests too. Pied Wagtails, commonly found around our buildings and farms picking up insects to eat, often take advantage of heated glasshouses for roosting, particularly in winter. And who can blame them! The trouble is that they often foul the crop beneath with their droppings. And while glasshouse vents can be closed until after dusk, this doesn't work in well-lit areas where the birds just wait until the vents are reopened. They're no fools those wagtails.

There are predictions, too, that other birds might become a big problem in the future. Ring-necked Parakeets – large birds, vibrant green in colour with touches of scarlet, which originally escaped from cage collections – are becoming increasingly common across southeast England. There are thought to be around 40,000 in London and the southeast of England, not a bad rate of increase from the first few that somehow got out in 1969. Birds of Southeast Asia and southern Africa, they're surviving in Britain perfectly well courtesy of our recent milder winters.

Fruit-eaters, one parakeet can consume an awful lot in a day so on the loose in Kent's orchards they could cause enormous damage. To experience how abundant they might become, it's worth a walk around Richmond Park in west London to watch follow-my-leader groups of them zoom from tree to tree, screeching as they go. Incredibly noisy, only the sound of airliners coming over low to land at Heathrow drowns them out.

From January 2009, these parakeets could be legally killed or have their eggs destroyed, though by humane methods only, a move as much to protect other birds (they often take over tree hole nesting sites) as fruit crops. So they have formally joined the ranks of the unloved … the bird pests such as Canada Geese, crows, Herring Gulls and magpies.

In the US, fruit crops are vulnerable to a range of different birds. Blueberries, grown in increasing quantities because they are now regarded as a 'superfood' by better-heeled western consumers, are a tempting juicy fruit about the right size to fit whole in the beak of several blackbird-sized birds.

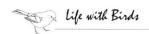

Oregon Berry Packing grows about 80 acres of blueberry bushes just west of Portland in Oregon. Will Unger is their Field Manager.

'Depending on the year, we have some severe bird problems, mainly the European Starling, mostly because when it does come in the field, it comes in large numbers, sometimes in the thousands. The other birds we struggle with are the American Robin and the Cedar Waxwing [an attractive cinnamon and yellow-coloured bird smaller than a starling] but although these two birds are common we don't get them in giant flocks like the starlings', says Unger.

'Like most farms around us, we used to chase the birds out of the fields with shotguns but that posed problems with safety so several years ago we changed to scaring devices and deterrents. Now we use propane cannons which make a gun-like boom and speakers that play recordings of hawk noises. We also spray on a product call RejeX-it which makes the blueberries unpalatable to the birds without harming them. This combination seems to be the most successful at keeping most of the birds out but still not all of them.'

'We've tried putting nestboxes in trees to encourage predator birds to nest and we have also used kites that look like hawks but both of those proved to be ineffective. The cost of netting isn't practical; many farms that considered it found it to be far too expensive to work', he says.

Some growers in California have homed in on a different tactic. Munger Farms, who have 1,600 acres of blueberries in the San Joaquin Valley, where most of the state's crop is grown, hire a falconer when the crop is getting ripe. He roams the fields in his pickup from sun-up to sun-down, scaring off the marauding starlings and waxwings with three trained Aplomado Falcons, dark blue-grey backed falcons a little smaller than a peregrine.

Some vineyards do the same. Hahn Family Wines in California's Napa Valley, a company that encourages wildlife in its vineyards, uses a falcon to keep grape-eating starlings away from the ripening crop. As with most fruit crops, there are many other ways of protecting grapes in vineyards against birds with a sweet tooth. Many growers stretch long strips of plastic tape along the rows above the vines. In the wind they vibrate, producing a sound that birds dislike. Long strips of cloth were traditionally used in the Middle East in this way.

Increasing numbers of vineyards, as well as vegetable and other crop growers, in many western countries are producing their products organically or at least trying to use natural means of controlling pests such as slugs and snails. One way is to let guineafowl, large domesticated ground birds derived from wild species found in southern Africa, roam amongst the crops to eat damaging bugs. They will even kill small to medium-sized snakes; they kill rats and mice to eat; scare away small birds that would otherwise take seed or fruit; and are good 'watchdogs', letting landowners know when something's in the area that shouldn't be there. And, as an extra, they lay eggs that make a good meal.

In the same way, domesticated geese and chickens are turned out into some vineyards in Chile in the spring to eat potentially harmful insects while other wineries encourage insect-eating birds. Frog's Leap Winery in California, for instance, encourages birds such as bluebirds (small dark blue and chestnut birds related to thrushes) and Tree Swallows (greenish-blue and white birds like House Martins) to eat up aphids and leafhoppers. Both nest in tree holes so putting up suitably sized nestboxes encourages them to stay around feeding their youngsters.

In the past, crop protection has sometimes gone too far. North America's only native parrot, the Carolina Parakeet, was once common across the eastern US where it had a liking for orchard-grown fruits and nuts. Farmers killed large numbers of them even though they also ate cocklebur seeds, thereby reducing the spread of this poisonous weed. Shooting was facilitated by the parakeet's endearing habit of gathering around a dead comrade, making it easy to shoot more and more in turn. On top of this their forest habitat was being cut down, they were being killed for their green, yellow and red feathers to decorate ladies' hats, and they were also kept as cage birds – all of which meant these stunningly attractive parakeets didn't stand much chance of survival. The last one was killed in 1904 and the last zoo-kept bird died in 1918.

But there is another way of protecting a valuable crop, one that's easy (and cheap) enough for a few raspberry or blackcurrant bushes in your garden to keep thrushes at bay, but incredibly expensive if you are a commercial grower.

Imagine putting bird-proof netting over 12 acres of grapevines! Like many of their neighbouring wineries, that's precisely what Gavin and Linda Perry have had to do at their B'darra Estate vineyard on the warm Mornington Peninsula in Victoria, Australia. They grow a range of white and red grape varieties including Sauvignon Blanc, Shiraz and Muscat and the netting is there to protect them against European starlings.

'It cost us AU$35,000 [c.£17,000] to buy and set up the netting plus another AU$3,000 [c.£1,500] a year in maintenance', comments Linda. 'But without it we simply wouldn't have a crop. The starlings would decimate it.'

In a classic case demonstrating the folly of introducing a species to a place where it is not naturally found, European Starlings were introduced to Australia in the late 1800s, supposedly to help protect crops from insects like leatherjackets. Highly adaptable birds, today they are common in much of southeast Australia and parts of New Zealand. And, surprise surprise, they don't eat just leatherjackets!

'It was a huge mistake. They cause millions of dollars of damage to various crops like grapes, stone fruits, olives, and berry fruits as well as digging up newly sown grain and aggressively out-competing native birds like parrots for nesting holes in trees and buildings', says Katherine Howard, a Threatened Species Network Regional Manager for WWF in Australia. They can also carry parasites and diseases which raises concern in food factories and in the livestock industry.

Netting fruit and other crops seems to be the only way of keeping them at bay, together with eliminating scrub and woodland that encourages them to roost in large numbers, though this damages populations of harmless birds too. Shooting and scare guns work only for a short time while trapping is unlikely to take sufficient numbers to have any significant impact on the damage they cause.

According to Australia's Invasive Animals Cooperative Research Centre (IACRC), Australia is host to 56 invasive animal species, although birds are certainly not the biggest culprits. The ones with the greatest impact (in order of damage) are European red fox, feral cats, rabbits, feral pigs, wild dogs, the house mouse, carp, goats, cane toads, wild horses and camels. Birds come lower in the damage pecking order!

'In a total farm and fruit-growing industry sense, the damage by birds to crops in Australia is low. Valuable horticulture crops, wine and table crops such as apricots are often netted. Broadacre crops are rarely protected because it's impractical. There is sensitivity about using bird killing chemicals while guns, bird scaring explosions, and kites shaped like hawks are all used to limited success', comments Mick Poole, a retired agricultural expert now living in Perth.

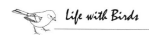

According to the IACRC, there are over a hundred bird species in Australia and New Zealand that can cause significant losses of fruit, nuts, grain and rice. Apart from European Starlings, other introduced pests that cause damage include European Blackbirds, sparrows and the Common Myna.

The Common Myna, native to India and much of Southeast Asia, is a starling relative, brown with yellow head markings, and a lively chap that's able to eat almost anything and live almost anywhere, including eastern Australia where it was introduced in the 1860s seemingly to try to control insect pests. Heard that one before?

But it's an avid feeder on fruits of more or less any description, too, as well as feeding on other farm crops, and the Australian government is attempting to halt its probably inevitable westward spread across the continent to try to prevent it developing into fruit-farming enemy number one.

Not all of Australia's crop-damaging birds are ones that naturally would never have darkened the continent's shores of course. Some native species can be a problem too, with silvereyes (greenish birds small enough to nip through fruit netting) being the worst offenders. Honeyeaters, with their curved beaks hiding a long tongue that can probe deep inside flowers for nectar, are common in Australia and also have a liking for fruit. Several parrots, cockatoos and their close relatives are also avid fruit-eaters, the archetypal five portions a day consumers that can be the bane of an Australian fruit grower's life.

Not surprisingly, some fruit growers in some countries have been known to take the law into their own hands. A Chinese news-site, www.sina.com.cn, in 2005 reported the controversy caused by the trial of Chen Jinsong, a grape grower in Changping District, Beijing, who had become so fed up with losing much of his crop to birds that he took action. Firecrackers and gongs didn't work for long so he laid sticky nets on some of the vines. When local police arrived, seemingly tipped off by concerned villagers, they counted 163 entangled birds including some of China's uncommon and protected species.

Chen argued that he couldn't afford more effective measures like gas cannons and that he was losing a considerable amount of his crop. He was fined and given a two-year prison sentence all the same!

European Starlings were also introduced to the US, in this case by a crank called Eugene Schieffelin (1827–1906). He decided that the US needed to have all of the birds mentioned in the writings of Shakespeare, part of a strange notion – though then more mainstream – that plants and animals should be distributed around the world. So it was that 60 starlings were released in New York's Central Park in 1890 and another 40 the following year. Today the birds are common across the whole US and much of Canada too! There might be 500 million of them. Thankfully, some of his other introductions failed.

Getting rid of bird pests is today a technological industry with netting, gas cannons, broadcast alarm calls, trained falcons and other means potentially available (at a price of course!). In the past, though, the best-known bird scarer – though often pretty useless – was the scarecrow.

No one is sure about their origin but perhaps the earliest mention is in the Japanese mythology compiled in *Kojiki* in 712 where a scarecrow appears as a deity, Kuebiko, who cannot walk but knows everything. Known in English as *The Records of Ancient Matters*, the Kojiki is the oldest surviving book in Japan.

Traditionally a human figure dressed in discarded clothes, today scarecrows are little used in the US or Europe but are still found in some Japanese ricefields and elsewhere in Southeast Asia. Because they are static, birds soon get used to them – as they do with most scarers – and scarecrows probably do more scaring of young children than of birds.

'In the old days, Thai rice farmers used to place scarecrows in their ricefields to chase away birds. Some still do but most put up empty plastic bags on a stick or stretch a line across the paddy with several bags on it. When a breeze blows, they make a loud noise. These may work well for a few days but soon the birds get used to the noise and will eat rice again!' comments Dr Choowaew.

Other commonly used more low-tech deterrents nowadays include CDs on a string which flash in the sunlight and turn in the breeze; 'hawk kites', attached to poles that hover in the wind above the crop to mimic a bird of prey; or tethered balloons decorated with large eye shapes.

Where farmers have no chance of affording such equipment – in many African countries and much of China for example – the alternative, and often very successful – bird deterrent is a small boy with a couple of pieces of wood to bang together!

Until even the early decades of the 20th century, young lads were often employed in Britain to frighten crows and rooks away from crops. In his autobiography, *From Crow-Scaring to Westminster* (National Union of Agricultural Workers, 1922), the then Norfolk Labour MP Sir George Edwards wrote:

> On coming out of the workhouse in March 1856, I secured my first job. It consisted of scaring crows from the field of a farmer close to the house. I was then six years of age and I was paid one shilling [5 pence] for a seven day week.

But Edwards soon got into trouble! In his second week of employment he fell asleep out in the fields, the marauding crows returned and the farmer gave him 'a severe thrashing' and deducted money from his wages. Employment laws were pretty lax in those days!

When it comes to birds causing crop damage, though, Chairman Mao had the answer – or thought he did! But Mao was no ecologist. And he obviously didn't get – or accept – any expert advice either.

It was in 1958 that Mao Tse-tung, then President of the People's Republic of China, launched his so-called 'Great Leap Forward', supposedly to improve the lot of millions of poor Chinese peasants. The central idea was that rapid development of China's agricultural and industrial sectors should take place in parallel. Part of the leap was the 'Four Pests Campaign': rats, flies, mosquitoes … and sparrows.

According to Mao, sparrows (mainly the Tree Sparrow in China, though other sparrows, finches and yet more small birds eat grain seed) were reducing crop productivity. Or so the Great Leader thought. And selling grain to the then USSR and other countries, at the expense of his own people who often starved, was a national priority in Mao's China to give the appearance of productivity to international observers. So it was that the 'Kill a Sparrow' campaign was launched.

Millions of peasants, the army, students and others were mobilised to bang pots and pans, wave red flags, put out 'scarecrows' and run about creating a general hullabaloo to stop sparrows landing anywhere. Nests were torn down. Eggs smashed. Nestlings killed. Birds were trapped and shot.

Keeping the birds flying for a day meant starvation for them. And as their energy ran out, they fell to the ground dead. Trailer-loads of sparrows – with probably many other birds amongst them – were collected up for disposal.

Sha Yexin, author of *The Chinese Sparrow War of 1958* (New Century Net, 1997), recalls a broadcast on Radio Peking on 5 May 1958:

> At 5 a.m. bugles sounded, cymbals crashed, whistles trilled. The massed students beat their kitchenware and advanced, singing rousing revolutionary anthems.

China's *People's Daily* exhorted the citizenry, 'No warrior shall be withdrawn until the battle is won. All must join battle ardently and courageously; we must persevere with the doggedness of revolutionaries'.

Nobody knows how many sparrows died but the number was in the millions.

'The massive extirpation force netted and scatter-gunned the exhausted birds or snared them with long, gum-tipped bamboo poles. Some 310,000 sparrows had fallen in Peking alone, and an estimated 4 million throughout the rest of China', recounts Yexin.

'The national hero was Yang Seh-mun, aged 16, of Yunnan. He had killed 20,000 sparrows single-handedly by sneaking around during the day locating nesting trees. At night, the *China Youth Daily* proudly reported, he climbed trees and strangled whole families of sparrows with his bare hands.' What a boy!

But Yang Seh-mun wasn't a hero for long. Because while the grain harvest improved initially, it then started failing. And failing on a grand scale. In 1960, China's National Academy of Science had found, rather belatedly, that sparrows ate more insects than grain. Mao issued another diktat to stop any more sparrow killing. But it was too late.

With no sparrows to eat them, it was boom time for locusts, grasshoppers and other crop-ravaging insects. Due to the crop failures that resulted, sometimes compounded by poor seasonal weather, and the leadership's determination to keep exporting grain, between 1959 and 1961 somewhere between 20 million (the official figure since given by the Chinese government and widely thought to be an underestimate) and as many as perhaps 50 million Chinese died. And all because of a crackpot idea their leader had.

Mao was forced by other senior party comrades to abandon the Great Leap in 1962 after admitting that he was partly to blame. He remained as Communist Party chairman but had lost esteem and passed the presidency to Liu Shaoqi, a more moderate leader, who, along with Zhou Enlai and Deng Xiaoping, took on a more active role in government to curb the excesses of the Great Leap Forward and begin to set China on a more acceptable and rational path of development.

According to Jung Chang and Jon Halliday in their *Mao: The Unknown Story* (Vintage, 2007):

> North Korea's Kim Il Sung [its President, 1948–1994] turned out to be less stupid than Mao on this issue. Mao had pressed him to emulate China's anti-sparrow campaign. To humour Mao, Kim drafted a '3-Year Plan for Punishing Sparrows' but then did nothing while he watched to see how Mao's campaign turned out.

The Chinese aren't the only ones who have tried to kill sparrows off. Mao should have studied North America's history of trying to eradicate House Sparrows. He would have saved himself a lot of trouble and the crops might not have failed, at least not as catastrophically as they did.

House Sparrows didn't live on the North American continent until organisations such as the 'Cincinnati Acclimatization Society', in the 1850s, released 4,000 European songbirds of at least 18 different species including House Sparrows in order to 'aid people against the encroachment of insects' and ensure that the 'ennobling influence of the song of birds will be felt by the inhabitants'. It was as if the US didn't have any good bird singers themselves.

The House Sparrow liked the look of its new home. Very soon it was considered an agricultural pest, eating grain and contaminating stores with its droppings as well as ousting some native hole-nesting birds such as bluebirds from their natural nest sites. As soon as 1887, less than 40 years after the sparrow's first introduction, some states had already initiated efforts to eradicate house sparrows.

In Britain, too, where house sparrows are native birds, they had long been considered vermin. Roger Lovegrove, in *Silent Fields: The Long Decline of a Nation's Wildlife* (Oxford University Press, 2007), describes the plight of many birds at the hands of farmers trying to protect their crops, their poultry and their livelihoods. He refers to the ubiquitous House Sparrow as a 'street urchin, scrounger and uninvited lodger … but there is no disputing its enormous success as it shares most aspects of its life with Man in both town and countryside'.

He goes on to comment:

> By the eighteenth century, the burgeoning populations of House Sparrows were recognised as serious pests on crops of ripening corn … and as a domestic nuisance particularly in their habit of burrowing into the thatched roofs of cottages to find nesting sites. Thus began an escalating war of attrition against the species. The irony is that however great the levels of annual killing, the impact on the population was inevitably negligible. As the record of bounty payments shows, however many were removed, the same numbers were there to be killed the next year. The reason for this fact is that most of the killing, notably at harvest time in late summer, involved huge numbers of young birds of the year that would anyway … be subject to natural mortality in subsequent months.

A rather determined lady in Victorian England went further. At a time when 'well-bred women' didn't mess with moths and maggots, Eleanor Ormerod (1828–1901) became a leading insect pest expert. In 1885 she wrote to *The Times* calling for the extermination of House Sparrows because of the agricultural damage they did. She didn't have quite the same power to get things done as Mao. Bird lovers of the day hanged effigies of her and someone, apparently, took a pot-shot at her.

And during World War I, the BBC broadcast government appeals to destroy sparrows, suggesting that their ecology was as poorly understood in Britain as it was in China.

Through the 17th and 18th centuries in particular, Britain's record for bird killing would have compared well with Mao's. The numbers slaughtered were huge, especially of crows, magpies, sparrows, rooks, cormorants because they took fish, any bird of prey – or anything resembling one – and even Green Woodpeckers that damaged wooden tiles on church towers with their pecking.

Few people gave a second thought to the rights and wrongs of all this slaughter; most birds that came anywhere near a crop were given no mercy by people who often struggled to get enough food themselves. And the birds they killed were frequently eaten too.

World War I, according to Roger Lovegrove, was something of a watershed; never again in Britain was there shooting and trapping of birds on the same scale. And the slow but steady development from then on of a conservation movement responded to changing public attitudes as living standards improved.

Today, the House Sparrow remains a pest of cereal crops and it can be legally killed US-wide. In Britain, where it has long been a protected species, and in much of mainland Europe, its numbers are steadily declining in the countryside because of substantial changes in farming practices while in towns and cities it might well be the insects they need for feeding their chicks that have become scarce (see Chapter 7).

Sometimes, though, taking action against pest birds can backfire spectacularly. Isaiah Berlin (1909–1997), the Latvian/British philosopher, once recounted that an acquaintance of his had been visiting a law court in Heidelberg in 1936 where a man was condemned to four months in prison for throwing a stone at a bird, contrary to the Reichsjagdgesetzbuch (the Reich hunting code introduced by Hermann Goering who was Reich Minister of Forestry, amongst much else, from 1934 to 1945) 'because that was bestial cruelty and the National Socialist Government was opposed to cruelty in every shape and form'! No further comment is necessary.

Growing crops – and trying to protect them against the ravages of certain birds – isn't an issue solely for land-based farmers. Fish farmers have similar problems to overcome too.

Fish farming involves raising fish commercially in tanks or enclosures in lakes, estuaries or coastal sea waters. The most important fish farmed in this way are salmon, carp, tilapia, catfish and cod. Because of considerable overfishing of many of the world's inshore sea waters and oceans, fish farming offers an alternative solution to the increasing demand for fish to eat and for fish protein to incorporate in animal feeds and other products.

A third of the seafood destined for dinner tables worldwide is currently produced by fish farms – 40 million tonnes per year – according to the Marine Conservation Society, who think that this will double to 80 million tonnes per year by 2030. Shellfish farming is also big business; in Britain it includes mussels, oysters, scallops, clams and cockles, and in Southeast Asia huge coastal areas have been put over to prawn farming.

Not surprisingly, these farms with their huge concentrations of fish or shellfish at various growth stages – and thereby sizes – are like the promised land for fish-eating birds such as cormorants and herons! Rather than the paraphernalia of methods often used to protect land crops, fish farmers with bird pest problems usually resort to nets and wires to protect their 'crop'. Another option is to keep valuable fish in tanks closer to where people work so that the birds are disturbed regularly. In some countries, such bird pests can be legally shot.

Several seabirds that consume fish have done rather well, too, from much of the world's ocean-fishing industry. Trawlers frequently throw some of their dead catch overboard because they haven't caught the right fish or they're the wrong size – the consequence of a pillaging rather than a well-managed fishing industry – while on-board processing has produced plenty of fish offal thrown overboard too. Several seabirds soon learnt to exploit this easy eating.

The Northern fulmar is one of many that's benefitted hugely. Pale grey and white seabirds that breed on cliffs, fulmars superficially resemble gulls but aren't related to them. Until the late 19th century they were birds of the far North Atlantic with only one breeding colony in British waters, at St Kilda off the northwest of Scotland. Increased fish trawling and whale-catching provided ample amounts of offal and discarded fish dumped at sea. Fulmars were quick learners. Their well-fed numbers increased and the birds started spreading south. Today there's hardly a sea cliff in the UK without them!

The ocean and inshore fishing industries, though, are bad news for many seabirds. Sometimes very bad news. Every year, according to the RSPB, about 200,000 seabirds in European waters alone are snared, entangled and drowned on hooks and in nets used by fishermen. It's a kill that the European Commission has for many years failed totally to address even though some technical fixes are available to reduce this mortality.

Birds aren't very discerning when it comes to picking out food. In one study published in 2002, some 80 per cent of floating plastic debris washed ashore on part of the Dutch coast had peck-marks made by birds. Being optimistic, it might be that most were simply testing it to see if it was edible. In reality, though, post-mortems of dead seabirds like the mighty albatrosses of the Pacific Ocean have often revealed a deadly mix of plastic objects in their guts: plastic toys, small tubes and sticks, and tiny plastic pellets for instance.

Conservationists believe that many tens of thousands of these huge seabirds are killed annually by eating plastic debris (it blocks their gut, leading to starvation, or poisons them), by getting tangled in discarded plastic fishing nets and by impaling themselves on the huge number of baited hooks attached to several kilometre-long fishing lines used by many fishing boats. As a result, several species of albatross are in severe decline.

In the western Pacific off Asia, there is what's come to be known as a floating garbage patch of plastic the size of the United States! It circulates here because of the way the sea currents trap it. A lot of it ends up on atolls and islands where albatrosses and other seabirds breed, some of it regurgitated by them. In 2008 on Kure Atoll in the Pacific's Hawaiian Islands, Lindsay Young and fellow researchers from the University of Hawaii who were examining these regurgitated plastic objects found the most unusual to be a sealed pot of face cream with the lotion still inside!

'We were sorting through these objects right after Christmas, and there were so many small plastic toys in the birds that we joked that we could have assembled a complete nativity scene with them', commented Young.

But let's finish this chapter on a more positive note. Not all birds that inhabit farmland, and use it for most of their feeding, cause problems for the farmer or grower. Some cause no damage at all. Others may be beneficial, like the ghostly pale Barn Owls that hunt over fields at night across much of the world and have a liking for devouring small rodents such as mice, thereby reducing the rodents' consumption of stored grain and other crops.

Pound for pound, Barn Owls consume more rodents than possibly any other animal, making them one of the most economically valuable farmland creatures. Farmers in Europe often find these owls more effective than poison in keeping down rodents and many encourage them by providing nestboxes in their farm buildings.

Across much of South America, southern Africa and Southeast Asia, white Cattle Egrets – in summer noticeable by their attractive orange-buff feathers on the back, breast and crown – follow cows, water buffalo and other livestock on pastureland, waiting to snatch grasshoppers and other ground insects disturbed by their hooves. But you might also see them on a cow's back! The Cattle

Egret is a popular bird with cattle farmers for its role as a controller of cattle parasites such as ticks and flies that they pick off their skin.

When they're foraging on the ground near a large animal these egrets are more than three times more successful in capturing prey than when foraging alone. Their performance is similar when they follow farm machinery, too.

Cattle Egrets aren't the only farmers' friends on pastureland either. In India and across much of Southeast Asia, drongos – all black, smaller than jackdaws and with a distinctive forked tail – feed on a variety of insects. They congregate in fields that are being ploughed, picking up exposed caterpillars and beetle grubs. I've watched them, too, sitting on the backs of cows and buffalo feasting on their parasitic ticks and lice, helping to keep the livestock healthier, something that more brightly coloured oxpeckers do on livestock and large game animals across much of central and southern Africa.

In Europe, the US and some other countries, there is a considerable area of habitat where a huge – and increasing – variety of birds are actively encouraged to have a free feed … and even, if possible, to set up home and breed. Gardens are becoming increasingly bird-friendly as millions of householders supply ever more millions of birds with an array of peanuts, seeds, suet and other delights on bird tables and feeders, a food supply the likes of which would astound the inhabitants of so many developing countries.

In Britain alone, the bird feed and feeder market was worth around £200 million in 2009 according to the British Trust for Ornithology (BTO), probably ten times what it was worth a decade or two earlier. When the BTO launched its Garden Bird Feeding Survey in 1971, gardens attracted an average of 16 or 17 species, according to its David Glue. These days it's between 18 and 23 species as the range of feeds, and feeders, has increased and as more species adapt to garden takeaways. The survey's record is a staggering 59 different species in a garden in west Wales!

The birds coming to British garden feeders in winter, when they most need supplementary food, are changing. Birds like elegant black, white and scarlet Great-Spotted Woodpeckers are today common garden bird table feeders. They never used to be. Plump Wood Pigeons are increasingly attracted, and Blackcaps, sparrow-sized greyish warblers that used to leave for Africa in the autumn, now stay put all winter long. It's apparently because Blackcaps from cooler continental Europe now winter in the UK instead of risking a long flight south and back again in the spring. Milder British winters and garden feeding are the reasons. There is even evidence from research by Dr Martin Schaefer of Freiburg University in Germany that British-bound Blackcaps are developing a slightly different beak shape to cope with the garden bird feeders they encounter!

Britain's obsession with garden bird feeding, in particular, has a long pedigree. In the harsh winter of 1890/91, national newspapers asked people to put spare food out for birds. People started visiting municipal parks and lakes and feeding birds there too. By 1910, *Punch* magazine was declaring it as a national pastime!

In British gardens, Blackbirds, Blue Tits, Robins and Dunnocks are usually the most abundant. In the US where an estimated 55 million people feed birds, the top attendees are stunning vermilion-coloured Northern Cardinals; slim, light grey and pink Mourning Doves; Dark-eyed Juncos (small, grey, sparrow-like birds); and little yellow and black American Goldfinches.

In Elizabeth City in North Carolina, Bonnie Hanbury-Calliotte has been feeding birds in the garden of her 1852 home, the oldest in this attractive town, for many years.

'I put feed out all year, suet, sunflower seed, and, of course, sugar solution in spring and autumn for hummingbirds', she says. 'We get a big range of birds feeding: Cedar Waxwings, Chipping Sparrows, Ruby-throated Hummingbirds, American Goldfinches, Northern Mockingbirds amongst others. It's great to watch them.'

In the US and in Central America, thousands of people put out special feeders filled with sugar water for hummingbirds on migration. They're a simple piece of glass or plastic first made commercially available in the early 1930s from which the tiny birds, their wings beating so fast they're hardly visible, suck up the sweet solution (one part white sugar to four parts water) for the energy they need. It mimics the sugar-rich nectar they naturally obtain from flowers.

Birds, though, don't confine themselves to raiding our crops of grain, fish and fruit for an easy feed. They are rather partial to our waste food scraps too, and that is the subject of Chapter 9.

9

A load of garbage

For as long as we have discarded food scraps and other detritus, birds have made
use of it to survive. Today, millions of birds worldwide make a meal of
our waste. Nowhere is that more evident than in our cities.

It's lunchtime on a warm summer's weekday in the heart of Bristol. In the city centre along bustling St Augustine's Parade, office and other workers are taking their lunch breaks, sitting around
the attractive water fountains, making the most of the sunshine and eating sandwiches or takeaways
from nearby cafes. I've joined them to watch what transpires here each and every day because these
human workers are not the only ones eating their lunchtime snacks.

Oblivious to the cacophony of noise from incessant buses and cars on the streets all around,
and dodging between the office workers' legs, are groups of plump birds, some slate-blue and white,
some pink and white. They are busily eating lunch too. They are humble city pigeons and hundreds
of them come here on weekdays to make the most of this city centre alfresco restaurant.

But theirs is not a very restful lunch break. Incessantly, they pick crumbs off the neat paving,
toss scraps of paper over to see if there are edible morsels underneath, and collect excitedly in lively
groups wherever someone has decided to share a little of their lunch with these virtually hand-tame
birds. And, frequently to the annoyance of local authorities in cities around the world, many people
enjoy scattering at least a few crumbs and watching the ensuing pigeon scramble for the best bits
to devour.

Very soon, though, the lunch break is over and people return to their offices or to construction
jobs locally. Now the pigeons scurry about, mopping up the last lunchtime scraps, making sure that
there isn't a crumb left on St Augustine's Parade. I walk its length and breadth and I can see none;
the pigeons have picked it clean.

Then they gradually move away too. On to another spot, perhaps, where the remnants of a Big
Mac have been dropped on a pavement or maybe where a shopping centre rubbish bin has been
overturned by something much larger than a pigeon, its motley contents scattered in the breeze.

City pigeons, descendants of pale grey-coloured wild Rock Doves (now renamed, rather plainly,
as the Common Pigeon) that breed mainly on the ledges of coastal cliffs and frequently interbred
with domestic and racing pigeons, are almost certainly the bird that is most instantly recognised by
everyone the world over. Even office workers in the world's largest cities – where their encounters
with birds are few and far between – recognise this bird, maybe the only one they do!

That's not surprising. City pigeons share much of their lives with us, in cities from Tokyo to New
York, London to Sydney, eating up our spilled scraps of food and breeding on the brick and concrete
ledges of our buildings, their substitute for the sea cliffs and crevices their ancestors still use.

They loaf around on roofs, in gutters, on ledges and windowsills, in and around railway stations, car parks, town squares and shopping centres. Anywhere, in fact, that they can scavenge some scraps of food. And although they are notoriously tolerant of people when they are sifting around for crumbs on the ground – and will readily feed from your hand – they like a bit of peace and quiet for breeding.

So their favoured spots for laying eggs in the scrappy nests they construct from grasses, bits of rag and paper, and maybe a few leaves, tend to be in abandoned buildings. A deserted seaside hotel with easy access to most of the rooms through broken windows perhaps, part of a factory that has fallen into disuse or on high ledges inside railway stations. Sometimes, too, they will nest in holes in trees.

Living for up to six years, city pigeons are arguably the most successful birds in the world, found in towns and cities across almost every continent. Look closely at some of the film footage of the dreadful New Orleans floods in August 2005 and the only bird that appears on screen is the ubiquitous town pigeon! Able to evacuate far faster – had it wanted to – than the city's human inhabitants, there must have been enough food scattered about to entice them to stay on!

They are unbelievably versatile. A few years ago I was with a group of fellow travellers in the Sahara Desert very close to its dead centre in the extreme southwest corner of Libya, where sand-blasted, dark red mountains devoid of any vegetation contrasted with the wind-smoothed contours of orange-yellow sand.

We had reached a temporary Tuareg settlement where the families kept some goats to graze on the spiny shrubs in nearby wadis and a few chickens fed partly on some corn these semi-nomadic farmers had carried out here with them.

But the scatter of grain in a little enclosure against a cliff that they had constructed to pen in a few young goat kids had attracted half a dozen 'city' pigeons and here they were, hundreds of kilometres from any permanent habitation! And while the flying distance would be no amazing test for a pigeon, how was it that they knew that there was a scatter of grain to be raided in otherwise so incredibly inhospitable surroundings?

For such a resourceful and successful bird – and one that's easy to study because they are so tame – it's ironic that ornithologists have paid it scant attention. Most serious birdwatchers disregard the common city pigeon. Regarding them as a bit of a 'Heinz 57' of the bird world, any serious ornithologist pays them almost no attention.

So it is that in the authoritative *EBCC Atlas of European Breeding Birds: Their Distribution and Abundance* (T & A D Poyser, 1997), the authors comment that few – if any – birds are as poorly known in terms of their distribution and numbers as the city pigeon and its Rock Dove (or Common Pigeon) ancestor.

So John Tully is a breath of fresh air. A retired deputy headmaster living near Bristol, and a very active amateur ornithologist, Mr Tully is putting the city pigeon on the ornithological map for the first time. Over the last couple of decades he has become the leading world expert on them.

'Birdwatchers want wild birds to look at', comments Tully. 'I suppose they think that city pigeons are sort of tainted but I think their success makes them even more worth studying. They are arguably the bird that has best adapted itself to live our urban life.'

'It's pretty easy to count them in winter because almost all of them are in towns and cities then', comments Tully. 'In summer, when they're breeding, they make forays out into the countryside for

food so it's harder then to get accurate counts. But unlike counting most birds, you don't even have to get up early in the morning. Pigeons rise late and roost early. That suits me! They even line up on building ledges like well-behaved schoolchildren', he adds wistfully.

'In the 1991/92 winter when I retired', he says, 'I counted 108 pigeon flocks in Bristol totalling 7,440 birds. I repeated the count ten years later and the total came to between 7,500 and 8,000 birds so it hadn't changed much, if at all. A few flocks had disappeared but many of the others had increased in number, some markedly. But they have declined a bit since then.'

Bristol, with around 420,000 human residents, covers an urban area of 110 square kilometres. So there is one city pigeon for around 50 or 60 human residents.

But what John Tully had spotted in his repeat survey was a big change in where the pigeons were living. No longer were they predominantly in the city centre where they were concentrated in 1991/92. Many of them had moved further out, not to the outer suburbs with their bigger gardens and leafy green spaces, but as far as the inner suburbs – still very built up – closer to the centre. Often where there are shopping centres, pavement cafes and other places where people drop food.

'Where houses are pretty tightly packed as they are in some parts of Bristol', comments Tully, 'there don't seem to be as many pigeons. It may be that, by coincidence perhaps, there are less food scraps or there are more cats to kill them off.'

'But I also think the pigeons like shopping places and piazzas, places where they can also get an open view. It might be something to do with spotting predators like cats, or Peregrines that hunt them or even Sparrowhawks, the females of which are big enough to kill them and carry them off. They don't seem to like being confined too much, where they can't see what's happening around them', he adds.

And the reason for town pigeons moving out to pastures – or more correctly buildings – new? John Tully reckons that it's because much more aggressive Herring Gulls and Lesser Black-backed Gulls have moved into the centre to grab all the scraps and to breed on warm city roofs and ledges where they are little disturbed.

'We have over 2,000 pairs of Herring and Lesser Black-backed Gulls breeding in Bristol now', he says. And they're still increasing. City pigeons have declined by about 28 per cent between 2000 and 2008 but Herring Gulls have increased by 66 per cent over the same time and Lesser Black-backs by 11 per cent. And the gulls nest on factory and office roofs, places often hard for people to get to.

Whether the increase in city gulls will continue is hard to say. They first began nesting on British city roofs in the 1920s. Many spend long periods feeding at refuse landfill sites, then return to their urban homes at night to roost and to breed in summer. They tend to live longer and produce more offspring than their cousins who confine themselves to the coast, their natural habitat.

But land-filling of domestic refuse is declining as more local authorities and consumer groups promote recycling and composting. So their food sources will decline, probably drastically. Their abundance might yet be short-lived and city pigeons might even re-take their city centres!

Gulls can be notoriously aggressive, especially when they have eggs or youngsters nearby. In coastal towns they sometimes even injure people by swooping down to take a sandwich from someone's hand as they are about to take a bite! They sometimes spray revolting vomit or faeces as they do, a tactic almost certain to cause the hapless individual to drop their snack.

Reducing city gull numbers, or attempting to remove them entirely, is fraught. They largely ignore bird scarers that frighten off other birds. Rooftop spikes, tensioned wires and similar means of deterring city pigeons prove pretty ineffective too. If their nests are removed and their eggs are taken, broken, or oiled to stop them hatching (all perfectly legal because they are listed as pests), the gulls will simply rebuild or re-lay, or choose another nest site in the same area and start all over again!

They might be intimidated by birds of prey but, in addition to being social birds with strength in numbers, gulls are large, powerful and aggressive so they are more than capable of fighting back against any potential predator, particularly if they consider their chicks to be at risk.

City pigeons, a much more delicate and more easily deterred bird, never great squabblers, wouldn't stand a chance of success competing with a noisy, beak-stabbing, bellicose Herring Gull at a newly discarded burger and fries. So, in the long run, city gulls will turn out to be a very much more difficult problem than city pigeons have ever been.

'You get around one town pigeon for every 50 people in most cities', comments Tully. 'I suspect it's higher in tourist areas. I did counts in Bath, a popular tourist destination, several years ago and there the ratio was one pigeon for every 44 people though in Weston-super-Mare it was only one for every 58, perhaps because, as a seaside resort, Weston isn't exactly popular in winter when I did the counts. Or the pigeons don't like the sea air', he adds.

'So much depends on how free of food scraps and other rubbish a town is', says Tully. 'Nailsea in North Somerset [population 18,000] has a pretty reasonable pigeon population and it isn't too spick and span', he comments. 'Thornbury in South Gloucestershire [population 12,000], on the other hand, has cleaner streets and better waste collection. There are almost no pigeons there.'

According to Dr Stephen Baillie, Director of Science at the UK's British Trust for Ornithology, British city pigeons might have shown an upward trend in numbers of perhaps 10 per cent since 1994 though, because there are few data, no one's sure! In the 1960s the best guess was that there were more than 100,000 pairs of them in Britain and Ireland. There has been no proper census to find out.

John Tully, though, is certain that this is a huge underestimate. He's estimated the numbers of human city and large town dwellers in Britain to be about 30 million out of the UK's total population and used his average of about 50 people for each pigeon. That gives a total of around 600,000 city pigeons in the UK! It might even be more.

To anyone who slips headlong on their slimy droppings or has their drying washing stained with the stuff, city pigeons are a pest. But they have their positive attributes too. Tully estimates that the Bristol lot consume between one and two tonnes of waste food every week, anything from discarded apple cores to Kentucky Fried Chicken.

'They don't re-deposit most of it where they feed either', comments Tully. 'Most of their droppings are at their roost sites, mainly dilapidated buildings with a plethora of holes in their roofs and smashed windows. It's only the demolition workers that need worry! Most city people don't come into contact with it', he adds.

But their diet doesn't consist entirely of human society's waste. City pigeons, like their wild counterparts, will also take seeds of garden plants and weeds growing in urban areas. And they make forays into the countryside in order to feed on grain or other plant seeds too. They pick up grit from roads and pavements, sometimes even small pieces of mortar as a source of calcium and to help physically in their crops to break down the food they eat. After all, British fish and chips can take some digesting.

In spite of emotive language used occasionally by the tabloid press, there is no evidence that city pigeons pose any significant human health hazard, and it's only possible to pick up infections like pigeon lung disease if you work with them in confined places such as pigeon lofts.

They do produce a lot of unsightly droppings discolouring ledges on buildings, and their accumulated guano, being acidic, corrodes the stonework and metalwork, the reason for many such ledges and windowsills now having upright plastic or wire spikes attached to them to prevent the birds landing. Not a modern invention, metal spikes were used for the same purpose in 1444 in Sandwich in Kent according to local church wardens' accounts.

Spikes plus netting to keep pigeons from landing where both pigeons and people are likely to congregate – railway stations for instance – are reducing the places that the pigeons can call home. If these measures become widespread, their numbers are almost certainly going to decline.

Another technique to try to limit them has been to build a modern-day dovecote (see Chapter 3) to entice them away from places where they might cause a problem and then remove their eggs as they get laid. It's been tried, for instance, at the University of Wales Hospital in Cardiff.

'We built a dovecote and two wooden sheds for the pigeons about eight or ten years ago because we had so many pigeons on flat roofs at the hospital', says Simon Williams, Head of Operational Services for Cardiff and The Vale Health Board. 'We're trying to keep on top of maintenance so that they can't get into roof spaces and other places and we also use spikes and netting to stop them landing.'

'I go there once a week to remove pigeon eggs in the sheds and dovecote and replace them with china eggs', comments Vicki Watkins of Fauna Wildlife Rescue who is contracted by the hospital. 'It's taken away about two-thirds of the pigeons from the main hospital buildings and their numbers have reduced overall. I've been doing it now for seven years. They use another contractor to remove gull eggs and I believe their numbers have dropped too.'

PiCAS UK, a Pigeon Control Advisory Service, advocate a mix of measures to reduce pigeon problems depending on the site. The mix often involves sealing any roof spaces, installing spikes and netting, building pigeon lofts or dovecotes where the birds are encouraged to breed and their eggs are replaced with dummies to keep the population limited, and, if possible, installing smooth, steep-sloped roof sections so the birds can't land on them.

PiCAS is also quick to point out that killing pigeons simply won't work and uses the example of Basel in Switzerland where around 100,000 city pigeons were shot over a number of years. It made no difference to the numbers in the city; more youngsters survived to fill the gap!

The issue about the mess made by city pigeons came to something of a climax at an otherwise rather ordinary railway bridge over Balham High Road in south London. It was never famous for much, apart from carrying trains in and out of London's Victoria Station but, since August 2000, it's become infamous for its pigeons!

The bridge has ledges on which large numbers of city pigeons roost. A High Court judge, Mr Justice Gibbs, decided that Railtrack (now Network Rail), which owns the bridge, should pay the 'reasonable' costs of dealing with the public nuisance claimed by Wandsworth Council who have to clean up their droppings on the pavements below.

'As early as the 14th century, Londoners irate with the pigeons at St Paul's Cathedral were throwing stones at them, thereby breaking windows, much to the Bishop's consternation', the judge said. 'But there is no evidence that the population of Balham has resorted to this form of self help.'

The council claimed that its annual cleaning costs had reached £12,000 whereas the one-off capital cost to pigeon-proof the bridge with mesh would be £9,000. An appeal against the decision was dismissed the following year. Network Rail has around 20,000 bridges in its UK rail system. Luckily for them, not all are home to pigeons.

If we want fewer pigeons in our cities, London's former mayor, Ken Livingstone, had the right idea. Where city pigeons are abundant and congregate – at well-known tourist spots like Trafalgar Square for instance – signs ask people not to feed them.

The mayor introduced a byelaw in 2002 making it illegal to feed them or to distribute feeding stuffs for them. The same anti-pigeon policy is being continued by the current mayor, Boris Johnson. The reason? Not because of any claims that they are a health hazard but in order to cut the costs of cleaning and repairing the monuments in the square.

In 2001, Bernard Rayner, whose family has sold bird seed in Trafalgar Square for 50 years, agreed to close his stall in exchange for a substantial payoff from the London mayor. After a brief High Court hearing about the withdrawal of his licence, during which Mr Justice Hooper admonished counsel for the mayor for making him 'spend an awful lot of time reading about pigeons', Mr Rayner, 47, said he was sad to leave the square.

'I've been concerned with the pigeons all my life, but everything comes to an end', said Mr Rayner.

If you walk around Trafalgar Square these days, you won't get hordes of city pigeons around your feet or flying up in front of you. According to the mayor's office, about 4,000 pigeons here in 2002/03 have been reduced to around 120 now. Many might have simply gone elsewhere in the city but some campaigners are appalled at the policy. Supporters of 'Save the Trafalgar Square Pigeons' claim to feed the birds every day outside the banned zone while still campaigning against the ban.

Julia Fletcher of Pigeon Alliance recently called the loss of pigeons 'the greatest wildlife cruelty catastrophe that London has ever known' and claimed that autopsies had shown that birds had died of starvation.

Most city authorities wanting to reduce city pigeon numbers quote a long list of 'pigeon problems' and refer to numerous complaints they receive from members of the public. The problems include a range of diseases that pigeons carry, allergies resulting from mites and other insects nurtured in pigeon nests, pigeon faeces damaging buildings, nesting materials blocking drains and gutters, and fire escapes and pavements becoming slippery because of their droppings – however correct or incorrect such assertions are.

And while RoSPA, the Royal Society for the Prevention of Accidents, lists 'slips, trips and falls' as a major cause of outdoor accidents they have no data on whether pigeon droppings are ever a contributory factor.

But most city authorities recognise that many people value having pigeons around and that they have become a generally welcome part of urban life. So most are trying to keep city pigeon numbers down but certainly not eradicating them, an impossibility in any case.

Venice, though, has a completely different attitude. The maritime city has a reputed 100,000 of them, more than its 60,000 human inhabitants. In the fabulous 12th century Piazza San Marco,

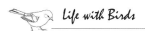

arguably the finest built square in the world, they congregate in swarms, picking crumbs from the cafes around and being fed by waiters and tourists alike. Since 2008 it's been illegal to feed them there but not everyone takes note.

'If you want to reduce city pigeons it's easy', argues John Tully. 'Stop feeding them, don't leave food scraps around, don't drop refuse, have an efficient refuse collection system and the pigeons will undoubtedly decline. Some cities like Bern have reduced them considerably but you have to be squeaky clean to do it. The Swiss are of course', he adds.

The anti-pigeon lobby generally gets more attention than their supporters, and connotations such as 'stool pigeon' and 'pigeon-toed' don't help. One of the less common supporters is Andrew Blechman, a US journalist who wrote *Pigeons: The Fascinating Saga of the World's most Revered and Reviled Bird* (Grove/Atlantic, Inc., 2007), a witty, quirky and sometimes entertaining account of pigeon loving and hatred. But does he fall into his own trap by referring to them as 'scruffy-looking birds with a brain the size of a lima bean'? Most city pigeons I've ever seen look decidedly well turned out and nicely groomed.

Pigeons doing pretty well in our towns and cities are one reason why many pairs of Peregrines have taken up residence on some of our tallest buildings around the world. They have a penchant for taking hapless pigeons in flight, carting them back to their high-rise nests and encouraging the young falcons to devour them.

Might pigeons do well as the result of the smoking bans that more and more countries are introducing? And will climate change benefit them? John Tully thinks so. As more and more people eat outdoors, more food scraps are dropped under their tables. Pigeons – maybe urban gulls too – are bound to benefit.

Most people seem to like having pigeons around. Perhaps it's because they are so tame, because their softly murmured cooing is endearing, or because they have, quite simply, been part of our city scene for so long. Today they are to be found on almost every continent and in most cities the world over … the most successful urbanised bird we have. They apparently first appeared in London in the mid 14th century, the time that a very much larger – and much more impressively coloured – bird held sway on London's streets.

To the throngs of 16th century pilgrims, most from the countryside, jostling their noisy way across London Bridge to Southwark Cathedral, the familiar stench of excrement would probably have surprised them less than the flocks of huge, rust-red birds encouraged by the city folk to feed off any stinking debris.

They were Red Kites. A bird of prey perfectly content to live off food scraps and small, dead animals rather than kill its own prey, the Red Kite is an impressive beast, surely all the more so at close quarters in a London street!

Well over half a metre in length, with a metre and a half wingspan and a deeply forked tail, in breeding plumage the red kite is a bright rusty red with a near white head. Graceful birds, adept at extraordinary manoeuvrings in the air, they made their nests of rags and refuse in the forks of city trees.

Medieval Red Kites apparently thrived in London as they presumably did in most European cities at the time. John Clark, Senior Curator (Medieval) of Early London History and Collections at the Museum of London, refers to two early mentions of their existence in Britain's capital.

One was by Baron Leo von Rozmital, a Bohemian nobleman who, with an entourage, visited London in 1465 during the reign of Edward IV as part of a tour of 'the western corners of Europe'.

He was well received and dined lavishly with the King, reputedly being presented with 50 courses of food! The Baron refers to clouds of kites in the city and also mentions that it was a capital offence to harm them because they were essential scavengers that helped to clean up the place, though John Clark has never found evidence to support any such ordinance.

The Italian Andrea Trevisano, Venetian Ambassador to England from 1496 to 1498, commented that Londoners tolerated not only Red Kites but crows, rooks and jackdaws too. The kites, he said, were so tame that they would take out of the hands of little children the bread smeared with butter in the Flemish fashion, given to them by their mothers.

'I suspect that the notion of a penalty attached to destroying them was a tale told to foreign tourists. There was of course a penalty for taking the royal swans, but I've never found any reliable reference to legal protection for the carrion-eating birds!' says John Clark. All the same, it was probably widely accepted that they should be left alone because of their usefulness.

But more of a clincher is the fact that Red Kite bones have been found in excavations in what is now the City part of London, the original area of the capital. Alan Pipe, Zoologist at the Museum of London Archaeology, has compiled the records that exist and they show that kites were present there from the 2nd century AD, through the Middle Ages, with the most recent evidence dating from 1340 to 1500. The bones have been found in excavations at Poultry, around the Guildhall, the Baltic Exchange (in what is today the City's financial district) south to Monument Street near the north bank of the Thames and west into Drury Lane.

Ravens were seemingly commonplace in medieval London too. Alan Pipe has numerous records of bone finds dating from AD 70 right through to 1710. Presumably they, too, fed off waste and dumped meat and slowly died out as the city became cleaner. Today, it would be unusual to see ravens in any half clean city. Those famously confined to the grounds of the Tower of London (with their wings clipped to make sure they stay put) would not live there naturally.

Like most growing cities, London was a pretty grubby place through the Middle Ages. But a lot of houses had their own 'privies', albeit often draining into open ditches. There were numerous public latrines for those that didn't, though with all of this effluent, and more, pouring into the Thames, the river was highly polluted and often stank.

'In general, popular writers exaggerate the stinks and filth; academic writers concentrate on the counter-measures adopted by the City', says John Clark. 'The occasional tipping of a chamber pot into the gutter I can imagine went on, but certainly not "households throwing their excrement into the streets" as some writers suggest. Rubbish was collected from the streets on a daily basis. I've noticed that the worst complaints about heaps of uncleared rubbish belong to the period around 1350 and later plague years when there was a fear of disease. Not surprisingly, the public services had broken down.'

'Butchers used to dump their offal onto the shore of the Thames where it would wait for the next high tide to wash it away. Later on they were made to empty it directly into the river from a jetty at high tide so that it wouldn't pile up. Presumably this was the sort of waste that carrion birds would particularly go for', he adds.

Both Chaucer (1343–1400) and Shakespeare (1564–1616) mention kites, though not specifically in London. In his plays and other writings, Shakespeare refers to kites no fewer than 15 times.

Roger Lovegrove in *Silent Fields: The Long Decline of a Nation's Wildlife* (Oxford University Press, 2007) points out that Red Kites were always detested in the countryside because they took farmyard poultry and young rabbits, both important as food for people. So they were frequently killed.

City tolerance changed too as drains started to be installed and some of London's refuse got taken to dumps on the fringes of the growing urban area. By the late 1800s, a huge underground infrastructure of main sewers had been installed at great cost under the direction of Joseph Bazalgette (1819–1891), an engineer still venerated by sewage and water engineers today, though hardly remembered by most people who benefitted.

With better sanitation and refuse disposal, city centre kites declined. Long associated with the squalor and disease that London's municipal engineers wished to eliminate, the Red Kite became the bird no one wanted to see. They were poisoned, trapped and shot, with bounty payments encouraging the carnage.

The last cockney Red Kite was seen flying over Piccadilly in 1859, though most of them had been killed off very much earlier. By 1870 they were extinct in England. In Scotland they hung on until 1900. Only in the wildest, least populated parts of central and west Wales did a few pairs survive.

From that tiny population – reduced at its lowest ebb to six breeding pairs – combined with reintroductions from continental Europe to Scotland and England, the Red Kite is once again on the increase. It hasn't yet attempted to re-establish itself in our towns and cities, where gulls and city pigeons have established a monopoly on discarded food. But who knows; one day they just might turn up on London's streets once again and start breeding in its parks. They've already been seen diving into streets in Leeds city centre!

Red Kites have a surprising habit of decorating their stick nests – almost always built in a large cleft in a tree – with coloured objects. Often it's clothes, underwear taken from washing lines, handkerchiefs, gloves, even hats. Sometimes it will be children's soft toys, crisp packets or other colourful items.

Shakespeare even wrote the habit into *The Winter's Tale* where the character Autolycus, himself a petty thief, says: 'My traffic is sheets; when the kite builds, look to lesser linen'. Henry Williamson (1895–1977), the natural and social history writer, even wrote a short story, *The Flight of the Pale Pink Pyjamas*, about a Red Kite's assault on a clothes line!

Kites the world over are humankind's free sanitary engineers, eating up huge quantities of food scraps in cities and wherever there are uncovered refuse tips. Most of them are Black Kites, arguably the most common bird of prey worldwide.

Not actually black but a rather dull dark brown in colour, and nowhere near as attractive as their red cousins, Black Kites inhabit most continents and many cities. From Bamako, Mali to Cairo, Egypt; from Mumbai, India to Kuala Lumpur, Malaysia, Black Kites are to be seen drifting in the warm air, waiting to plunge to the ground to seize some discarded food scrap or anything edible from a market stall. Flocks of them congregate at refuse tips.

Visiting sprawling Mumbai's huge municipal refuse tip in its eastern suburb of Deonar is not something I would recommend. It certainly isn't in any of the tourist guides. But, accompanied by a security guard nervously tapping his lathi, the long truncheon-stick carried by Indian police, it proved possible, though difficult, to get permission to walk over the huge dump. It is not an experience for the sensitive.

The squalor and stench is stomach-churning. Rabid dogs abound. And some desperately poor people eke out a living of sorts by sifting through every lorry load that arrives. Mostly these people live in the squalid shanty towns surrounding the dump, the whole site a disgrace in a country with one of the most vibrant economies in Southeast Asia. Begun in 1927, it's the oldest and the biggest open refuse dump in Asia, taking 70 per cent of the city's refuse.

While most such dumps are 'retired' within 30 years, Deonar has exceeded its saturation point and the garbage piles as high as nine-storied buildings and covers well over a hundred hectares. Around 1,200 trucks from all over the city come here daily, disgorging around 8,000 tonnes of garbage to add to the piles. Proposals to close it and install a modern facility, something talked about for a decade, were again rejected in May 2009 'for further studies' while around 2.5 million people remain affected by the pollution from it.

All this detritus, though, attracts plenty of birds. Squabbling parties of Black Kites take to the air as I approach them, then circle ominously before landing to sift through another new pile of refuse nearby. Phalanxes of snow-white Cattle Egrets, standing incongruously neat as choirboys on a knave of putrid discards, compete with the more aggressive kites for scraps of food. And flocks of delicately coloured Yellow and Citrine Wagtails pick off insects from the clouds that this urban horror breeds.

Vultures the world over will eat food scraps too, but many of them specialise in searching out the corpses of dead animals as they drift effortlessly on warm air high above. A pack of a hundred or so aggressive, hungry vultures can reduce a farmer's dead cow to bones in an hour. In keeping all manner of diseases at bay as a result, they are probably more important in many poor developing countries in Africa and Southeast Asia than antibiotics are in combatting human disease.

Not as showy as kites, and often not as obvious as pigeons, sparrows are great city cleaners too. Sit in an outdoor cafe in Madrid or in Marrakech's famous gravel-covered Djamaa El Fna square and chirpy House Sparrows picking up crumbs under the tables are as guaranteed as a good cup of coffee.

In Marrakech's case, though, they are likely to be accompanied by House Buntings, far more colourful, orange-brown sparrow relatives. Virtually worldwide in their distribution – though introduced to the Americas, Australia and New Zealand – House Sparrows will often take crumbs from your hand, so tame are they at pavement cafes.

Denis Summers-Smith, a life-long expert on sparrows and the ubiquitous House Sparrow especially, in his *On Sparrows and Man* (The Thersby Group, 2005), describes the close interrelationship between us and the cheeky but loveable little bird, which probably began at least 10,000 years ago when early hunters started to grow crops. House Sparrows began associating with wheat farmers in the Middle East ... and Tree Sparrows with rice farmers in China. They've lived close by ever since!

Other birds eat up our discarded food and associated detritus from human society too. Tree Sparrows, tidier-looking but similar to their house cousins, are the most common sparrow in cities in China, Japan and parts of central and Southeast Asia. In hectic Bangkok, they are extremely common around many of its streets, picking up whatever morsels they find in spite of the vast numbers of lorries and cars so close by.

Sparrows are not known to be very noisy and their vocals fade into insignificance alongside what must be one of the noisiest city birds in the world. The house crow, a rather scruffy black and grey crow larger than a jackdaw, makes its presence felt in villages, towns and cities all across India, Nepal, Pakistan and wider afield where, in some places, it's become established after hitching rides on ships! As its name suggests, nowhere does it live outside urban areas.

The House Crow is an aggressive scavenger that will eat almost anything, from discarded food in refuse bins (which it will ransack) to road-killed rats. In a day, the House Crows of Mumbai probably mop up thousands of tonnes of waste that would otherwise make the city's backstreets even more squalid than they often are.

But its downside is that this crow leaves a trail of destruction – plastic bags and other debris – in its wake. And it also decimates local wildlife, aggressively snatching many birds' eggs and chicks as well as taking frogs, lizards and other small mammals, sometimes raiding people's homes to see what it can get and dive-bombing people carrying food.

This is a bird to watch! Its spread might be unstoppable. It has got as far as the Middle East, into Australia (where it has since been eradicated) and even into parts of the Netherlands. It hasn't yet made it to the southern US or South America where the climate would suit it just as well. But it might.

Much less aggressive, the Australian White Ibis – a large wading bird found naturally in wetlands, grasslands and estuaries where they feed on frogs, crayfish, fish and large insects – has, rather peculiarly, turned its attention to city life on that continent.

These days you are likely to encounter groups of these black-headed white birds with their long curved beaks raiding garbage bins or stealing food at picnic sites in Australian cities. While they are quite harmless, some people find their large size, and particularly their beak, intimidating. They also make quite a slimy mess wherever numbers of them roost. But they might not have become city slickers had it not been for the diversion of so much water from inland rivers for the irrigation of farm crops, reducing the amount of damp habitat in which they can feed. It was a case of adapt or perish for the Australian White Ibis.

In Indian cities, Common Mynas – brown, starling relatives – are abundant, frequenting railway lines and both urban and suburban areas where they feed aggressively on any food scraps, taking food from rubbish bins and collecting at picnic sites. Where they've been introduced, in eastern Australia and New Zealand's North Island for instance, the Common Myna is regarded as a serious pest.

Maybe the bird owes its success in the urban and suburban settings of Sydney and Canberra to its origins; having evolved in the open woodlands of India, this bird is cut out to live in habitats with tall vertical structures and little to no vegetation on the ground. And that sums up many a city street!

Crows in particular are ardent road scavengers – Magpies and Carrion Crows in Europe, House Crows in much of Southeast Asia. Several different species of vulture across the world do the same. After all, why do all that searching for a meal if there's a takeaway just along the road.

In the countryside, it's usually not possible to get very close to birds. In cities, it's easier. Urban birds, those that make a meal out of our discarded food scraps especially, can be extremely tame and confiding. So it is that most of us admire those cheeky sparrows brave enough to hop onto our picnic table. And the city pigeons that scramble around our feet if we accidentally drop a few crumbs from a lunchtime sandwich.

It's only in our towns and cities that people can experience wild birds up close and intimate. Otherwise, the closest we can get is by looking at their images … on television and in art. And that is the subject of the next chapter.

10
The art of using birds

Birds – their colours, their songs, their wildness and flight – have inspired artists,
composers and songwriters. They still do. They've also inspired poets and other writers,
even designers of wallpaper and postage stamps. And advertising agencies as well.

I'm standing in scorching midday heat, the nearby sun-drenched rocks too hot to touch. Behind me in the pale ochre-coloured sand is a dry wadi full of prickly shrubs and small acacia trees nurtured by some long-past showers of rain that rarely wet this parched landscape.

In front of me, though, is an art gallery. A very unusual art gallery in a very unusual place. Close to the centre of the Sahara Desert in the very south of Libya, I'm admiring walls covered in artistic images of crocodiles, giraffes, elephants, herds of antelope, and of hunters giving chase with spears and clubs. Amongst these images are unmistakeably those of ostriches, once a common bird hereabouts and now long gone. What I'm looking at are some of the oldest examples of wildlife art in the world.

The walls are small cliffs at the base of the Akakus Mountains and amazingly clear images of these animals are drawn, or sometimes carved, on their orange-brown sandstone. They date from a time, between 8000 and 5000 BC, when the Sahara was not a desert but a lush, fertile land supporting a vibrant and extensive human community. And some of the members of these communities – hunters and herders – clearly fancied themselves as artists.

The detail they show is often stunning. Of people herding domesticated livestock. Of chariots. Of a couple holding hands as if attending some ritual. Even of a young woman having her hair combed by another, ready for her wedding perhaps. Of groups of palm trees. And of the feather patterning on the backs of the ostriches.

Two German explorers, Heinrich Barth and Gustav Nachtigal, were the first westerners to 'discover' these drawings in the late 19th century, a time when being PC was not yet dreamt of. So impressed were Barth and Nachtigal with the quality of them that they were utterly convinced that only Europeans – and not 'barbarians' as they so indelicately put it – could have drawn them!

That myth was first dispelled by Professor Fabrizio Mori, an expert on early cultures at Rome University who began the first systematic studies of them in 1955 and who attributed them to forebears of the Tuareg, the remaining desert inhabitants. The Tuareg – a few families of which are still semi-nomadic hereabouts – are incredibly proud of the rock drawings which they treat as a precious inheritance handed down to them by their forebears.

Most experts agree that the paintings were done using crude brushes made of feathers or animal hair or by using a stick, a bone spatula, or just fingers. The outlines are thought to have been done first, then coloured in.

But this incredible resource of rock art, distributed here at well over a thousand scattered sites, is not just a unique record of early life in the Sahara but a documentation of a past era of climate change and its human impacts that have a resonance for life on our planet today.

Over the last few decades, archaeologists have identified a rough time sequence illustrating a major transition in lifestyle for the people who originally settled in the Sahara around 10,000 BC when the climate was more humid. The first colonists were hunter-gatherers. By 5000 BC they were combining hunting, fishing and gathering with pastoralism, herding cattle, sheep and goats, maybe the ostriches too, as the climate became drier.

Sometime after this, the climate became drier still, any permanent water disappeared and seasonal lakes and streams became few and far between. The Sahara's farmers dwindled as their animals died out. Ostriches became rare and survive now only in the tree-dotted semi-deserts of parts of Mauritania and Sudan.

Birds have long featured in the art of other, much better-known civilisations too. In ancient Egypt for instance. Tourists visiting its fantastic temples and tombs might assume that the outlines of animals and birds carved into stone monuments, or drawn on papyrus, are some primitive art form. In fact they are hieroglyphics, pictures that make up words, the earliest form of Egyptian script dating from around 3000 BC.

But there is absolutely no doubt that even the early Egyptian civilisation possessed extremely talented artists. About 80 km south of modern-day Cairo, in the fertile Nile Valley, the tomb of Atet, wife of Prince Nefermaat who died in 2589 BC, has a series of amazing, coloured frescos. One of them shows three species of wild geese, all accurately drawn and worthy of inclusion in one of today's bird identification books.

There are plenty of examples of Roman bird art too, together with other wildlife, mainly in the form of colourful floor mosaics. Some of the best preserved are from the Villa Dar Buc Ammera, a Roman villa dating from the 1st century near Zliten on the north coast of Libya – not far from the famous Roman city of Leptis Magna, where a number of such villas are preserved almost intact because they got buried under sand when they were abandoned.

Dar Buc Ammera's floor mosaics, long ago taken to the Archaeological Museum at Tripoli, incorporate exquisite details of birds feeding youngsters in their nests, men killing wild ostriches, an array of ground birds such as partridge and cockerels, and water hunting scenes in which duck and geese figure prominently.

Ancient China, Japan and Korea had a long tradition of wildlife painting too, most of it done using living specimens rather than the often dead ones that western artists tended to rely on. Many of their artists specialised in particular birds and captured extremely life-like images because they observed them so thoroughly.

Hand-drawn and coloured monastic manuscripts dating from the early Middle Ages in Europe often contained drawings of birds – many of them recognisable as particular species – decorating the margins of religious texts. In later medieval art, birds sometimes make an appearance in works by some of the great European masters. But it's usually just a bit part. And their presence is almost always symbolic of some aspect of Christianity.

Stand in front of Carlo Crivelli's *La Madonna della Rondine* (The Madonna of the Swallow), painted around 1490, in its rich gilded frame in London's National Gallery and you might not readily spot the swallow. The bird is perched, rather discreetly, on a cornice above the Madonna's head. Art experts think it was intended as a symbol of the Resurrection of Christ.

Vincenzo Catena's *Saint Jerome in his Study*, painted about 1510, has a silent and tranquil atmosphere partly conveyed by a lion sleeping so peacefully on the floor that a quail is content to walk nonchalantly past it. The quail, apparently, symbolises truth.

White doves figure in several of the National Gallery's masterpieces. They are usually to be found hovering above someone or other, over Mary for instance in Nicolas Poussin's *The Annunciation* painted in 1657. Not surprisingly, they represent the Holy Spirit and represented peace as the dove still does the world over.

Peacocks appear quite frequently in scenes depicting the Nativity at Jesus's birth or the Annunciation when Mary was told by the angel Gabriel that she would conceive the child. This symbol of immortality puts in an appearance, for instance, in Botticelli's *Adoration of the Magi* painted around 1476.

Strangely, though, although vast numbers of depictions of birds in paintings are included because of their religious significance, fewer than 40 different species are mentioned in the Bible out of about ten times that number to be found in the Holy Land!

Centuries back, the pretty little European Goldfinch was adopted by the Christian Church to symbolise the Passion of Christ even though the bird fails to get even a passing mention in the Bible. It's in several religious paintings held by London's National Gallery, such as Benozzo's 15th century altarpiece *The Virgin and Child with Angels* in which an angel is shown giving the Christ Child a goldfinch, and Bastiani's badly worn *The Virgin and Child*, painted around 1480, where there's a captive goldfinch held on a string!

A little more recently, some European artists began to paint birds for their own sake rather than incorporating them in some greater religious masterpiece. Roelandt Savery, a Dutch artist, was one of the first. Of his many works, his most famous is of a Dodo (the long extinct pigeon-relative found only on the island of Mauritius), painted in 1626, and he depicted it as an ugly, overweight and squat bird, now believed to be very inaccurate.

Other paintings were more accurate. Though over a century later, George Edwards' hand-coloured engraving of a Rainbow-billed Toucan, a showy and colourful South American bird with a huge beak, done in 1747, is accurate and life-like. Many ornithologists consider Edwards as 'the father of British ornithology'; he was well travelled for the time and he was a keen observer of the many birds he painted.

Other paintings, though, while accurate in colour and many details, sometimes lacked realism, possibly because they were painted from dead specimens, usually birds that had been shot. An example is Giovanni da Udine's male Red Junglefowl, the bird from which our domestic chickens were derived, painted around 1550. The colours are pretty accurate, the detail clear, but the poor bird's legs are set a bit far back so he looks as if he might tip over.

Some of the National Gallery's paintings have reason to be rather well endowed with wildlife. Roelandt Savery's *Orpheus* – the Greek mythological character who supposedly has the power to enchant with his music – contains a veritable cornucopia of wild creatures. It was painted in 1628, and I managed to identify a cockerel, numerous parrots, pelicans, swans, ducks galore and at least two different species of crane. The odd thing about Savery's *Orpheus* is that the good chap is playing a violin instead of the customary lyre to do his enchanting. The birds and a menagerie of other animals don't appear to mind one bit.

In non-religious paintings, there are depictions of a much wider variety of birds. Hieronymus Bosch in his *The Garden of Delights* in Madrid's Prado relies on several birds to convey a sense of the paranormal; an evil and foreboding owl or a myriad of swallows flying between skull-like rocks. And with foreboding in mind, it's difficult to disassociate Van Gogh's ominous black Rooks flying over a cornfield against a leaden sky, now housed in Amsterdam's Van Gogh Museum, from his suicide a few hours later.

Predictably, perhaps, certain birds figure much more commonly than others in art. The dove, used universally as a symbol of peace, is one of Picasso's most famous bird images.

John White (*c.*1540–*c.*1593), who drew the birds of Florida and Virginia while on a voyage with Sir Walter Raleigh, can arguably claim to be Britain's first bird artist, though his drawings – some in London's British Museum – are today not well known. He was closely followed by Francis Barlow (*c.*1626–1704) who became much better known in his time for his lively game bird and bird of prey drawings including illustrations for *Aesop's Fables* first published in 1666.

Thomas Bewick (1753–1828) was a Northumberland-born, self-taught wood engraver and bird expert and the first artist to properly include bird habitats in the engravings he made. By engraving on hardwoods using very fine tools used mostly by metal engravers, he achieved the incredible detail for which he became famous.

There's no doubt, though, that the finest bird illustrator, and the best known ever, was an ex-storekeeper who gave drawing lessons in his spare time in the then American frontier town of Louisville, now a large city in Kentucky, where he settled temporarily.

The illegitimate son of a former French sea captain, trader and slave dealer and a French chambermaid working on the island of Hispaniola, now Haiti, his name was modified a few times from its original Jean Rabine to become, eventually, John James Audubon (1785–1851). His first drawings – rather stiff pencil and pastel studies of common European birds – were made at the age of about 20 in France where he was raised by a doting stepmother. But his future work back in America, backed up by brilliant observation in the field coupled with his good aim at shooting birds (commonplace then in order to draw them), eventually paid dividends.

Jonathan Elphick, in his thorough and extremely well-illustrated *Birds: The Art of Ornithology* (Scriptum Editions, 2004), takes up the story:

> In the end, each copy of *The Birds of America* contained 435 huge colour plates … from the first, a proud Wild Turkey cock, to the final plate of a pair of plump little American Dippers. Artistically Audubon's paintings are superb; ornithologically they have some serious limitations. These were partly connected with his usual method of drawing not from life – which he often claimed to do – but from birds he had just killed.
>
> But Audubon's approach to depicting birds represented a quantum leap forward. In contrast to many of the static images of previous bird artists, his birds are full of life: his hawks, kites and eagles swoop down on prey or rip it apart; songbirds reach up to pluck berries or snatch butterflies. The background was also carefully designed, and often showed the bird's typical habitat in detail.

Today, only 120 complete copies of *The Birds of America* survive intact. The sale of a copy in March 2000 at Christie's, New York reached almost $9 million (£5.4 million), making it one of the most expensive books ever sold. Ironically, Audubon himself died of ill health in relative poverty, partly perhaps the result of being worn out by years of epic struggles to get his work recognised and published. But maybe the greatest irony is that it had to be published in London because no one in America at that time was interested!

Since Audubon's time there have been many other outstanding bird artists. People like the Scot, Archibald Thorburn (1860–1935) who worked almost exclusively in watercolours and of whom Sir Peter Scott, himself an excellent artist and naturalist, said that 'he portrayed the texture of feathers more brilliantly than anyone else before him'. As a young man Thorburn was keen on shooting but apparently gave it up when he heard the awful screams of a brown hare he had wounded.

Thorburn was one of the first bird artists to work, free of charge, for the growing RSPB, doing the artwork for 19 of its Christmas cards up to 1935 when he painted the last one – a tiny Goldcrest, Europe's smallest bird – while bedridden and in pain shortly before he died.

And then came Charles Tunnicliffe (1901–1979), brought up in Cheshire in England but who settled in Anglesey in northwest Wales and, based there, did most of his brilliant, painstaking work predicated on detailed field sketches prior to producing final portraits in watercolour or oils back at home. One of the greatest of all British bird painters, he also produced fine drawings, engravings and paintings of a wide range of British wildlife, farm animals and country life, much of it to illustrate a huge array of books and other publications including cards to go inside packets of tea and work for the RSPB.

In the United States, with the legacy of Audubon still looming large, Roger Tory Peterson (1908–1996) took bird painting in a different direction, to the mass market. Hailed as the inventor of the modern field guide to help average birdwatchers identify what's flitting about restlessly in front of them, his straightforward but accurate style of painting has probably helped millions the world over. Peterson was most certainly a brilliant naturalist and observer. Rather than flamboyant and over-artistic, his paintings provided clarity and showed the fundamental points an observer needed to concentrate on in order to stand a good chance of identifying a bird.

With so many excellent bird artists and illustrators to choose from, who would Jonathan Elphick select as his 'all-time greats' of the last century? He came up with Tunnicliffe and Eric Ennion (1900–1981), renowned for the liveliness of his subjects; Richard Talbot Kelly (1896–1971), whose technique involved flat colour washes within skilfully drawn outlines; Richard Richardson (1922–1977), who painted extraordinarily accurate pictures for field guides; John Busby who creates expressive images full of life in watercolour and pencil; Robert Gillmor, a prolific producer of masterful line drawings, watercolours, linocuts and silk screen paintings; and Bruce Pearson who does dramatic paintings of wildlife in evocative landscapes in several media.

'It was extremely difficult to choose a shortlist. There are so many outstanding names. If you extend the choice across Europe I'd put at the top two Swedes, Bruno Liljefors [1860–1939], with his dramatic oil paintings, and Lars Jonsson, one of the greatest of all bird artists. Add in North America and I would have to choose Louis Fuertes [1874–1927], a superb artist with an ability to distil the character of the bird, and Roger Tory Peterson [1908–1996]. But I could very easily include others too. There are so many excellent artists to choose from', he says.

Birds aren't depicted only in paintings and book illustrations of course. They are pretty thoroughly represented, for instance, in porcelain (usually known better by its more common title of chinaware), in fabrics and wall coverings, on postage stamps and in other media too.

Taxidermy is often regarded as an art and to practise it, you must be very familiar with anatomy, sculpture and painting, as well as tanning because it basically involves removing the whole animal's skin, treating it to preserve it and mounting it in a life-like way for display. It has always been popular using birds as subjects, though today more of the mounted specimens are done for museums than for private homes.

One modern taxidermist – 29-year-old Polly Morgan working in East London – has taken the age-old practice into the realms of expensive and often unnerving tableaux which she creates using animals and birds that have met a natural or accidental death.

Two of her creations, *Dead Blue Tit on a Prayerbook* and *Dead Quail in a Matchbox*, were bought by Kate Moss for a reputed five-figure sum. That's each! Others include a dead magpie standing in an aggressive pose on the handset of an antique Bakelite telephone, warning against answering it in case it's bad news! Many of her works regularly fetch prices of between £8,000 and £30,000. Nice money, you might say, for a dead bird.

On a more classically artistic note, the Chinese had mastered the production of porcelain long before the west became aware of it, and by the 17th century oriental porcelain had become a valuable export commodity from China. But in 1708 it was developed in Meissen, near Dresden in Germany, and, this being the great age of the decorative arts in Europe, it was sculpted to make intricate figurines.

Not all of them were of then popular saints. Birds became a feature of Meissen porcelain, reaching high prices affordable only by the aristocracy of the day, and Meissen-ware influenced a growing band of manufacturers. Cockatoos and parrots, rather predictably, but also swans, cockerels, peacocks, even small finches and large vultures, were just some of many turned out. A plethora of other manufacturers followed suit and all manner of porcelain bird figurines can be bought today, from the cheap and kitsch to the expensive and rather exquisite depending on your taste ... or lack of it.

Whether it's a desktop 'wallpaper' for your computer screen or the paper sort that you glue to the inner walls of your home, birds feature in some of their designs. For the former you'll find anything from a close-up of a Herring Gull's head (who wants that staring at them from their screen?) to the vibrant colours of a macaw or the shimmer of a peacock's fanned tail.

While computer 'wallpapers' are a more recent arrival, the more traditional paper wall covering has been around much longer. The Chinese had painted landscapes and birds on rice paper as early as 200 BC although it took until the 16th century before these oriental prints were imported to Europe. Vibrant plumages of birds such as peacocks, ducks and other waterfowl painted by Chinese artists were the first to arrive in Europe in the 18th century.

The development of a repeating pattern on wallpaper was introduced by a Frenchman, Jean Papillon, in 1675 and by the early part of the 18th century, the papers were available in strips with the pattern applied using wood blocks cut by artists. By the mid 1800s there were machines printing it.

Postage stamps have long been another market for bird artists. James Chalmers, a Scottish inventor, and Lovrenc Košir, an Austrian civil servant, laid claim to inventing them and the first ones were introduced in the UK in 1840 as part of postal reforms promoted by Rowland Hill, an English teacher, inventor and social reformer.

Birds started appearing on them as soon as 1845; Switzerland was the first, with one issued in the Canton of Basel featuring a white embossed dove carrying a letter in its beak. Printed in black, crimson and blue, it's also the world's first tri-coloured stamp.

Others soon followed, for example Japan in 1875, and the following year Colombia issued a stamp with a very recognisable Andean Condor, a huge South American bird of prey. The first United States bird stamp, an eagle with wings outspread, was issued in 1911.

Oddly, the UK – where very many people have long had wildlife interests – didn't issue any until the 1960s although some then British colonies had done so earlier; for example, Kenya, Uganda and Tanganyika issued a set in 1935 showing the head of King George V flanked by two Crowned Cranes. Britain's first in 1963 celebrated 'Nature Week' but went somewhat overboard with a Long-tailed Tit, a Woodlark and a Great Spotted Woodpecker, together with a badger and a roe deer fawn and some flowers, all crowded on the same stamp.

Kjell Scharning has been collecting bird stamps for more than 30 years and has compiled a website (www.birdtheme.org) with a mind-boggling picture-list of every stamp that he can trace with a bird on it issued anywhere in the world at any time. And that's a staggering 27,000 stamps illustrating 3,500 different species.

Some are rather surprising. The Marshall Islands, a republic of 34 tiny Pacific islands and atolls, has issued dozens of them, mostly, and predictably perhaps, of a variety of seabirds and shorebirds. Malta, the Mediterranean island country with a terrible reputation for shooting and trapping almost any bird that moves, has issued more than 40 stamps depicting a range of birds from little Tree Sparrows to huge Mute Swans. And the Maltese have probably trapped or shot every one illustrated.

It's easy to understand why many countries might incorporate colourful kingfishers or showy birds of paradise on their stamps, but who would have thought that five countries in the world would show off the dull brown little Dunnock on its postage stamps – not that I have anything other than admiration for such a plain little bird getting due recognition.

According to Scharning, the most frequently depicted bird in the world is the impressively large, white-headed Bald Eagle found all across the US and Canada, followed by the Peregrine (found across much of the world) and the charming Emperor Penguin, found only in Antarctica but probably recognised worldwide. These three might be a tad predictable but it isn't, for instance, because the US and Canada have flooded the market with Bald Eagle stamps. Many countries where the bird is never seen – Sri Lanka, Tanzania and Sierra Leone for instance – have produced stamps with Bald Eagles on too!

You might assume that those countries with a good wildlife conservation record would have produced the largest number of postage stamps with birds on – Denmark perhaps or the United States. But no. Top of the list, with 456 stamps, is the Gambia, a tiny West African country, closely followed by another, Liberia, where postage stamps might not have been a priority in a country suffering decades of murderous civil war in the recent past.

The US weighs in at number 11 beneath Cuba and North Korea. The Falkland Islands with 239, the tiny Channel Island of Alderney (8 square kilometres with a population of less than 2,500 people) with 130, and the Isle of Man with 124 all outdo the UK with its 97. Maybe the numbers simply reflect the personal interests of some senior postal officials.

Walk around any town or village in many countries and you might not realise how frequently the names of birds feature as place names or street names. There's Ravenscraig, North Lanarkshire; Cranesville, Pennsylvania; or Peregrine Street in Darwin, Australia for example.

A bit like place names, the names of public houses might not often be considered as works of art. But pubs often have somewhat artistic signs to denote them and birds have often been used – some still are – to name British pubs. Out of around 55,000 of them countrywide, more than 3,000 are apparently named after birds or have a bird's name incorporated in them. The signs are of particular importance on older pubs because many of their earlier customers would not have been able to read.

A 2007 survey by CAMRA, the Campaign for Real Ale, found that pubs with 'swan' in their name are the fifth most common in Britain (451 of them), some way behind 'crown' with 704 but well ahead of most. And there are plenty of other bird names too.

So we have 'The Swan', 'The Black Swan' (well over a hundred of those), or even, disturbingly, 'The Swan with Two Necks'; also 'The Bird in Hand', 'The Dog and Duck', 'The Three Feathers' and 'The Falcon's Nest'. Then there's 'The Spread Eagle', which hopefully refers to the bird not the clientele; 'The Goose and Cuckoo', an odd combination; 'The Sociable Plover'; 'The Winking Owl'; 'The Flamingo and Firkin' in Derby and 'The Strawberry Duck' in Entwhistle, Lancashire.

Sometimes, though, pub names aren't what they might seem. 'The Ostrich' at Wherestead outside Ipswich, Suffolk has been renamed 'Oyster Reach' on the basis that the locals a couple of hundred years back with their strong accents couldn't be understood and the name got corrupted! True, oysters were better known locally than desert birds, but the new name sounds rather twee. The pub was called 'The Ostrich' in 1893, according to the Queen's Chaplain who visited it then, so perhaps the answer is that a sailor returning to Ipswich's port from far-off lands told amazing stories of ostriches and the pub was named in the bird's honour!

Many pub names have good stories attached to them, as you might expect. One is that, in the days of horse and coach travel at Stoney Stratford, roughly halfway between London and Birmingham, the London coach changed horses at 'The Bull' and the Birmingham coach did the same across the road at 'The Cock Inn'. The passengers from the respective coaches would swap news while waiting for the changeovers and it's supposedly from this that the phrase 'cock and bull story' is said to have originated!

It may or may not be considered as art – rather like Tracey Emin's unmade bed – but many video games contain images of birds. *Zoo Tycoon 2*, released in 2004, is a video game in which the player may create and operate a zoo by managing its finances, employees and animal exhibits. Originally released for Microsoft Windows, it includes a flamingo, a peacock and an ostrich.

Super Mario World 2: Yoshi's Island, is a platform video game developed and published by Nintendo for the Super Nintendo Entertainment System console released in 1995. It includes a stork carrying babies and a character called 'Raphael Raven', the leader of the ravens … though he doesn't look much like the real thing!

Birds have appeared in films, though mainly with distinctly bit parts, as background sounds or as caricatures. So, *Mary Poppins*, released in 1964, starring Julie Andrews and Dick Van Dyke and produced by Walt Disney Studios, has four penguins depicted as cheerful waiters carrying water glasses and menus.

But there are exceptions! In Alfred Hitchcock's infamous *The Birds*, released in 1963 and based on a novella by Daphne du Maurier, they have star billing. The film involves parties of highly aggressive birds, mainly crows and gulls, attacking people with such ferocity that real-life assaults by some seaside holiday resort gulls seem trivial by comparison. Crows generally in films are more typecast as villains than many actors ever become, playing the conveyor of danger, death, evil … and the Devil Incarnate.

In *Finding Nemo*, a 2003 animation for children, 'Nigel', a Brown Pelican, helps tiny Nemo, an unusually small clownfish. And then there was the highly successful *March of the Penguins* which won several awards in 2006 for best documentary. It shows the extraordinary breeding cycle of the Emperor Penguin (the heaviest penguin species, standing at over 120 cm tall) filmed over a year in extremely tough circumstances in the Antarctic … though it presents it in a rather cloying way by giving the birds human-like characteristics.

Birds have appeared in a huge range of comics, in puppetry, animation generally and in nursery rhymes, often developing huge followings for the character concerned. Think of 'Daffy Duck', the animated character in the Warner Brothers' *Looney Tunes* and *Merrie Melodies* series of cartoons. Daffy is known as the best friend, but occasional self-imagined rival, of Bugs Bunny. Or 'Woody Woodpecker', another Warner Brothers animation; 'H. Ross Parrot' who promoted using the alphabet in the educational children's series *Sesame Street*; and 'Graculus', the ever sensible green bird in *Noggin the Nog*, a cult classic chidren's animated television series devised by Peter Firmin and Oliver Postgate.

Birds crop up in everyday sayings and proverbs, most of them said without giving a thought to their origins. So we have 'up with the lark' because they start singing early; 'as bald as a coot', referring to the white patch that looks bald on the front of its head; and 'as dead as a dodo' (extinct!). There are countless others.

The very attributes that make birds seem so familiar to us – their flight and song – at the same time retain for them an air of mystery that sets them apart from other animals. They remain wild, unpossessed by humans, as the English poet and critic Matthew Arnold (1822–1888) wrote. It's a theme that Leonard Lutwack (1918–2008), formerly Professor Emeritus of English at the University of Maryland, explores in one of the rare studies of the subject, *Birds in Literature* (University Press of Florida, 1994).

His examples – both expected and surprising – come in some measure from Greek and Roman writers but primarily from the poetry and prose of American and British writers of the 19th and 20th centuries. Lutwack describes examples of birds in poetry and as metaphor, including the classical swan representing love and fidelity or an owl representing wisdom, and the birds of such poets as Emily Dickinson and Walt Whitman. He mentions birds that are trapped, hunted, or killed in sacrifice such as the injured duck in Henrik Ibsen's play *The Wild Duck* written in 1884 and the shot seagull in Anton Chekhov's *The Seagull* written in 1895.

Birds as part of erotic writing are mentioned by Lutwack too, with special emphasis on D.H. Lawrence's juxtaposition of birds and lovers, the association of white birds with chastity, and the traditional identification of women with docile birds and men with birds of prey.

Shakespeare mentions birds rather frequently. Caroline Spurgeon (1869–1942), an English literary critic, in her detailed analysis of Shakespeare's imagery, found mention of 64 different species spread over 606 occurrences.

James Fisher (1912–1970), a leading British ornithologist and broadcaster, once commented that Shakespeare

> … provided quotations of unprecedented beauty. As far as I can discover Shakespeare saw birds well, and remembered them, as he remembered an incredible amount of things, with precision.

Shakespeare, for example, refers to 'the owl, night's herald' (in *Venus and Adonis*) and, in *Titus Andronicus*, says that 'The eagle suffers little birds to sing, And is not careful what they mean thereby, Knowing that with the shadow of his wings, He can at pleasure stint their melody'.

Birds often get a mention in literature as part of painting a palette of countryside bucolic charm, real or imagined. Surprisingly, maybe, because so much of his writing portrays gloomy Victorian life, Charles Dickens (1812–1870) in *Nicholas Nickleby* describes a scene as '… heaven above was blue, and earth beneath was green; the river glistened like a path of diamonds in the sun; the birds poured forth their songs from the shady trees; the lark soared high above the waving corn; and the deep buzz of insects filled the air'.

And, of course, birds appear in many a children's story, such as J.M. Barrie's *Peter Pan* in which Peter asks delightfully, 'Do you know why swallows build in the eaves of houses?' then adds: 'It is to listen to the stories'. There's Beatrix Potter (1866–1943) and her endearing *Tale of Jemima Puddle-Duck* first published in 1908 but still read by, or to, many a child. And, more recently, Roald Dahl (1916–1990) and his *Danny the Champion of the World* in which a father and son try to steal their landlord's pheasants by stupefying them with raisins spiked with sleeping pills.

From Edward Lear's (1812–1888) great fun in *Mr and Mrs Spikky Sparrow* to the romanticism of W.B. Yeats (1865–1939) in *The White Birds*, or Ted Hughes (1930–1998) writing about *Swifts* screaming past buildings with lines as full of verve as the birds themselves, these creatures have inspired very many poets. Their elegant colours, their songs, their ability to fly, the close association some have with people, their care for their offspring, the mystery of their migration; it's little wonder that birds have long been a natural vein to tap.

Works by ancient Greeks like the oral poet Hesiod, who lived in the second half of the 8th century BC, and the poetic playwright Aristophanes (446–386 BC) are probably some of the earliest containing references to birds. But for poems covering the widest possible range of birds, from the ubiquitous sparrow to the fantastical phoenix, it's hard to beat a recent anthology edited by Simon Armitage and Tim Dee entitled *The Poetry of Birds: A Collection of Avian Verse* (Viking, 2009). Nearly 300 pages of poems include examples by Chaucer, Wordsworth (who mentions robins in 14 of his poems), Philip Larkin, Emily Dickinson and Marianne Moore.

You won't find many poems about crows, presumably because they aren't pretty and they don't sing. But American writer Edgar Allan Poe's (1809–1849) *The Raven* is an exception. It tells of a talking raven's mysterious visit to a distraught lover, tracing the man's slow descent into madness. It's a good one for a Halloween party!

John Clare (1793–1864), the English poet and son of a farm labourer who came to be known for his wonderful representations of the English countryside, mentions more birds – some reckon up to 145 different species – in his verses than almost any other poet. Some that he mentions are rarely named anywhere else; snipes, for instance, the night-calling Corncrake, the common or garden Blue Tit, and the 'little trotty wagtail he went in the rain'.

John Skelton (1460–1529), too, had much earlier incorporated a great number of birds in his poetry. A sarcastic wit and public gossip critical of many clergy of his day (although for some years he was one too!), he referred to no fewer than 75 birds in his 1,400 line poem, *The Boke of Phyllyp Sparowe*. It's a lament for schoolgirl Jane Scroop's dead pet sparrow when it was killed by the nunnery cat where she resided near Norwich, though, in truth, Skelton was more interested in Jane than her sparrow … or the cat.

Some poets could never have seen the birds about which they wrote. Not that such detail stopped Samuel Taylor Coleridge (1772–1834) writing about an albatross – which the Mariner killed with a crossbow – in *The Rime of the Ancient Mariner* in 1797. The great poet never travelled outside western Europe, while albatrosses are huge seabirds restricted to the Southern Oceans and North Pacific.

Some birds crop up more frequently than others in poetry; the Barn Swallow is a good example because it gets welcomed back in springtime. The Skylark singing in the summer dawn, an evocation of joy and optimism, gets into many poems. And so does the Nightingale, now rather less romantically called the Common Nightingale, which has inspired poets and songwriters alike with its loud song of melodic whistles, trills and gurgles which is as often sung at night as it is by day.

Ode to a Nightingale by John Keats (1795–1821), a lengthy poem, was apparently written in one day in May 1819 in a garden in Hampstead, London where one had built its nest. In those times, this now north London suburb was partly wooded countryside.

But the song 'A Nightingale Sang in Berkeley Square', with lyrics written in 1940 by Eric Maschwitz and which was made famous in World War II by Vera Lynn, is almost certainly stretching reality. Tree-framed and pleasant though it is, this Mayfair square in central London is not likely to have been host to Nightingales, at least not in 1940. Sweet-singing Song Thrushes more probably.

A huge range of popular singers have recorded songs about birds or with birds in the lyrics. Some are awfully predictable: eagles soaring on massive wings; doves bringing hope and peace. Some are silly, some are serious, but they each reveal a little bit about how we relate birds' traits and qualities to ourselves and different facets of our daily lives.

There are romantic analogies of course, as in Portuguese-Canadian singer-songwriter Nelly Furtado's Grammy Award-winning single 'I'm Like a Bird', part of her debut album *Whoa, Nelly!*, released in 2000.

A lot of the song lyrics relating to birds emphasise their freedom, their ability to fly away, that everything will turn out alright in the end. 'Three Little Birds' by Bob Marley & The Wailers from their 1977 album *Exodus* is one of his most popular songs. It's a happy, upbeat tune telling the tale of three birds who help remind Marley that 'every little thing is gonna be alright'.

'Freebird', part of US rock band Lynyrd Skynyrd's first album, *Pronounced Leh-nerd Skin-nerd*, released in 1973 and still considered a rock and roll anthem, exploits this theme of freedom and independence and suggests that some people will never change their ways.

Annie Lennox wrote and released 'Little Bird' in 1993 as a single taken from her 1992 debut solo album, *Diva*. It peaked at number 3 in Britain and it describes how in times of trouble and sadness we can be envious of a bird's ability to fly away from it all. It's not to be confused with a

1968 song with the identical name – but startlingly simple lyrics – released by the American pop band The Beach Boys.

Many other solo artists and bands have used birds in their lyrics, some euphemistically. An example is 'Blackbird' by The Beatles, written by Paul McCartney and released in 1968, which draws attention to black women in the US suffering race discrimination, 'bird' being British slang for a woman in the 1960s. 'Chick', another bit of 1960s slang for girls, is still in use. Think of 'chick-lit' and 'chick-flick'!

Classical music has used birds for inspiration too, though maybe not as frequently as you might imagine. Antonio Vivaldi's (1678–1741) Flute Concerto in D is usually referred to as 'The Gold-finch' because it challenges the flute to imitate the bird's silvery trills and sweetly warbled phrases, even its more plaintive notes. George Frideric Handel (1685–1759) wrote an Organ Concerto in F major entitled 'The Cuckoo and the Nightingale', two birds for the price of one, using maybe the most versatile instrument ever invented when it comes to the mimicry of their calls and songs. Cuckoos, because of their call, and Nightingales because of their shrill, highly musical song have made their way independently into a number of pieces of classical music.

The Carnival of the Animals by Camille Saint-Saëns (1835–1921) is arguably much better known although its bird sounds are restricted to a cuckoo, represented by a clarinet playing its repeated two-note call, an aviary of strings, piano and flute with the flute taking the part of a trilling bird while the pianos provide occasional pings and trills of others unidentified in the background, plus some pecking hens and a rooster!

The Austrian Gustav Mahler (1860–1911) incorporated some birdsong into his work, although apparently their singing so distracted him while he was composing that he was known to shoot them!

Arguably less well known, the composer who incorporated more birdsong transcriptions into his music than any other was the French composer Olivier Messiaen (1908–1992), who was also an organist and ornithologist. He found birdsong fascinating; he believed birds to be the greatest musicians and considered himself as much an ornithologist as a composer. His piece for flute and piano, *Le merle noir*, is based entirely on the song of the European Blackbird.

The birdsong episodes in his work became increasingly sophisticated, and with *Le réveil des oiseaux* this process reached maturity, the whole piece being built from birdsong: in effect it is a dawn chorus for orchestra.

Prokofiev's (1891–1953) children's classic *Peter and the Wolf* contains a duck – gulped down by the big, bad wolf – neatly represented by the oboe (in addition, of course, to Peter's sidekick, a little bird who flies around the wolf to distract him, represented by a flute).

Larry Blakely, Emeritus Professor of Biological Sciences at Cal Poly Pomona in California, has compiled a list of classical composers of instrumental works who have been inspired by birdsong and reflected it in their compositions.

'I came up with around 30, from the Englishman Giles Farnaby [*c*.1563–1640], who wrote a piece for the harpsichord based on the call of the "Woody-Cock" [the Eurasian Woodcock, a ground bird related to snipes] to the Finnish musician, Harri Viitanen [born 1954], who composed a work he called *The Blackbird for Solo Oboe* over the period 1999–2001. Although some of the composers on my list are American, most are European, and the Nightingale, cuckoo, and Skylark figure prominently among the compositions', says Blakely.

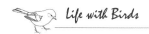

'One of the most frequently played pieces of bird-inspired classical music is Ralph Vaughan Williams' *The Lark Ascending*, in which the Skylark [now called the Eurasian Skylark] is portrayed delightfully by a violin, while the nightingale and cuckoo appear, together or separately, in many works.'

'The American composer John Luther Adams [b. 1953], who composes in a one-room log cabin in Alaska, wrote a series of short pieces for piccolos and percussion, which he called "songbirdsongs" which environmental guru Edward Abbey, in a letter to Adams in 1978, wrote, "Your musical evocation of the Hermit Thrush … moved me to tears"'.

'But the piece that's inspired me most', comments Blakely, 'is *Cantus Arcticus, Concerto for Birds and Orchestra*, by Finnish composer Einojuhani Rautavaara [b. 1928]. This avian symphonic work is different from others in that actual bird sounds are melded with the music of the orchestra throughout the three-part piece. The bird sounds were recorded by Rautavaara in the Arctic regions of Finland', he says.

If birds have inspired writers, poets, classical and popular music composers, sculptors, wall-paper designers, even postage stamp and pub sign makers, is it any wonder that they have been exploited in advertising too? They can be endearing. They can be charming. Cheeky and intriguing. Indeed, a few birds have featured in some of the industry's longest running ads or have become symbols for the very products themselves. They can be a great way of surrounding a brand with associations other than how much the product is costing us. And while some trained live birds appear in ads, many are merely images.

'Swan Vestas', Swedish-made matches composed of aspen wood, have an outline of a white swan on every box and have used the bird's name and outline since they started life in 1883 as 'Swan Wax Matches' made by the Collard & Kendall match company near Liverpool out of cotton wicks dipped in wax.

These days Swan Vestas are not marketed as 'the smoker's match'; that slogan was removed in the 1980s! A novel promotion was introduced between 1914 and 1917 where a free life insurance policy was inserted into every box. Among the conditions of the insurance was that the box of Swan Vestas must be on the person at the time of the accident and that the death must be due to an injury received while travelling! Death in World War I obviously didn't count.

'Penguin' paperbacks were the brainchild of Allen Lane, then a director of The Bodley Head. After a weekend visiting Agatha Christie in Devon, he found himself on a platform at Exeter station searching its bookstall for something to read on his journey back to London but discovered only popular magazines and reprints of Victorian novels. With an idea planted, he wanted a 'dignified but flippant' symbol for his new business.

His secretary suggested a penguin and another employee was sent to London Zoo to make some sketches. Seventy years later Penguin is still one of the most recognisable brands in the world. Not to be confused with Penguin biscuits with their famous 'P-p-p-pick up a Penguin!' slogan and a stylised penguin on every wrapper. They've been made since 1932.

The first Penguin paperbacks appeared in the summer of 1935 and cost the same price as a packet of cigarettes. The way the public thought about books changed forever – the paperback revolution had begun. Within 12 months the imprint had sold a staggering 3 million paperbacks. The offshoot 'Puffin' was born in 1940 as a series of non-fiction picture books for children.

Penguins have been used to advertise a huge range of products including, very recently, Skoda cars; also, not surprisingly, for in-car air conditioning and for other vehicle features such as traction control for a better grip (penguins mostly live on slippery ice), as well as toothpaste and refrigerators and even for career advice companies, printing paper and, more predictably, in campaigns about climate change.

Penguins are popular because they are so cute, so human, so funny. According to some advertising gurus, though, penguins aren't good messengers because, unlike lions, horses or owls, they stand for no specific feature except allusions about ice, cold and heat. Most penguin species have featured in one ad or another around the world but Emperor (the largest), King (with its bright orange ear patches) and Adelie Penguins (smaller and entirely black and white) are most often used.

The Red Grouse, symbolic of Scottish moors, made it onto 'The Famous Grouse' Scotch Whisky as a label in 1896 when Matthew Gloag took over the established business and got his daughter Phillippa to draw the bird. Initially called 'Grouse brand', the word 'Famous' was added in 1905.

In 1956, NBC, the National Broadcasting Company in the US, adopted a technicolour peacock with 11 plumes in its tail as its mascot and logo. He was retired in 1975 and replaced by a strange triangular design resembling the letter 'N' and then reinstated a few years later with a more modern look. Today, in more stylised form – and with just six coloured plumes – the peacock is still the NBC logo.

Aflac Incorporated is the largest provider of supplemental insurance in the United States, founded in 1955 and based in Columbus, Georgia but operating in several countries. Since 2000, the company's identity has become more widely recognised as the result of commercials featuring the Aflac Duck, a white, park-pond duck who frustratedly quacks the company's name to unsuspecting prospective policyholders to jog their memory. It's a real, trained duck, though not a wild one.

The duck concept and all of the Aflac commercials to date have been created by Kaplan Thaler Group, an advertising agency based in New York City. Struggling to come up with a concept to make the big but relatively obscure insurance company's name memorable, one of the agency's art directors stumbled upon the duck idea while walking around Central Park at lunchtime uttering 'Aflac, Aflac'. He soon realised how much the company's name sounded like a duck's quack. The Aflac Duck character has now starred in more than 30 commercials and he's enshrined on Madison Avenue's Walk of Fame as one of America's Favourite Advertising Icons. He also appears, in modified form, in Japanese ads for Aflac, and the company logo was changed in 2005 to include him. For anyone interested, the duck has 'his own' Facebook and Twitter pages!

There are numerous companies supplying trained animals, including birds, for making adverts. 'Animal Acting' promotes itself as Europe's leading supplier. Set up in 1979, the company reckons that it can supply 'all types of birds' from eagles to sparrows, all of them trained and accompanied by highly qualified handlers.

With changing attitudes to animal rights and welfare, avoiding the charge of exploitation is becoming increasingly important for advertisers. Popular opinion might in future see the use of animals in advertising as undignified, in spite of its popularity until now. The Captive Animals' Protection Society (CAPS), founded in 1957, is opposed to the use of animals in entertainment.

Its main focus has been to end the use of animals in circuses but it campaigns also to ban the use of captive wild animals in advertising and films.

One bird (an image again and not the real thing) that, although not in use today, in large part shaped a product's marketing for many years was Guinness's toucan. The bitter black stout still brewed in Dublin was promoted by a toucan as black as its stout. Toucans are large birds with outsize beaks found mainly in South America, well away from Guinness's Irish origins.

'The toucan character was one of a family of animals, otherwise called the "Guinness Menagerie", created by the artist John Gilroy, who worked for S.H. Benson, the first advertising agency appointed by Guinness in 1929', comments Eibhlin Roche, the Guinness Archivist in Dublin. 'He got the idea while watching a performing sea-lion at a circus and had the curious thought that the animal would be smart enough to balance a glass of Guinness on its nose!'

'The toucan [which started out as a pelican] was the first of the "Guinness Menagerie" to appear in poster form. The theme of the ad was a "Guinness-a-day", and it showed a pelican with seven pints of Guinness Stout balanced on its beak. It carried the rhyme: "A Wonderful bird is the Pelican, Its bill can hold more than its belly can, It can hold in its beak, Enough for a Week, I simply don't know how the hell he can".'

'Dorothy L. Sayers [1893–1957], who worked for Benson for nearly a decade, changed the bird to a toucan, and the number of glasses of beer to a more abstemious two, so that the actual advert which appeared was as follows: "If he can say as you can, Guinness is Good for You, How grand to be a Toucan, Just think what Toucan do"', says Roche.

Something much more amusing is an advert made in 2006 for 'Windex', a spray-on window cleaner popular in the US and Canada. Clear glass panels account for numerous bird deaths when birds fly into them. In the ad, two computer-generated images of crow-like birds turn the tables on the house-owner by getting him to respond to a doorbell they ring. He forgets that the all-glass patio door is closed and thuds into it. The crows fall about laughing.

Some adverts, though, have used or focussed on live birds. One for VISA cards in 2005 showed Richard Gere walking in Jaipur in northwest India and using the ubiquitous card to pay for the release of a flock of pigeons from confinement in a wooden cage. Freeing them is supposed to bring good luck – to whoever pays up – not just the birds.

Very much cleverer is a charming ad made for a range of natural juice fruit squashes for Robinsons released in 2009. It shows an obviously highly trained canary flying into a nestbox in which the inside turns out to be a dwarf version of an average living room and kitchen. The trained canary does a bit of tidying up and tries out the TV channels before opening up the fridge to reveal bottles of … you guessed it.

Another recent ad is one for HSBC filmed on the Li River in Guilin, southwest China, showing traditional, night-time fishing using cormorants diving underwater to catch fish. The theme is about always making the most of local experience. The advert neglects to mention, of course, that such fishing these days is done almost entirely for tourists, not for food.

So our admiration for birds has been a source of inspiration not just for artists, poets and advertising agencies. Birds have helped decorate wallpapers, porcelain figurines and thousands of postage stamps. With their, in many cases, wonderful songs and calls plus plumage colours to die for, it's little wonder that since time immemorial we have kept them as close to us as we can in cages and aviaries. And that is the subject of Chapter 11.

11

The beauty stakes

It's because of their vibrant colours, their cheery songs – and sometimes because
they can be taught to talk – that birds have long been kept in cages. But it's an age-old
practice that has spawned a damaging, illegal, and
often sinister, international trade.

In the blazing hot Saturday afternoon sunshine in Bangkok, it's quite a relief to get into the albeit airless shade provided by the vast rows of stalls at what is reputedly one of the largest outdoor markets in the world. With more than 8,000 stalls setting up here every weekend, Chatuchak Market in the Thai capital has a reputation for selling almost everything you could ever wish to buy. Certainly there seems to be everything on sale: furniture, books, jewellery, CDs, any size of Buddha statue you might care to have, aquarium fish, puppies and much much else.

But I'm here to find birds – not, you might imagine, the best place in Thailand to look, in this crush of humankind and goods for sale! But the sounds of bird calls and songs echoing between the stalls in one section of this vast market tell a different story. A very different story indeed.

Row after row of stallholders are selling caged birds. Not just the very familiar budgies and zebra finches almost always bred in captivity, or even aviary-reared cockatoos. But bamboo cages of illegally trapped birds taken from the Thai countryside or from much further afield.

Many of them contain a single Red-whiskered Bulbul, gorgeous brown and white birds with scarlet face patches and a black crest. And they are popular not only for their looks but for their lively song, a double whammy that confines all too many of these common countryside birds to a life of captivity. In theory, though, they are protected by Thai law. They shouldn't be captured and caged at all.

There are more exotic captives here too, and many of the stallholders, knowing that what they're doing is illegal, are keen to ban any photography. Tiny owls looking abject and scared in bamboo cages so small they can hardly move. Stunning golden yellow and black orioles; a Hill Myna, glossy black with yellow ear patches and an orange beak; a young Black-shouldered Kite, a small grey bird of prey of open savanna country, tethered to a perch. And all of them supposedly protected against capture.

There are plenty of others, from African hornbills to toucans and macaws from South America to cages full of small finches. Whether any of these have been obtained legally is questionable. From the attitude of the stallholder who wanted no photographs taken – and managed to pour water over me as I did – that's pretty doubtful.

Yet there is no sign here of any police or other law enforcement presence even though it's well known that Chatuchak Market in Bangkok is a place to go if you want to buy illegal cage birds. Passing laws to protect wild birds is easy; implementing them seemingly less so.

Worldwide, there are precious few studies which have tried to calculate the scale of this sort of trade. One of the few is by Chris Shepherd of TRAFFIC Southeast Asia, published in 2006. TRAFFIC is the wildlife trade monitoring network, a joint initiative of WWF and IUCN (the International Union for the Conservation of Nature).

Shepherd went to the three bird markets in Medan, the provincial capital of Sumatra, part of Indonesia, every month from 1997 to 2001 where a total of around 50 individual stallholders sold birds. He counted the birds of each species for sale.

What he found was an eye-opener in a country where a plethora of national laws exist to protect many birds and to limit their trade. Like Thailand, Indonesia long ago signed up to international controls, including CITES, the Convention on International Trade in Endangered Species.

Altogether, 300 different bird species were for sale at the Medan markets, with more than 3,500 individual birds available each time TRAFFIC did its monthly survey. What's more, 56 of the 300 species had total legal protection in Indonesia – or were supposed to have – so their sale was illegal. Many of the not fully protected birds were being sold far in excess of the numbers that the Indonesian quota system requires, an attempt to try to limit, seemingly ineffectually, the amount of trade in them.

Over the five-year period, in excess of 200,000 wild birds were being offered for sale. And this is in just one large Indonesian town! In Shepherd's conversations with the traders, many freely admitted that some of their birds were trapped in protected areas and that they could get much higher prices for the rarer ones. It comes as no surprise to realise that the Indonesian police and other supposed law enforcement authorities were taking no action.

During the 60 monthly visits over this period, TRAFFIC counted, for instance, nearly 11,000 Zebra Doves, more than 2,500 Coconut Lorikeets (colourful parrot relatives), more than 12,000 Magpie Robins (small, black and white insect-eaters) and more than 30,000 Scaly-breasted Munias (small finch-like birds with large beaks). The vast list included wild-caught ducks, birds of prey, numerous cockatoos, crows and tiny finches.

Indonesia has long had a poor reputation for controlling bird trade. According to Dr Richard Thomas, Communications Coordinator at TRAFFIC International based in Britain, of the 116 red-listed bird species in Indonesia (those closest to extinction), 59 are affected by trade in one way or another, not just for pets but also for food.

The exquisite, almost all-white Bali Myna is a starling relative confined to forests on the one island of Bali in Indonesia. Found nowhere else – not naturally anyway – it's now one of the rarest birds in the world. Why? Because there are more of them in captivity than are left living wild. Habitat destruction has done the rest as Bali gets more and more urbanised. So the Bali Myna is critically endangered.

'It's a status symbol for some Indonesian officials to have a bird, preferably one that's wild caught, in a cage on your desk', says Richard Thomas. 'And there has been a flourishing illegal trade in them as cage birds even though they are, supposedly, fully protected in Indonesia and internationally.'

In 2009, BirdLife International estimated the species' wild population at around 50 individuals in its one protected forest on Bali. It fell as low as six birds in 2001. In the early 1900s there were a thousand or more. A nearby island on which they have been released to try to guarantee their survival possibly has between 50 and 100 whereas about a thousand survive in captivity either as cage birds or in zoos around the world!

According to BirdLife International, the Bali Myna's decline to virtual extinction in the wild is primarily attributable to illegal trapping in response to worldwide demand in the cage-bird trade. This threat continues despite the fact that the whole population is now confined within a national park and has been the subject of a specific conservation programme. The park and programme have, however, suffered from repeated mismanagement and corruption. In 1999, while black-market prices soared (£1,500 for a bird in the mid 1990s), an armed gang stole almost all the 39 captive individuals in the park which were awaiting release into the wild.

What's happening to the Bali Myna, though, is just the tip of the illegal trade iceberg. BirdLife International reckons that almost 4,000 bird species involving several million individuals annually are subject to illegal domestic or international trade. Heavily affected groups include finches, weavers, parrots and birds of prey. Trapping for the international bird trade has been identified as a threat affecting one in 20 threatened and near-threatened bird species. Some are close to extinction as a result.

Most people that keep cage birds do so because they admire their beauty or their calls and songs, often all three. And they get a buzz out of successfully breeding their birds, raising them from eggs and nondescript chicks to become often gorgeously coloured adults. Birds have almost certainly been kept as pets since time immemorial, almost anything from young cassowaries in New Guinea to small but highly coloured, almost tail-less pittas in other parts of Southeast Asia.

Many bird-keepers in western countries specialise in one particular species or in a particular variety of that species while others keep a wider range. Margaret Johns and her husband, who live in the Medway area of Kent, are more typical of the latter, keeping a range of birds including parrots, parakeets, macaws, lovebirds and budgies in an outside aviary. They have all been bred in captivity for generations.

'We've kept birds most of our lives. I suppose we have a hundred or so at any one time but we only sell the youngsters we breed, not the older birds. We keep them. They're so fascinating. You start with one or two birds, then you see others you'd like to have and you go on collecting. They're so intelligent, specially the parrots of course, and they're wonderfully coloured. We admire their calls, pretty noisy sometimes. And the budgies are such endearing little things', comments Mrs Johns.

But others who keep cage birds, unlike Mr and Mrs Johns, are more interested in rarity and in possessing something beautiful that no one else, or very few people, can possibly have. And it's that human greed which drives much of the illegal trade in rare wild birds.

For one bird, Spix's Macaw, greed has exterminated its wild population. Vibrant blue in colour and more than 50 cm long, this gorgeous bird inhabited a part of Brazil where it was pretty well dependent on just one species of tree for nesting. Its decline is attributed mainly to hunting and trapping, although destruction of its habitat and the introduction of the Africanised bee (the so-called 'killer bee'), which competes for nesting sites and has killed breeding macaws at the nest, have not helped.

The last three wild birds were captured for the cage-bird trade in 1987 and 1988 and none have been seen in the wild since. Tony Juniper, in his *Spix's Macaw: The Race to Save the World's Rarest*

Bird (Fourth Estate, 2003), constructs an account of the capture of these highly intelligent and curious birds from the facts he has gleaned where they once existed in Brazil:

> The birds were shocked to full alertness by a startling shrill screeching sound. It was the scream of a distressed parrot. The macaws' curiosity was aroused. They were compelled to respond.
>
> The noise was coming from some distance away on a bend in the creek. The three birds approached. As they drew nearer they could see on the ground a struggling parrot. It appeared unable to move … even though it was violently writhing. The single Spix's Macaw approached while the pair remained at a distance. His natural curiosity overtaken, the parrot descended to a low perch closer to the bird struggling on the ground.
>
> As he settled, two men burst forth and ran towards him. Terrified, the macaw took to his wings, but he couldn't fly. The spot where he had perched was covered in bird lime, a glue used to trap birds. It had trapped him.
>
> Seconds later he was inside a nylon net. The men snapped the branch he was involuntarily gripping and wound the mesh around it, trapping him. Seconds later the blue macaw … was caged in a wire mesh-fronted crate. He lay panting on the floor covered in glue, tangled in the net where he had no choice but to grip the branch to which he was stuck. He called out, but there was no answer. His companions were already far away. It was the end of April 1987.
>
> Unlike some common parrots, this one was not destined for a run-of-the-mill pet keeper. A member of the world's bird-collecting elite would have this one. There were plenty of people who would happily part with a fortune for such a parrot and he would be sold to one of the real connoisseurs, a collector who would fully appreciate the rarity and value of such a trophy.

And while a number of Spix's Macaws have since been bred successfully in captivity by breeding centres around the world as part of a programme to eventually reintroduce the bird to its native part of Brazil, and some land has been bought for that purpose, keeping the illegal trappers at bay might be depressingly difficult.

'The cash value of this kind of illegal trade is extremely hard to come by because, by its very nature, it's clandestine', comments TRAFFIC's Richard Thomas. 'Parrots are probably the most high-value birds in illegal trade. I've heard the figure of £50,000 for a pair of Spix's Macaws.'

Even the Mafia has got in on the act, particularly with the rare parrot trade, simply because there's plenty of money to be made. Richard Thomas says that he understands the phrase for an informer 'to sing like a bird' has its origins in this link! Certainly Spix's and other large macaws, like Hyacinth and Blue-throated, are worth thousands of dollars on the black market which uses major smuggling routes through Bolivia into Peru and beyond.

Hyacinth Macaws, a metre long, are the largest parrots in the world. Vibrant cobalt blue with a yellow mark near their large fruit- and seed-cracking beak, these magnificent birds can be found in the more open parts of the forested Amazon basin in South America.

BirdLife International estimate that 6,000 or so remain but that maybe 10,000 were captured for the illegal bird trade in the 1980s with half of them destined for the Brazilian market. In 1983–84, more than 2,500 were flown out of Bahía Negra, Paraguay, with an additional 600 in the late 1980s. Although these numbers are now much reduced, illegal trade still continues. For example, ten passed through a pet market in Santa Cruz, Bolivia, between August 2004 and July 2005, where birds were changing hands for US$1,000 (£604) and were destined for Peru.

Add in habitat loss as forest is cleared for cattle ranching, a bit of local hunting for food, and fires which burn older trees (the ones with nesting cavities) and it's no wonder that this magnificent bird struggles. Thankfully, there are signs that the pressures are declining and the birds' chances improving, if only a little.

It's slightly smaller Blue-throated cousin is a startling blue and yellow macaw at home in palm-dotted open country in Bolivia where it's down to maybe a couple of hundred survivors. Like the Bali Myna, there are far more of them in captivity than exist in the wild. An estimated 1,200 or more wild-caught birds were exported from Bolivia during the 1980s, suggesting that the population was formerly much higher. Since 2000, collection for this illegal trade seems to have reduced considerably and there are huge efforts at education, protection, bringing landowners on side and other initiatives to try to secure a future for this amazing bird.

These, and very many other birds, are supposedly protected against international trade. And most are supposedly protected in their home countries too. CITES, the Convention on International Trade in Endangered Species of Wild Fauna and Flora, came into force in 1975 and has more than 170 countries signed up to it. Its aim is to protect animals and plants by preventing or controlling international trade in them.

Species listed on Appendix I of the Convention are considered to be threatened with extinction and are not allowed to be traded commercially, while those on Appendix II can only be traded under specific circumstances. Each country is supposed to set a sustainable quota for those on Appendix II so that their natural populations aren't reduced. Currently 163 bird species are listed on Appendix I and more than 1,274 on Appendix II. And that's a fraction of the total number of plants and animals (around 34,000) covered by CITES.

Every two or three years, signed-up governments meet to review the Convention's implementation and assess progress in conserving the species listed on its appendices. These conferences offer an opportunity to amend the list of species in the appendices.

So far, so good. But, and it's a very big but, everything depends on how keen signatory governments really are in implementing the requirements and on how keen they are to enforce it using their enforcement agencies such as police and customs.

Writing CITES needs into law in the countries concerned is the easy bit. Indonesia is fully signed up to CITES. It has all the laws in place … on paper. But it doesn't appear to take its obligations very seriously and do anything with them. That's why organisations like TRAFFIC and BirdLife International are constantly lobbying such governments to do more.

For the 2007 meeting of signatory governments held in The Hague, BirdLife International produced a short dossier which included this damning paragraph:

> The illegal trade in wildlife remains one of the biggest sources of unlawful income globally. National and international enforcement of wildlife trade rules requires much greater priority. Greater international cooperation in the implementation of CITES is needed. Contracting Parties should develop effective implementation strategies, providing additional incentives and financial support where needed, particularly for training and technical assistance in species identification and enforcement measures. The enforcement of CITES processes appears to be regularly neglected at present. Export quotas are often exceeded, as in the case of the now near-threatened African Grey Parrot. It is time for quotas to be routinely curtailed in order to compensate for levels exceeded in previous years. Further effort must be put into reporting the use of 'fraudulent' documents, followed up by measures that will act as a significant deterrent.

CITES, having been in operation now for well over a quarter of a century, has achieved a great deal in stopping or limiting trade in many species but it is still a very imperfect tool. BirdLife International says that, because it's only partly effective, some birds have been driven close to extinction and could go the same way as Spix's Macaw. The Yellow-crested Cockatoo, a large white cockatoo found only in East Timor and Indonesia, is one.

In its case, a fashion for keeping this particular bird was triggered completely inadvertently. The American television detective series *Baretta*, which ran on ABC from 1975 to 1978, was based around Detective Anthony Vincenzo 'Tony' Baretta as an unorthodox plainclothes cop with the 53rd precinct who lives with Fred, his Sulphur-crested Cockatoo, in an apartment at the rundown King Edward Hotel in an unnamed eastern US city.

This cockatoo, widespread in parts of Australia, is very similar to its rare Yellow-crested cousin in Indonesia. And, guess what, popularity drove collectors to capture the Indonesian birds where controls are slack rather than attempt anything in Australia where they aren't!

Other birds threatened by legal and illegal exploitation for the bird trade include the gorgeous little scarlet and black Red Siskin in northern South America; the Java Sparrow, a small grey, black and white seed-eater found in Indonesia; and the Grey Parrot of West Africa, one of the world's most intelligent birds. According to BirdLife International, since 1988 the international wild bird trade has been the primary driver in the worsening status of 15 species of birds.

Malta in the Mediterranean has an unenviable reputation for slaughtering large numbers of wild birds and of trapping them for the cage-bird trade. In 2008, GozoNews (a news service on the adjacent Maltese island of Gozo) reported that two undercover operations conducted by BirdLife Malta found that the illegal trade in wild birds is rampant in Malta's capital city, Valletta.

A raid by the Maltese authorities on Valletta's bird market found several dealers illegally selling wild-caught birds including linnets, greenfinches, serins and chaffinches. BirdLife stated that the birds could have originated from local trappers or from traders illegally bringing them in from neighbouring countries.

Geoffrey Saliba, BirdLife Malta's Campaigns Coordinator, applauded the swift actions of the police in acting on the reports, and added: 'While it is vital that these individuals are apprehended, it is equally important that they are dealt with seriously in the courts. We know that the bird market in Valletta has been raided several times in the past, but these traders still feel comfortable enough to openly break the law. It is pointless apprehending people unless they are given substantial fines which would act as a real deterrent in the future.'

Bird smugglers will go to extraordinary and almost farcical lengths to make money. In 2009 a man was arrested at Los Angeles airport with 12 rare songbirds strapped to his socks! In a scene straight out of *Monty Python*, customs officials uncovered the smuggled stash when they noticed an unusual amount of bird droppings on Sony Dong's shoes!

'He had fashioned these special cloth devices to hold the birds', said US Attorney spokesman Thom Mrozek. 'They were secured by cloth wrappings and attached to his calves with buttons. The birds are rare and there are collectors who are willing to pay top dollar for them.'

It's thought that Dong picked up the songbirds for less than $50 (£30) each in Vietnam and smuggled them to the US, where they usually sell for more than $500 (£300). Dong has been charged with conspiracy.

Customs and border protection authorities in Australia cracked their third wildlife smuggling attempt in Western Australia in September 2009 with the arrest of two men in Perth. The first man, a 53-year-old Australian, was arrested for allegedly attempting to smuggle 39 parrot eggs into Australia through Perth International Airport. He was stopped when he arrived in Perth on a flight from Bali.

During a baggage examination, officers became suspicious that the man may have been concealing prohibited items under his clothing. He was! The eggs were concealed in a specially made vest. He was arrested and charged with attempting to smuggle wildlife into Australia.

The incident followed some months after Australian authorities smashed an international wildlife crime syndicate based in northern Victoria which was making millions of dollars smuggling endangered and exotic bird eggs in and out of the country. Homes were raided and more than a dozen syndicate members interviewed including well-known licensed bird-keepers. They were apparently employing couriers wearing specially modified vests and underwear to carry up to 500 exotic bird eggs into Australia every month, each courier able to carry 30–50 eggs at a time.

Investigators told Melbourne's *The Age* newspaper that some of the couriers were in wheelchairs in a bid to avoid suspicion and that they travelled mainly to South Africa, the Philippines and Singapore where they exchanged native Australian birds' eggs (especially a wide range of cockatoos and lorikeets) stolen from nests for exotic eggs prized by Australian collectors. Some of the rare cockatoos can be worth £55,000 on the black market.

The Australian eggs were exchanged for those of rare and exotic birds such as macaws, the white Salmon-crested Cockatoo, and a variety of parrots and others. The eggs were smuggled back into Australia where the syndicate mostly enlisted women with either a nursing or animal husbandry background to hand-raise the birds after the eggs had hatched. The birds were then sold on the black market for huge prices. Legitimate bird breeding businesses were used as a front for the syndicate's operations which had been going on for over five years.

Australian customs national manager for investigations, Richard Janeczko, said that wildlife smugglers preferred bird eggs to live animals because they were easier to smuggle.

'Egg smuggling has grown over the years, but it's been a traditionally smuggled commodity for a long time', Mr Janeczko said. 'When people are smuggling eggs they try to bring in as many as they can because you don't have to worry about feeding them and they're easier to protect.'

The CITES Secretariat estimates that maybe 1.5 million wild birds are illegally bought and sold each year worldwide, a cash value of perhaps £35 million. Les Beletsky, in his *Birds of the World* (Collins, 2006), estimates that around 230 of the 1,180 bird species under threat worldwide are threatened because they are captured for the illegal bird trade, either locally as cage birds or as part of the illegal international pet trade.

But the greed exhibited by those people who will pay large sums of money to obtain a rare bird threatened with extinction in the wild seems poles apart from the more commonplace image of people keeping a pair of canaries or budgies in their city centre flat because they admire their colours, get cheer from their songs or wonder at their ability to imitate human speech.

In Britain, keeping locally available songbirds such as linnets or goldfinches was commonplace until around the 1930s. Hundreds of thousands were trapped each year. Singing competitions between caged chaffinches were common among the working classes in British cities in the 19th century. An account of one such needle contest, between the 'Kingsland Roarer' and the 'Shoreditch Bobby', held at the 'Cock and Bottle' pub in London's East End, is recorded in some detail in *The Avicultural Magazine* of 1896. The landlord was the judge and, incidentally, the 'Roarer' won … just!

Skylarks were popular singers too, sometimes even being cruelly blinded (as were other singing birds), usually by a hot needle pushed into their eyes, in the mistaken belief that this would enhance their singing – an obviously cruel practice deplored at the time by many people. Trapping finches was banned by law in 1896 but, with foreign trade and travel increasing in the 18th and 19th centuries, travellers were already spotting more exotic alternatives to these good old British songsters.

'Budgies' were first brought from their native Australia to Britain in 1840 by John Gould (1804–1881), a more able biologist than Darwin and a fine illustrator. Budgerigars are less popular than they were but, as cage birds, they are not only pretty but affectionate, friendly, and able to imitate people into the bargain. In their native arid habitat, budgies live in flocks and are yellow and green in colour. In captivity, though, all sorts of colour combinations have been bred. Name a colour, or colour combination, and you will almost certainly be able to get a budgie in it.

Whether they are tiny Zebra Finches – grey, cream and orange singers originally from Southeast Asia and Australia – or vibrant yellow canaries derived from the less brightly coloured natives of the Canary Islands and Madeira first captured and taken to Europe in the 16th century, almost all these common cage and aviary birds in western countries are now bred in captivity. In many cases, they haven't experienced a wild habitat for generations. They probably couldn't even survive in the wild. So keeping them has no relevance to what's happening to their wild relatives.

Some birds ended up in cages because they were attractively coloured … and because you could teach them to talk. It certainly was – and is – a novelty! A unique novelty at that because no other wild animal, not even amongst our closest relatives the apes, can be taught to talk.

But it is a novelty seemingly confined to relatively few birds such as parrots and their allies, budgies, myna birds, crows to some extent and a few others. Birds develop human speech almost only when they are in close company with people rather than with their own species. Just as young birds pick up the songs and calls of their parents, so birds kept as pets pick up many of the commonly used human sounds.

Their ability to learn to talk was one reason why parrots were popular with sailors. That's why Long John Silver, the pirate created by Robert Louis Stevenson, had one on his shoulder!

A budgerigar named 'Puck' holds the world record for the largest vocabulary of any bird, an amazing 1,728 words. Puck, a male budgerigar owned by American Camille Jordan, died in 1994, with his vocabulary first appearing in the 1995 edition of *Guinness World Records*.

Even more amazing was 'Sparkie', a talking budgie who sang in a Geordie accent! At the height of his fame in the 1950s he starred in adverts promoting bird seed, appeared on television and released a record that sold over 20,000 copies. In 2009, an hour-long opera about him – *Sparkie: Cage and Beyond* – by Michael Nyman and Carsten Nicolai was premiered at the MaerzMusik festival in Berlin. His stuffed body, which normally resides in the Great North Museum in Newcastle, was on stage, reminiscent, for the cognoscenti maybe, of the *Monty Python* infamous dead parrot sketch.

Sparkie and his owner Mrs Mattie Williams rose to fame when he won the BBC International Cage Bird Contest for talking budgies in 1958. There were 3,000 contestants but Sparkie's talent for imitating both in 'Geordie' and 'refined' English clinched it. By the time he died in 1962, he could recite ten rhymes and 383 sentences.

Sometimes, though, talking birds seem to get to know how to influence their 'master'. Graeme Gibson in his *The Bedside Book of Birds* (Bloomsbury, 2005) recalls a parrot he bought – apparently illegally from a Zapotec Indian boy, indigenous people in southern Mexico – who said little except Gibson's sons' names and imitated the noises of a vacuum cleaner and barking dogs. A year later Gibson gave him to Toronto Zoo to join a female of his own species. Gibson turned to leave and the parrot, in a voice his children might have used, called out 'Daddy'. He kept calling the one word, and looking expectantly as Gibson abandoned him. He had never said it before!

A plethora of bewildering varieties of these and very many other cage and aviary birds have been produced by individual breeders; the more unusual they are, the greater their value. Huge numbers of people buy and sell cage birds. There are even eBay-like websites devoted to their sale and purchase.

Take a look in *Cage & Aviary Birds*, the UK weekly newspaper with a circulation of more than 15,000, and the classified listings have a huge range for sale: the ubiquitous budgies of course, but rosellas (parrot relatives), lovebirds, firetails (small Australian birds like Zebra Finches), canaries, even Golden Pheasants, Aylesbury ducks and some British birds (captive bred) such as bullfinches and goldfinches. In the edition I looked in there were even two rheas for sale at £100 each. Flightless, ostrich-like birds from South America as tall as a fair-sized person, far from being cage birds, rheas require a large fenced area and shelter. They are not a bird for the faint-hearted to keep.

Large numbers of people keep doves and pigeons, not for racing but, like fantails and pouters, for their appearance or, like tumblers, for some unusual behaviour they possess. Less common than they once were, tumblers were bred for their peculiar ability to tumble or roll over backwards in flight. They were known in India before 1590 and Charles Darwin, interested in pigeon breeding because it developed different characteristics in the birds, refers to the short-faced tumbler in his famous book, *On the Origin of Species*, published in 1859. It's a breed still found at pigeon shows today.

In Britain, the National Pigeon Association is the governing body which sets out the rules for all show pigeons in the UK. There are more than 200 different varieties and pigeon shows are held countrywide. The biggest pigeon show of all is held in Nuremberg, Germany; the 2006 show had more than 33,500 different pigeons exhibited. Show pigeon-keeping is extremely popular, too, in Australia and the United States.

Beauty, elegance and song – or unusual behaviour – are not the only reasons for keeping birds. Sometimes it's more a case of companionship. And there are few birds that can become better companions, often with a bit of human speech thrown in, than several members of the intelligent crow family.

Jackdaws, Carrion Crows, even the larger Raven, can be very good companions indeed. The poet John Clare had a pet Raven; Charles Dickens had two, the models for the character 'Grip' in his *Barnaby Rudge*. Not many people would keep them now but until maybe the 1930s or later they were often popular as such in Britain.

Until the late 19th century, European Starlings could be bought in London for keeping as pets, apparently to be taught to speak and swear. Brilliant mimics, they will most certainly copy musical sounds they hear, from telephone ringtones to parts of concertos. Mozart kept one as a pet, though how much of the composer's prodigious output the bird could mimic is not clear.

Very rarely kept by individuals but often prominent in larger collections and zoos, a huge range of larger birds like flamingos, emus, ostriches and penguins perform much the same role as cage and

aviary birds. Although their keeping is sometimes dressed up as some form of captive breeding for supposed 'conservation' purposes, the main reason for having them is to delight visitors who pay for the privilege of seeing them.

Since they first appeared in European zoos in the mid 19th century, penguins have always been popular entertainers. Perhaps it's their endearing characteristics: standing upright, waddling around in groups, chattering amongst themselves … and going for the occasional swim. Who does that remind you of?

In some places, the daily return journey of penguins from their nests to the sea and back has itself become a tourist attraction. At Phillip Island, near Melbourne, Australia, large numbers of tourists turn up to watch the daily parade, where tiered seating can accommodate more than 3,000 spectators. The colony has an equal number of penguins (these are Little Penguins, the smallest species standing just 40 cm tall) and they generate a sizeable income for the local economy, bringing pleasure to huge numbers of people whom they seemingly disregard as they waddle past!

Visiting the Stafford Bird Show, now the premier cage and aviary bird show in the UK and held annually, you soon realise how popular cage-bird keeping is. According to the Parrot Society who organise it, 6,000 people made it there on the October day on which it was held in 2009. The huge exhibition halls were full of rows of cages and a few larger aviaries containing an amazing range of birds including noisy macaws, lovebirds, cockatiels, finches, even quail and doves. And there were unending supplies of bird feeds, cages, aviaries, bird bedding and a variety of everything else the discerning bird-keeper might – or possibly might not – need.

How many people keep cage or aviary birds in Britain is like asking how many people keep pet cats or hamsters. No one knows because they don't have to be registered but the Pet Food Manufacturers Association estimated 1.39 million bird-owning households in 2004. The Parrot Society has 4,500 members although its John Hayward is quick to point out that some people who keep parrots don't let anyone know because the birds are valuable and the stealing of them not uncommon. Not surprisingly, there is a good business in specialist insurance for cage and aviary bird-keepers.

Under British animal welfare law, all captive birds, like all animals, must be provided with appropriate living conditions including sufficient space. Anyone keeping them has a responsibility not to cause unnecessary suffering. And there are a number of controls and licence requirements enforced by the government or government agencies in Britain that have to be complied with if any bird not native to the UK, a parrot for instance, is being imported here.

But how many keepers of cage birds are interested in wild birds? Kim Forrester, editor of *Cage & Aviary Birds*, says that it's been its long-standing editorial policy to write pieces about wild birds on their news pages.

'Our readers are genuine bird-lovers and are interested in all kinds of birds, whether wild or caged, which is why we tend to cover wild bird stories. However, wherever possible, we try to focus on the connections between wild birds and aviculture, for instance, captive breeding programmes', she says.

There are, though, several organisations that regard keeping birds in cages as inherently cruel even when they have been bred as cage birds and have never ventured into the wild.

PETA, People for the Ethical Treatment of Animals, with more than 2 million members and supporters, is the largest animal rights organisation in the world. It's concerned that before being shipped, many illegally captured birds are force-fed, their wings are clipped, their beaks are taped shut, and they are crammed into everything from spare tyres to luggage to hide them. It's not unusual, they say, for 80 per cent of the birds in a shipment to die. But PETA is also concerned that caged, captive-bred birds show unnatural behaviour and that they are sometimes housed in confined cages with little space to exercise.

Animals Australia, Australia's national animal protection organisation, has a strident view too.

'We have been conditioned to think that keeping birds in cages is acceptable. We convince ourselves that the bird doesn't suffer as it knows no other life and was bred in captivity. The motivation for caging birds has not changed throughout the centuries – it is about what they contribute to our lives – and their needs are forgotten and denied them. Caged birds often exhibit destructive, abnormal behaviours directly related to mental suffering such as feather plucking, excessive vocalisation, fear and aggression. This is not surprising when natural behaviours such as flying, choosing a mate, belonging to a flock, building nests and dust bathing are denied to them', it says.

CITES doesn't only cover trade in whole animals and plants; it covers trade in some parts of animals and plants too! One of the best-known examples is rhino horn used in traditional Chinese medicines and to make dagger handles in Oman and Yemen. Birds' parts don't figure highly in traditional Chinese medicines, though parts of owls and other birds of prey such as eagles and hawks are sometimes sought after.

In 2009 there were reports from Nepal of Eurasian Eagle-Owls being captured and killed for sale for some supposed medicinal use. According to a 2008 report in *Thaindian News*, a Thailand-based Indian online news service, owls like these traded illegally could be worth between $7,000 (£4,200) and $12,000 (£7,200) each.

'After munias [small finch-like birds] and Rose-ringed Parakeets, it's now the owls that are being targeted', comments Jose Louis, who works with the enforcement department of the Wildlife Trust of India. 'There are some known areas where the illegal trade continues but detection is very difficult. Besides the owls, Rose-ringed, Blossom-headed and Alexandrine Parakeets are the preferred choices of buyers who keep them as pets.'

Getting involved in trying to reduce the illegal wild animal and bird trade is not an occupation for the faint-hearted. For instance, in 2008 Malaysian officials made a gut-wrenching discovery in a raid in the town of Muar. Along with more than 7,000 live monitor lizards, over 900 dead owls – plucked, frozen and plastic wrapped for easy cooking – and other wild animals were seized. The haul comprised 796 Eastern Barn Owls, 95 Spotted Wood Owls, 14 Buffy Fish Owls, eight Barred Eagle-Owls, and four Brown Wood Owls. The owls had their heads and feet attached, a sign that they were to be sold as food but maybe also to satisfy demand in Guangzhou, China where they are sold in wine as tonics and cures for headaches.

'It's the first time we've ever seen a big shipment like this of owls', said TRAFFIC's Chris Shepherd. 'The scale of these hauls indicates that Asian wildlife smuggling is growing more sophisticated, organised by syndicates rather than just opportunistic individuals trying to make a buck off a few animals. Apparently there have been a number of shipments of owls that went undetected. One wonders how long we will have owls in that part of Malaysia!' he adds despondently.

A local man was arrested at the raid. But after pleading 'not guilty' he was released on bail and, by early 2010, he was still to come to trial. There have been other raids, and yet more dead owls

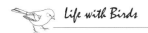

found in a similar state. Needless to say, all owls are fully protected by Malaysian law and they are listed on CITES. Enforcing it is, as usual, seemingly very much harder than passing the law.

So, rightly or wrongly, birds have long been kept for their beauty, either of appearance or song, sometimes both. And in some cultures the feathers of certain birds are very highly valued for their beauty too, so much so that the birds themselves are killed so that particular feathers – or in some cases, whole bodies of birds replete with their full complement of feathers – are used to decorate human bodies much as make-up is used today in western societies. In New Guinea, bird feathers are still used for personal decoration.

According to Dr Chris Healey, an anthropologist formerly at the Northern Territory University in Darwin, Australia, and an expert on the exploitation of birds for trade in New Guinea and Borneo, most bird of paradise skins (complete with feathers) came from the northwestern part of New Guinea and some outlying islands.

There is an account by Alfred Russel Wallace (1823–1913), the British naturalist, explorer and anthropologist, of paying local tribesmen in New Guinea to capture birds of paradise (*The Malay Archipelago: The Land of the Orang-utan and the Bird of Paradise*, Singapore/Oxford, 1989).

Exquisite Red Birds of Paradise, large and gorgeously coloured, were snared in traps or killed at his request, then if captured alive, tied onto perches or stuffed into primitive cages where almost all of them died from their injuries or starvation within days. It reads like something from the Middle Ages!

'By the time Europeans became interested in the most impressive, long feather plumes as a major commercial operation around the turn of the 19th century, they generally took over all aspects of the trade, becoming hunters themselves or supplying local New Guinea tribespeople with guns and ammunition as well as managing the export of plumes', says Healey.

He goes on to say that bird of paradise plumes had long been traded between tribes within New Guinea. The Kundagai Maring, for instance, were adept at trapping birds of paradise and exchanging their plumes for other commodities like pigs with tribes in the central highland valleys in the east of the island who wanted them for decorations.

'The uses for the plumes varied between different language groups and tribes but they were widely used as decorations in ceremonies like the massed dancing and display accompanying ceremonial feasting and gift exchanges between local communities. In some of the central highland groups, plumes were also included in "brideprice", the payment of valuables given by a husband's kin to the bride's kin along with other gifts such as axes, seashells, pigs and occasionally live or cooked cassowaries [very large, dark and often vicious ground birds]. More recently, money has largely replaced all other valuables except pigs and cassowaries', comments Healey.

'Plumes are still used as decoration by some groups but there has been little collecting for a couple of decades. The Catholic Church has encouraged traditional decorations as part of church marriage ceremonies, and local agricultural shows promote dancing competitions. It's mostly the men who get decorated as it always has been.'

'The particular birds used vary across New Guinea, partly reflecting availability, but also cultural variation. The Lesser [with flowing yellow and white tail plumes] and Raggiana Birds of Paradise [with gorgeous pink to red ones] are widely used, usually whole skins with their wings and tail removed and flattened to display them to best effect.'

'The Princess Stephanie's Astrapia [named after Princess Stephanie of Belgium] is another favourite, usually its stuffed body (minus wings) plus its long glossy black central tail feathers. The Black and the Brown Sicklebills [which are also birds of paradise] are used too, though they're quite rare, as well as plumes of sundry other species including parrots, hawks and eagles, domestic fowls – indeed, almost anything may be added to a head-dress', comments Healey.

Killing birds of paradise for decoration is nowhere near as common as it once was, either for local use or for the international plume trade before it was banned a century ago. The bigger threat most of these incredibly coloured, plumed birds now face is deforestation destroying the very habitat most of them need to survive.

Native American Indian tribes traditionally made considerable use of feathers, not only to represent brave acts (see Chapter 12) but also for ornamentation. Tribes in the forests of tropical South America still exploit a huge range of birds for decorative feathers used in dances and other ceremonies – toucans, parrots, macaws and eagles amongst others. The feathers might be used to decorate their arms, legs and necks but they might also be pushed through perforated lips, cheeks, ears and noses. Beauty knows virtually no limits.

African tribes have a history less bound up with feather ornamentation although ostrich feathers were often commonplace for decking out people's heads and shields. It has its equivalent in the peacock feathers formerly used across much of Southeast Asia.

But the illegal killing of birds for the feather trade hasn't by any means stopped. At least not in some parts of the world.

In 2009 the Air Intelligence Unit in India seized 27 kg of peacock feathers (of the Indian peafowl, the country's national bird; the well-known male with its exquisite tail) from a Malaysia-bound passenger at Chennai airport. Noohu Mohammed, an Indian national, had hidden in his luggage bundles of peacock feathers covered by a cloth, artificial flowers and newspaper.

The seizure by customs officials confirmed that the national bird continues to be poached in villages in India's poor Tamil Nadu State. The local people, who often kill the birds for meat and oil, are now increasingly garnering an income from killing peacocks for their feathers that are much sought after in several East Asian countries for decoration.

Well before there was any protection for birds in Britain and a long time before international measures such as CITES were even a twinkle in some conservationist's eye, Britain was the centre of an enormously destructive trade in feathers.

Walk today around the impressive Fletcher Moss Gardens in Didsbury, Manchester – part botanic garden with a wealth of trees and shrubs, part wildlife habitat – and the large, ivy-covered house named 'The Croft' overlooking the place isn't immediately obvious. Donated to the people of Manchester in 1919, the house is arguably of greater historic importance than the gardens themselves.

You might wonder what on earth 'The Croft' has to do with birds at all. But it was here in 1889 that Emily Williamson, the owner's wife, formed a group called the Plumage League to campaign against the then enormous slaughter of birds for feather plumes to decorate ladies' hats.

Towards the end of the Victorian era in Britain, and in other European countries and the US, some birds were threatened with extinction because fashion 'demanded' particular ornamental feathers to decorate hats. The only way to obtain them was to shoot the birds. Men selected fedoras with feather trim while women's hats became larger, hat ornamentation became more lavish, and the feather trade expanded its enterprise to include, in the US, marketing the remains of some 64 different bird species.

Egret and heron plumes, the long feathers draping from their heads in summer, were particularly sought after. In one year alone (1902) some 1,608 packages of these plumes came under the auction hammer at the London Commercial Sales Rooms. That probably represented around 200,000 birds shot for their feathers! In the first quarter of 1885, three-quarters of a million egret skins were sold on the London market alone.

The Audubon Society in the US offered public lectures on such topics as 'Woman as a bird enemy' and erected Audubon-approved millinery displays. Frank Chapman (1864–1945), a US ornithologist, noted in 1886 that as many as 40 species of birds were used in about three-quarters of the 700 ladies' hats that he observed in New York City! The stunning Roseate Spoonbill from the southeastern US was hunted for its vibrant pink wings which were used to make ladies' fans! Not surprisingly, the spoonbills became rare and were first given protection only in the 1940s, the start of their comeback.

American women in the 1880s sported egret plumes, owl heads, sparrow wings, and whole hummingbirds; a single hat could feature all that, plus four or five warblers for good measure. The booming feather trade was decimating the gull, tern, heron and egret rookeries up and down the US east coast. In south Florida, plume hunters would nearly destroy the Great and Snowy Egret populations in their quest for the birds' long spring mating feathers. 'That there should be an owl or ostrich left with a single feather apiece hardly seems possible', *Harper's Bazaar* reported on the winter hat season in 1897.

Most of the tiny hummingbirds were captured on Caribbean islands, many moving through on migration. On Trinidad, there are suggestions of 15,000 hummingbirds stuffed and exported every week around that time to the hatters and dressmakers of Europe.

Great-crested Grebes (elegant birds that breed on lakes) were brought to the edge of extinction in Britain because a few of their head feathers provided comely decoration on clothes and hats for well-to-do ladies and because their down (the soft insulating under-feathers) became a useful fabric for hats, capes and muffs. In the 18th century the grebes were common across the UK but by 1860, when the trade was in full swing, only 40 or so pairs remained countrywide. Around the same time, Kittiwakes – delicate-looking gulls that breed in colonies on sea cliffs – were massacred on Lundy Island in the Bristol Channel because their wings were wanted for the fashion trade.

Punch magazine railed against the killings and on 14 May 1892 commented:

> One dealer in London is said to have received, as a single consignment, 32,000 dead humming-birds, 80,000 aquatic birds, and 800,000 pairs of wings. We are told too that often 'after the birds are shot down, the wings are wrenched off during life, and the mangled bird is left to die slowly of wounds, thirst, and starvation'.

Large numbers of white egret head plumes were imported to Britain from Florida. In the US, vibrant green, yellow and red feathers from stunning Carolina Parakeets were used for decorating ladies' hats, the killings contributing to the demise and eventual extinction of that bird. And even more extraordinary decorative plumes from extravagantly coloured birds of paradise found in New Guinea were popular across Europe with those who could afford them.

Mrs Williamson's fledgling – excuse the pun – Plumage League joined forces in 1891 with the Fur and Feather League created by a Mrs Phillips in Croydon near London to become the Society for the Protection of Birds.

The little society attracted attention. In 1899, Queen Victoria confirmed an order to prohibit the wearing of feather plumes by the military and in 1906 Queen Alexandra wrote a letter to the society expressing disapproval at the wearing of plumes for fashion. Importing plumes from overseas was finally banned by law in Britain in 1922. It had taken 33 years from Emily Williamson's original initiative!

Feathers are still used in fashion clothing today. In New York's 2009 Fashion Week, there were crowns of black ostrich feathers, spiky black feather chokers and gowns sprinkled with sequins and feathers, all of them, though, from captive-reared birds including ostriches, cockerels and peacocks.

According to fashion commentators, feathers showed up surprisingly frequently on coats, dresses and hats, stimulating one retailer to say, 'Feather clothes are instant drama. They throw back nicely to Victorian or flapper looks. Feathers are great for a bit of fun in the office or for being coquettish on a date'. It's a reminder of Coco Chanel's famous quote: 'Every girl should be two things: classy and fabulous'.

In the meantime, though, the society started by Emily Williamson gathered increased momentum. In 1904 it became the Royal Society for the Protection of Birds, the RSPB, today the largest wildlife charity in Europe with over a million members. Its humble origins are recorded on a plaque on the wall of 'The Croft'.

Of course, if most birds weren't as attractively coloured, and weren't able to call and sing, their international trade would hardly be worth a second thought. But then their association with all sorts of myths, traditions, sacrifice, potions and even magic – the subject of the next and last chapter – may not have developed either.

12

All myth and superstition

Tales of superstition and witchcraft, magic and sacrifice. Birds, imagined or real, have
been involved in them all. Some still are today.

It's a fittingly grim, overcast and cold winter's afternoon and I'm standing in front of a small, rather
sombre stone memorial crowned with a sculpted metal spade and pickaxe. Around me is the
industrial complex of the Corus steelworks in Port Talbot on the South Wales coast; the sea is close
by and the hill-slopes opposite between the Afan and Ogmore valleys are murky with mist and rain.

One of the worst ever coalmining disasters in Britain occurred here, deep beneath where I'm
standing, on 10 March 1890. No fewer than 250 men and boys were working underground in what
was then the Morfa Colliery when there was a huge explosion. Eighty-nine of them, including one
rescuer, were killed. The majority of the dead left widows, children and dependent relatives in
poverty. And many bodies were never recovered, sealed forever, deep in pitch black coal and rock.
A number of pit ponies, stabled underground, were either killed in the blast or had to be left down
there to die of slow starvation.

It wasn't the only explosion at Morfa, just one of the then many South Wales coalfields. Four
men had been killed in another explosion in 1858; 40 more in 1863; and in 1870, another 29.
The pit, with its harrowing death record, was closed in 1913. Over the period 1850 to 1930 the
South Wales coalfield had the worst disaster record in Britain, with a total of 3,119 people killed.
Coalmining was an exceedingly dangerous occupation.

But what, you might ask, has this to do with birds? The answer lies in superstition. Morfa Colliery
became widely known in its day as the 'Pit of Ghosts' because reports of strange happenings and
ghostly sightings prior to these explosions were apparently commonplace. And Welsh coalminers
were incredibly superstitious.

The *South Wales Weekly News* of 14 September 1901 records that, in the colliery districts of
Wales, the 'robin redbreast' was regarded as a harbinger of calamity. A robin singing close to a
window meant 'vexation, sorrow, or annoyance'. But if it ventured over the threshold and indoors, it
was a certain harbinger of illness or death.

Prior to other mine explosions, a robin had apparently been seen underground and many miners
believed it to be an ill-omen of coming disaster. They always caught any such bird and released it
outside to fly off. A crow, or two black crows flying east and west, were held to be a certain sign of
coming accidents and had apparently been noticed on the eve of several mine disasters too.

But it was at Morfa Colliery where the greatest concern was created over portents and auguries.
Shortly before its big explosion, the men had been disturbed by strange noises and tappings
underground.

'A bird had been seen in the mine, and crows had flown over the colliery. The workmen were in a state of consternation for some time, and a meeting was held secretly at dead of night to discuss the subject and decide what should be done. Either from fear of being laughed at or in dread of offending the "spirits" which wanted to warn them of 'the wrath to come', those who were present at the meeting kept silence and would not speak of it', the *South Wales Weekly News* noted in its reports of the Morfa disaster.

A dove had also been seen hovering around the mine entrance before the big explosion, as one had immediately prior to major explosions – and deaths – at other collieries in South Wales. Rather oddly, although in most places doves were generally associated with good news, this seemingly wasn't the case in Wales!

Adele Nozedar in *The Secret Language of Birds: A Treasury of Myths, Folklore and Inspirational True Stories* (Harper Collins, 2006) mentions a report in the *South Wales Echo* in 1902 of a dove spotted hovering near the mouth of a coalmine which caused 300 men not to clock on for work that day.

In coalmining areas, many birds seem to have been associated in local folklore with disaster, a reflection, maybe, of the decidedly pessimistic outlook of most Welsh coalminers and a long Celtic tradition of myth and superstition.

Another legend associated with mine disasters, and other deadly events too, was that of the 'Seven Whistlers'. Often allied with the Gabriel Hounds and other semi-mythical beliefs, they are imagined to be seven spirits, death portents like the banshee of Irish folklore (itself an old hag of a woman or a crow; although she is not always seen, her mourning call is heard, usually at night, when someone is about to die).

Belief in the Seven Whistlers was common among coalminers and seamen in the 19th century. They were heard only on dark nights – a wailing sound that some people attributed to the wind, others to birds flying over – Curlews perhaps with their haunting calls, or geese – while others said they were the souls of dead miners or seamen. If they were heard, some workers would not turn up for a day or two. They were heard, it was claimed, before some of the worst coalmining disasters in Britain.

Soaring through the sky, rising above the earth, birds have been symbols of power and freedom through the ages. In many myths, birds link the human world to the supernatural. Sometimes they are seen as messengers of the Gods, of doom and gloom perhaps. They play a major role in some creation and other religious myths. They appear as tricksters and oracles and they are often associated with the human soul after death.

Many of these birds are entirely mythical. The Quetzalcoatl, a feathered serpent god, was worshipped throughout much of what's now Central America, though he was sometimes known by different names in different places. To the Aztecs, Quetzalcoatl was related to the gods of the wind, of Venus, of the dawn and much else as well as being the patron god of their priesthood. Important indeed.

Another supernatural bird with power and strength was the mythical Thunderbird richly depicted in the songs, art and oral history of several native North American peoples. Southern

Russia once had its Sirin, an altogether less aggressive entity, half beautiful woman, half bird. And while Sirins sang beautiful songs to the saints, to everyone else they posed a danger by luring men to their deaths.

Garuda, a gigantic bird of prey, was supposed in Hindu mythology to carry the sun god Vishnu on his daily journey across the sky. He was probably derived from observations of real birds of prey like the larger eagles and vultures. Versions of Garuda were developed across much of Southeast Asia.

There was the Phoenix, a bird-like creature based perhaps on a composite of several very different real birds, and the ancient Greeks believed in their hideous, destructive harpies, ugly bird women with their bird faces and claws.

And then there's the least romantically named, Nine-headed Bird –sometimes called the Nine Phoenix – worshipped in China's central Hubei Province since the 1st century BC together with the Chinese dragon, two of the most worshipped mythical creatures throughout Chinese history. The number nine was thought to possess mysterious power in Chinese culture and the Nine-headed Bird was, and still is, thought to be a symbol of wisdom and good fortune. In the rest of China the people of Hubei are commonly known as 'nine-headed birds'!

Many mythical birds are linked to the story of the creation of the world. In ancient Egyptian mythology, there's the Benu bird, a long-legged wading heron that created the whole lot single-handed. In Borneo in Southeast Asia the Iban people tell of Ara and Irik, two bird spirits who between them made the sky and the earth. And a number of countries – Indonesia, the Polynesian Islands, and some northern European countries like Finland – have stories telling how the universe began with a 'cosmic egg' which hatched to give us all we have.

In several Southeast Asian countries where Buddhism and Hinduism are the dominant religions, much attention is paid to a mythical Kinnara, half human and half bird, a creature symbolising everlasting love. The Kinnari is female; a Kinnon male.

The Griffin is another. With the body of a lion and the head and wings of an eagle, it was considered a powerful entity, not to be messed with. The first Griffins date from the 5th century BC in Central Asia. But it was adopted by the Christian Church early on as a symbol of Jesus and it's commonly found sculpted out of stone on churches today such as at St Mark's Basilica in Venice, its veneration no doubt bolstered because Griffins were said to mate for life and, if their 'partner' died, would live alone for ever.

Rather more prosaically, the Griffin is also the logo of Vauxhall, appearing on all of their vehicles. The all-powerful chap has been adopted as a logo by other companies too.

Griffins put in a very regular appearance in heraldry, the tradition of using an emblem to indicate the status of a person and his or her influence within a society, or as a symbol – a coat of arms – of a town, city or university perhaps. The Griffin's amalgamation of lion and eagle is used to denote strength and military courage, and it is always drawn as a powerful and fierce monster.

A form of heraldry was in use in ancient Egypt but it's the use of it in Europe during the Middle Ages and – in a different form – today that's best known.

Its origins lie in the need to distinguish participants in combat when their faces were hidden by iron and steel helmets – the knights in their suits of armour. Today, heraldry rules on questions of rank and protocol, granting 'coats of arms', a kind of badge of a person's rank, still seemingly an issue of importance to some people in many western societies, Britain particularly.

The rules of heraldry are complex, archaic and difficult to understand. But several birds commonly feature in coats of arms, rather like the emblems showing allegiances in ancient Egypt in which cranes, falcons and other animals figured. During the Middle Ages, coats of arms remained popular for visually identifying a person other than in battle, impressed in sealing wax on documents, carved on family tombs, and flown as a banner on 'important' country homes for instance.

Doves, again, are popular as symbols of peace-bringing while the pelican, apparently as a Christ-like figure, is common in the heraldry of ecclesiastics! Many other birds appear as puns on the name of the bearer. If your name is Larkin or Sparrow, for instance, the depictions will be rather predictable.

Many real birds appear, too. The eagle is apparently the most common followed closely by the falcon, both reminiscent of the battle origins of much heraldry. But less bloodthirsty birds are present too. Cornwall's coat of arms has a Red-billed Chough, an attractive crow of coastal pastures. Liverpool's incorporates cormorants. Perth has Black Swans. Powhatan County in Virginia in the US has a Wild Turkey.

Among individuals with coats of arms, Ronald Reagan (1911–2004) had arms that included a falcon. Theodore Roosevelt (1858–1919) incorporated ostrich feathers in his. In Britain, the arms of Sir George Martin (the record producer, arranger and composer famous for producing the Beatles' hits) include a House Martin!

Those of Sir Christopher Frayling (educationist and writer known for his study of popular culture) incorporate three owls and, incredibly, the long extinct Dodo. While these might be a little quirky, some can be exquisite for their beauty and detail; one such is that granted to Dame Sonia Proudman, a British High Court judge. It's dominated by a resplendent peacock with a magnificent tail fanned to reveal its full beauty.

Many cultures around the world have long venerated certain birds, sometimes real ones rather than mythical ones like the Griffin. The raven is the chief deity of the Tlingit people of Alaska, a kind of culture hero who brings the light, provides fire and so on. A raven story from the Puget Sound region describes the bird as having originally lived in the land of spirits that existed before the world of humans. One day the raven became so bored that he flew away, carrying a stone in his beak. When the raven became tired of carrying the stone and dropped it, it fell into the ocean where it expanded until it formed the land on which humans now live.

Waterbirds such as ducks and swans play something like this role in the creation myths of native North Americans. A Navajo myth about a great flood tells that the people fled to a higher world leaving everything behind. A turkey dived into the lower world to retrieve seeds so that people could eventually grow crops again. You might be familiar with the story in a different context!

Impressive birds like eagles were usually associated with whoever sat at the pinnacle of importance in society. So it is that the Magyar people (today known generally as Hungarians) claimed that a giant eagle, falcon or hawk – perhaps they weren't too good at bird identification – had led their first king into Hungary where he founded their nation.

The Roman Empire sported an eagle as their imperial standard, carrying it with them wherever the emperor of the day went, and the Nazi Party in 1930s Germany certainly made considerable use of its imagery too. Adolf Hitler sported an eagle emblem on his peaked cap or his sleeve.

The United States has the Bald Eagle as its seal or emblem of its president, used to mark all his (or one day maybe her) correspondence. It represents peace and freedom though it has an olive twig in one talon and 13 deadly arrows in the other. But look carefully and you'll notice that the eagle always faces the olive branch not the warlike symbolism of the arrows. The image was drawn in 1782; its symbolism might not always chime well with a few modern-day events in which the US is much involved.

Owls, though, are a surprisingly mixed bag in mythology, sometimes not all good, sometimes not all bad. They are often symbols of wisdom, patience and learning – just look at their faces and those big eyes and you can see why. 'Brown Owl', the adult leader in a group of Girl Guides, has a mothering context. Yet, because most owls hunt at night, they attract darker associations too. How many films or TV dramas have you watched in which the calls of owls or a sudden image of one taking flight are used to suggest mystery, suspense, evil and ghostliness? All rather predictable.

The screeches of a Barn Owl's night-time calls are almost guaranteed to frighten. Because the light-coloured Barn Owl breeds in ruins, it's sometimes thought to bring ruin whereas, for a farmer at least, owls are actually useful for catching rodents. In spite of this usefulness, in Britain up until maybe the 1950s it wasn't unusual to find one killed and nailed to a farmyard barn 'to keep storms away' or suchlike!

In China, owls spell misfortune to come, while the South African Hottentot culture believed that their hooting was an omen of death! Early Mexican cultures regarded them as sacred but the later Aztecs thought they were evil night demons. Sometimes it's just hard to get it right!

Birds have long been associated with birth. Many of us still refer to 'the stork bringing the baby', and the return of White Storks to the rooftops of buildings in central Europe where they nest is greeted very positively!

The mythological bird, the Phoenix, is a symbol of eternal rebirth. In China and Japan, for instance, the Phoenix was reborn during times of good fortune. Jewish mythology has a phoenix-like bird, the equally fictitious Hoyl. It was the only creature to refuse to eat the fruit in the Garden of Eden which God decreed must not be touched. As a reward, the Hoyl was given eternal life. It goes to sleep, and fire destroys it. But an egg remains and a new Hoyl hatches out. Not too difficult then!

Ravens and crows, presumably because they fed off the human corpses that littered all too many battlegrounds (and still do), are often symbols of war, death and misfortune. Other birds have certainly played a major role in accompanying a dead person's soul on its journey. They're an obvious choice … if only because they can fly!

In Syria, for example, figures of eagles on tombs do it; the ancient Egyptians thought the hawk the best and built tombs with narrow shafts leading out so that the nimble bird could enter and leave. In Jewish tradition, doves have the task. In Islamic tradition, all dead souls remain as birds until Judgement Day, while Christian tradition has it that the dove became a symbol of the immortal soul ascending to Heaven. Doves don't seem to have an easy time of it!

Some cultures believed that people could sometimes change into birds, a notion that raises a rather indelicate point about whether the individual might ship up as a gentle thrush – or dove – or transform into an irascible magpie! In Siberia and Indonesia, for instance, shamans (intermediaries between the human and spirit worlds who often treat illness), priests and prophets were believed capable of changing into birds during trances or other mystical states.

In some myths, people acquire the ability to fly, a rather nice thought. Norse tales tell of the goddess Freya's feather cloak that enabled her to do just that. And Christian teaching is peppered with pictures of angels having bird wings … though devils usually had bat wings. Religious symbolism can be awfully unfair.

And that's not all. Mythological birds apparently sometimes speak, though not always in a language humans comprehend! They might be messengers from the Gods, or Gods themselves. Either way, their advice was apparently very sound and humans would ignore it at their peril. Sometimes a rather drastic event was needed before the deprived human could understand this bird talk. After tasting the blood of a slain dragon, the imaginary German hero Siegfried apparently knew what the forest birds were saying.

Some folklore says that many birds are equipped to foretell the future, magpies, ravens and … wait for it … doves included. One of them, the curiously flat-headed, brown, heron-like Hammerkop (the name means 'hammer-head') was reckoned by the Khoikhoi, the native people of southwestern Africa, to be able to see reflections of the future in pools of water. It's a nice tale because this odd bird has a habit of standing bolt-still and gazing into water to spot something to catch and eat.

Lucky symbolism is commonplace too. Enter the dove, again! A symbol of purity, grace and unconditional love, it's the bird revered in most cultures around the world as a bringer of peace and love, a world away from the disregard or hostility with which many people treat its very close relative, the city pigeon!

The Torah, the Old Testament and the Koran describe a story in which a dove was released by Noah after the Great Flood in order to find land. The dove came back carrying an olive branch in its beak, proof for Noah that the water had receded. So a white dove flying overhead is a very good omen, except seemingly to Welsh – and maybe other – coalminers, who thought the opposite!

White doves as peace symbols are frequently 'released' at public occasions such as the Olympic Games, at weddings, funerals, sporting events and celebrations. Most are provided by hire companies who keep them solely for that purpose. After release the doves fly home again ready for their next event!

In the Far East the equivalent might be the Red-crowned Crane, a tall, long-legged wading bird, all white with a red head patch. Not that the bird is 'used' directly; rather folded paper cranes are carefully made after an origami tradition begun by Sadako Sasaki, a young Japanese girl who had leukaemia because of the Hiroshima atomic bomb. She died in 1955 but the origami paper crane is linked to her as a symbol of peace.

The crane in Japan is one of the mystical or holy creatures (others include the dragon and the tortoise), and is said to live for a thousand years bringing long life, happiness, luck and peace. So origami cranes are popular gifts for special friends and family.

The Common Cuckoo, when it arrives in Europe in spring from its African wintering grounds, has always stimulated lots of superstition. On such a 'cuckoo day' you can turn your money over so you won't be short of it, or you may have a wish and if you count the number of times it calls 'cuckoo', you'll know how many years it is before you marry, the number of children you'll have or some such life-changing event. Even more famously, the term 'cuckold' – an unfaithful wife producing children unrelated to the husband who helps raise them – arises from the bird's habit of getting other species to incubate its eggs and raise its young!

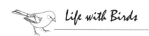

The tiny brown wren, now known for some reason as the Winter Wren and found across Europe, Asia and northern North America, has one of the most elaborate folk rituals of all associated with it, a ritual that still occurs in a few places in Europe, including Britain. It's an event that takes place on 26 December or thereabouts.

It consists of 'hunting' a fake wren, and putting it on top of a decorated pole (it used to be a real wren which was killed). Then the crowds of 'mummers' or 'strawboys' celebrate the wren by dressing up in masks, straw suits and colourful motley clothing and, accompanied by traditional céilí music bands, parade through towns and villages in remembrance of a festival that was celebrated by the Druids. The precise antics depend where the celebrations take place.

To the ancient Druids the wren hunt probably represented the death of the dark earth powers at the end of the year and the beginning of a new time of more light. Christianity took over this representation and suggests that the hunt might reflect the alerting of St Stephen's guards to his escape from imprisonment, causing the death of the first English martyr.

Most enigmatic of all birds in superstition, though, is the albatross, those huge-winged seabirds of the cold southern oceans and the Pacific that nest mainly on islands and glide huge distances over the waves. Sailors have always seen them as the deliverers of good luck.

Kill an albatross and you will incur misfortune, maybe even a curse or death, something that many ocean fishermen might like to think over as vast numbers of these elegant birds continue to be killed and maimed in fishing gear, throwing many albatross species into decline. An incredible 100,000 a year might be killed this way and 19 species are under threat as a result.

In our supposedly sophisticated, high-tech, western society, a lot of people remain incredibly superstitious. Crows and magpies give some people the jitters. Some fear seeing a single crow whereas two together is often regarded as good luck ('one for sorrow, two for joy'). Some people seeing a single magpie cross themselves, raise their hat to the bird or spit three times over their right shoulder and say 'devil, devil, I defy thee'! If you know anyone who does, don't walk on their right. Just in case a magpie comes along.

Magpie folklore might well stem from the fact that it was apparently the only bird not willing to go inside Noah's Ark, preferring to perch on the roof and chatter and 'swear' as the land drowned around them! Or that it was supposed to be the only bird not to mourn at Christ's crucifixion. Magpies have never been conformers!

Some people will still snap a cooked chicken's wishbone, the brittle, curved bone across its chest. It might sound rather bizarre but, along with the horseshoe and the four-leaved clover, it's supposed to bring luck. The two people snapping it each make a wish; the one getting the longer part is deemed to have their wish come true!

Swallows are treated as harbingers of spring and summer yet to come. The arrival in Europe of the first Barn Swallows of the spring (from southern Africa where they overwinter) is frequently commented on; likewise the return of the similar-looking Cliff Swallow to California from winter in South America. Their return every year to the Mission San Juan Capistrano in California on (or around) 19 March is celebrated with a festival even when, as in recent years, they don't turn up to nest there as they used to!

European Robins with their red breasts have always had Christian associations that are recalled on a very high proportion of Christmas cards. The story is that, when Jesus was on his way to be crucified, a robin picked one of the thorns from the crown on his head, injuring himself by piercing his breast, or the bird was splattered with Christ's blood when he got too close. Other stories claim that the bird's breast was singed while taking water to sinners in hell, or while fanning a fire to warm the baby Jesus at Christmas.

A much less romantic version suggests that the Victorian postmen in their red uniforms who delivered Christmas cards were nicknamed 'robin redbreasts' and the association stuck.

There are superstitions about robins doing a bit of weather forecasting too. Supposedly, if one sang on top of a bush the weather would be warm while if it sang from within the branches, rain was on the way. Some people still pay more attention to such things than they do to a TV weather forecast.

Referring to someone's 'swansong', meaning some kind of final gesture or performance before they die, is still commonplace. It has its origins way back in the time of the ancient Greeks who believed that swans only sing before they die! Swans can do pretty good snorts, grunts and hisses but singing isn't something that comes naturally to them. It may have arisen because Whooper Swans (all white with yellow beaks), migrating to the Arctic north to breed, produce a slightly more musical call, at best a kind of nasal honking, as they fly off, not to be seen again for at least half a year.

Some historic events might have turned out completely differently if only people had watched birds! The Emperor Napoleon I (1769–1821) of France, Napoleon Bonaparte, marching his army north to Moscow in 1812, might have considered why large numbers of storks and cranes were flying to the warmer south. His subsequent defeat by the Russian army and his ignominious retreat in murderous winter weather decimated his – until then – invincible army and paved the way for his downfall.

Many farmers and country people still hang up dead birds, crows and magpies especially, often impaled on fence wire, to supposedly discourage more of the birds from coming near – a kind of scarecrow. Needless to say, they don't!

A few years ago I talked to shepherds in the high mountains that dominate the core of the island of Madeira off the west coast of North Africa. A few of them were aware of the haunting, almost child-like wailing calls that they only heard on very dark nights in summer high up on the incredibly steep Madeiran mountainsides.

They were the calls of Zino's Petrel, a very rare, pale grey and white seabird that scrapes its own nesting burrows 6,000 feet up on these daunting slopes but only visits them in pitch darkness to avoid any predators. Some of the local shepherds, though, remained convinced that the ghostly wailing was the call of dead shepherds who long ago had lost their footing on these dangerous slopes.

Many people still believe that a bird tapping at a window – worse still, one getting inside your house – is an impending omen of death to an occupant. They apparently suggest frantic, wandering human souls. Russian tradition has it that a chicken crowing at you three times before noon means that the death of a close family member can be expected within a fortnight. The chicken should be killed, but not eaten, as consuming it will bring about further misfortune!

Russia is, though, the country with another deep-seated belief, that when you have alcohol, it must be drunk until it is gone, a recipe for over-indulgence if ever there was one. And where, bizarrely, if one or more birds defecate on you, it brings good luck!

At the Tower of London, Ravens have been kept in the grounds (ten in total with six on duty and four spare) for 900 years. They have their flight feathers clipped to make sure they can't leave

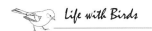

and they're well looked after at government expense. Superstition has it that, if they hopped off, the Tower would fall, and that maybe the monarchy and the whole country would collapse too. No wonder they clip them annually. In World War II, almost all of them died from shock during heavy German bombing raids but they were replaced with new birds in 1946 when the Tower was reopened to the public.

In Liverpool, two so-called Liver Birds have come to symbolise the city. Vaguely resembling cormorants, they crown twin clock towers on the Liver Building, constructed in 1911 at Liverpool's Pier Head overlooking the River Mersey. They rekindled an earlier belief that the Liver was a mythical bird that once haunted the local shoreline but its shape has varied, sometimes more eagle (as in Liverpool Football Club's badge) than cormorant.

According to popular legend, they are a male and female pair, the female looking out to sea (watching for the seamen to return safely home) while the male looks towards the city (making sure the pubs are open!). Local legend also has it that the birds face away from each other because, if they were to mate and fly away, the city would cease to exist!

There are plenty of stories about birds killing people, most of them myth rather than fact. Eagles picking up babies to devour. Cassowaries using their vicious claws to disembowel people. Ostriches killing with a single kick. Packs of vultures descending on someone sleeping in a field. And so on. Cassowaries are generally considered the most dangerous and the only birds to have certainly caused a human death, in Australia in 1926 when one pierced the jugular vein of a man with its viciously sharp claws. The man had been trying to kill the bird so there was a strong element of self-defence!

In many cultures around the world, a person's head is considered to be the most important part of the body, to be protected and respected. Its significance derives from the belief that the head is where the soul or spirit resides. Because of such beliefs, head-dresses are often an important part of daily and ceremonial attire because they draw attention to this key body part. And head-dresses are often made from birds' feathers.

The feathers are acquired by rearing birds, by hunting or by trade, so the production of head-dresses is often expensive or labour-intensive. The head-dresses themselves are fragile and often too delicate for daily use. Feathers are therefore frequently a status symbol, worn on ceremonial or ritual occasions. And they have probably been worn in some cultures since time immemorial.

Arguably the best known is their use by Native American Indians. One of the classic images of a Native American, mainly from TV westerns, is the tribal chief with a full eagle feather war-bonnet draped over his head. They were actually only ever worn by a dozen or so tribes in the Great Plains region of the central US such as the Sioux, Crow, Blackfeet, Cheyenne, and Plains Cree. And they were of different shapes and designs depending on the tribe. All of them, though, were made from eagle tail feathers. And it was the dark-tipped but predominantly white tail feathers of immature Golden Eagles that were the most valued.

A warrior would earn a single feather with each truly brave act he did, and often he would have to earn his first feather before he was considered to be an adult in the tribe. In some tribes, earning a feather was necessary before a man could take part in tribal councils or marry and have children.

He would only wear one or two of his eagle feathers – his most treasured ones – in battle. The rest would go onto a pole to walk with on special occasions. When he collected 30 or so feathers, he would have enough to begin a head-dress.

Each feather a warrior had earned had special meaning to him, so binding them together into a headpiece was even more special. The warrior would ask his best friends to help him with the task, men only. Together they would create the bonnet, and add to it as the warrior earned more feathers.

So Indian chiefs with great bonnets of feathers were not 'given' those like a crown is given to a king. Instead, they earned every one through brave acts, and it is because of those acts and the honour of his actions that he is then elected chief. Native Americans were in tune with nature and would never waste any aspect of it so the warrior awarded a feather would explore his lands until he found a suitable nest with an adult eagle in it, trap the eagle without harming it and remove a single feather, releasing the eagle back into the wild, thanking it for the gift.

Native Americans believe that the first birds were naked and that they asked the Creator if they could have something to cover up with. The Creator agreed, but said that the new clothing was far off and had to be fetched. The Turkey Vulture, a rather clean bird at the time, offered to do this for all the birds. He raced off quickly, and instead of stopping to eat normally along the way, just scavenged at whatever he found so as not to slow himself down. When he got there, the Turkey Vulture decided he should get the very best outfit for himself but, as a result, the Creator decided to teach him a lesson.

When the vulture got back home with his collection of coats, the Creator told all the birds that each of them could choose the coat they wanted but that the Turkey Vulture would have to choose last. So he became the ugliest of birds with his sooty-brown coloured feathers. And that's how the Turkey Vulture in the US looks today!

In the 1800s, Native American men from other tribes sometimes began to wear Plains-style war-bonnets. In part this was because the youthful American tourist industry expected Native Americans to look a certain way and partly because many Native American tribes were forced to move to Oklahoma and other Indian territories, so tribes that used to live far apart began adopting customs from their new neighbours. For the tribes adopting them they became a matter of fashion or a general symbol of authority rather than a display of honour and courage.

Today, eagle feathers are still sometimes awarded to descendants of Plains Indians who serve in the military or do other brave deeds. The 'US Eagle Feather Law' provides exceptions to federal wildlife laws to enable Native Americans to continue their feather gathering. Only individuals of certifiable Native American ancestry enrolled in a federally recognised tribe are legally authorised to obtain them, an issue that causes continuing controversy.

The Aztecs who dominated much of Central America in the 14th to 16th centuries, and many of the Maya Indians of Mexico, were also famous for their feather head-dresses, but these looked very different from the Plains Indian war-bonnets. They sewed together a large fan of feathers and attached it to the back of their head with straps and a headband or metal circlet. Another difference is that parrot, macaw and quetzal (similarly colourful, large bird) feathers were used instead of eagle feathers.

According to the Pitt Rivers Museum at Oxford University, the most striking examples of feather head-dresses come from the Amazon area of South America, from Hawaii and Papua New Guinea in the Pacific, and from Africa.

According to the Museum, feathers have been used in parts of South America to ornament the body since before the Spanish conquest in the 16th century, and the more remote tribes continue to use them as part of everyday life. They are used partly for decoration but they also have their own symbolism and meanings which are different for different tribes. The brightly coloured feathers of the macaw, parrot and toucan are the most popular choices and their long tail feathers are specially prized.

Often, birds are reared in captivity for their feathers by rural tribespeople so they have a continuous source of feathers which grow back on the birds after being plucked. Birds tamed in this way include parrots, macaws, curassows, guans, toucans and rheas. They're worn at initiations, at funeral rituals, by shamans, for social visiting, to express group identity, to mark life stages, or to exercise political power. They are often a sign, too, of a successful hunter and food provider and, as in Native American cultures past, it's only when a boy becomes an adult that he's entitled to wear an impressive feather head-dress.

Head-dresses are often constructed with the layers of feathers mirroring where the birds are found in nature; the white of the high-flying eagle at the top; the red or yellow of the tree-dwelling macaw or toucan in the middle; and the black feathers of the ground-dwelling curassow at the bottom.

Elaborate head-dresses are worn by many Pacific cultures, particularly in Papua New Guinea where there are often many different types for different occasions. Usually made out of vegetation, the designs often include birds of paradise feathers, including those from the highly sought-after King of Saxony Bird of Paradise, known to local tribes as the 'Kisaba'.

It's a thrush-sized bird, black and orange with two incredibly long enamel-blue plumes that drape back from the male bird's head. Like all 44 different birds of paradise (found only in New Guinea, eastern Australia and a few nearby islands), they have legal protection and hunting is only permitted at a sustainable level to fulfil the ceremonial needs of the local tribal population.

In the case of the King of Saxony plumes which the birds lose by moulting each year after breeding, bowerbirds frequently pick them up to decorate the bowers they build out of twigs and other materials on the ground to impress their mates! Tribespeople are allowed to retrieve them from any bowers they find.

In some parts of the New Guinea highlands, people engage in colourful local rituals that are called 'sing-sings', sometimes to re-enact a legendary battle for instance. They paint themselves and dress up with feathers, pearls and animal skins to represent birds, trees or mountain spirits. Bird beliefs are deeply ingrained in folklore among most of the tribes of New Guinea and Borneo, and different birds are associated with different traditions.

Like the Papua New Guineans still do, New Zealand Maoris used to wear feathered head-dresses to symbolise power. Feathers from a black bird with a white-tipped tail and an unusually shaped beak, the Huia, were particularly highly prized, with chiefs wearing white-tipped Huia feathers to symbolise power over chiefs wearing monotone feathers.

Huia feathers were revered as 'taonga' or treasures by Maori and in later times by the European settlers to New Zealand. The Huia feathers were often grouped in twos and were usually accompanied by a cloak made from the feathers of that better-known New Zealand bird, the dull brown kiwi. The entire carcass of a Huia was sometimes worn suspended from the ear and its feathers were also used for decorating the dead.

But human greed did for the Huia. They became extinct around 1910, the result of too much collecting to decorate people, the impact of introduced predators like dogs and rats that killed many, and forest destruction by the Maoris.

Hawaiian chiefs are another culture that wore spectacular feathered capes and helmets – uniforms denoting their rank: shiny black plumage from one species, scarlet from another, green and, the rarest, yellow from the Hawaiian Mamo, striking starling-sized birds with long curved beaks and black and yellow plumage. The Mamo was found nowhere else.

Reputedly, the yellow cape worn by Hawaiian chief Kamehameha the Great (1758–1819) was made from the feathers of 80,000 Mamos! You are going to guess the upshot of this of course; the bird became extinct (by 1899) because so many were trapped with a sticky paste plastered around the flowers they frequented, and because much of their habitat was destroyed.

In some rituals using birds' feathers, then, the birds were not always killed to get them. Sacrifice, though, has no happy ending for any of the birds involved. In some parts of the world it's still practised by many religions as a means of appeasing a god or gods or for changing the course of nature.

Animal sacrifice has turned up in almost all cultures at some time or other. It was practised by the Hebrews, Greeks, famously by the Romans as well as by the Aztecs and Hindus. There are numerous early records of the sometimes huge scale involved, such as more than 50,000 pigeons being sacrificed to the ancient Egyptian god Ammon in the reign of Rameses III from 1186 to 1155 BC.

In early Christian sacrifice, too, doves or pigeons often met their end on some altar or other. There is the story in the Gospel of John in the Bible's New Testament of Jesus castigating the dove sellers in the temple where the trapped birds were sold for sacrifice or for eating. It was a pretty awful business. They used a 'stool pigeon', a decoy blinded using a red hot needle before being tied to a stake so that it could be seen by other pigeons. When these came close to investigate its pathetic calls, a net would be thrown over them.

Chickens have long been popular victims. Today, much of the urban Hindu community in India disapproves of animal sacrifice which has been phased out in many towns and cities though it's still common in conservative rural communities where attempts to stop the practice have been met with resistance. In Tamil Nadu State, for instance, where the state government's attempts to clamp down on it over the last few years have been met with much disapproval, sacrifice of goats, buffalo and cockerels at Hindu deity shrines and temples is often commonplace and follows a long tradition.

Every five years, in what is thought to be the largest ritual animal sacrifice in the world, around 200,000 animals and birds are slaughtered in the name of the Hindu deity Gadhimai at a temple in the village of Bariyapur in southern Nepal. Pigs, buffalo, goats, wild rats and birds including chickens and pigeons are all killed by having their heads hacked off. It's an extremely bloody sight.

Thousands of visitors from India and Nepal attend the occasion in spite of frequent calls by animal rights groups worldwide to ban it. In November 2009 the *Kathmandu Post* carried a letter from Maneka Gandhi, widow of Indian politician Sanjay Gandhi, appealing to the people of Nepal to abandon the killing of animals at the festival later that month.

'Priests frighten villagers into believing that terrible things will happen if the goddess is not placated with animal sacrifices', she wrote. 'The festival is a business, and profit is the motive for killing so many animals. Villagers go into debt to buy the animals to be sacrificed. Debt leads to bankruptcies, and when the small farmers' lands are confiscated to become the property of large landowners, then the former farmers become day labourers', wrote Gandhi.

But the festival went ahead as usual, and in this deeply rooted tradition many Nepalis believe that the sacrifices will bring them prosperity. Visiting believers often bring their own animal or bird to sacrifice at the event. They also believe that by eating the meat, which is taken back to their villages and consumed during feasts, they will be protected from evil.

Birds – or parts of them – have been used in a huge range of medicines in the past and still are in potions administered by traditional healers (often referred to disparagingly in the west as 'witch doctors') in many developing countries.

In Britain, past uses of owls include owl broth to cure whooping cough, while charred and powdered owl eggs were used to improve eyesight … a piece of powerful symbolism considering the amazing eyesight of owls. Crushed swallow broth was used to supposedly cure epilepsy and stammering, the latter presumably related to the somewhat stuttering, quivering calls of these birds.

The foul-smelling, yellow- or orange-coloured oil ejected forcibly from the beaks of sea cliff-nesting Northern Fulmars to deter a predator from attacking their eggs or chicks was even exported from the distant Scottish island of St Kilda in the 18th and 19th centuries. It found its way to the cities where it was used to treat dental abscesses, sprains, rheumatism and boils! Whether it cured anything or not, you would have smelt pretty rotten as a result.

According to that famous medieval herbalist, Nicholas Culpeper (1616–1654), eating the brain of sparrows 'provokes the lust' while dried pigeon dung was used to make poultices to cure baldness and gout as well as being swallowed as a medicine or used as an enema. In the US, the vast slaughter of Passenger Pigeons (see Chapter 1) provided large amounts of such medicines.

In parts of Southeast Asia, Tree Sparrows are known to eat cannabis seeds, so it's often called the 'hemp bird'. Eating them is supposed to improve your sexual potency, presumably a cheaper alternative to Viagra.

Highly respected in their communities and usually women, sangomas – traditional healers in the Zulu, Xhosa, Ndebele and Swazi cultures in southern Africa – are consulted by most people of such tribal origins before consulting a western trained practitioner. And wildlife is an integral part of a sangoma's ritual medicine. For example, in training and for sangoma graduation ceremonies, the ritual animal sacrifice of a chicken, goat or cow is meant to seal the bond between the ancestors and the sangoma.

Vulture parts are prescribed for various ailments including headaches and are also supposed to be effective for providing clairvoyant powers, foresight and increased intelligence. By eating the brain of the vulture, the sangoma is said to receive greater powers to communicate with the dead. The foot of a vulture is believed to bring good luck in gambling. Vulture parts are often ground into a medicine (known as muti) which is smoked, drunk, inhaled, smeared on the body, given as an enema or rubbed into an incision. Taste-wise, it would surely make a western cough medicine very popular in comparison.

The problem is also that these practices are having an impact on South Africa's vultures which is extremely serious. Experts at Ezemvelo KZN Wildlife, the government agency in KwaZulu Natal Province responsible for wildlife, estimate that it could drive vultures to extinction in South Africa within 30 years. Seven of their nine native vulture species are already endangered and their use in muti is proving disastrous.

Traditional healing might be very long established but so, too, is another practice – witchcraft! The use of supposedly supernatural or magical powers, it can be used to inflict harm or damage upon members of a community or their property. But it might be used to heal someone from bad witchcraft too. The concept of witchcraft is a means of explaining human misfortune by blaming it either on a supernatural entity or a known person in the community, a witch!

Belief in witchcraft, and in consequence witch-hunts, are found in many cultures worldwide, today mostly in Africa south of the Sahara. But it was historically commonplace in Europe between roughly the 14th to the 18th centuries, where it came to be seen as a vast conspiracy against Christianity and where accusations of witchcraft led to large-scale witch-hunts.

Birds, mostly owls and ravens, are among the animals associated with witchcraft which include a varied selection such as the frog, serpent, pig, stag, goat, wolf, cat and many more. Hardly a charm or potion would work without a bit of owl in it, maybe something linked to the fact that an owl's flat, round face resembles a human face! Famously, the witches in Shakespeare's *Macbeth* include an 'owlet's wing' in their vile brew while in *Julius Caesar*, an owl hooted and shrieked before Caesar's death.

A witch's animal was known as his or her 'familiar' and was thought to be an associate of the devil. Obsession with the witch's familiar was most prevalent in England and Scotland and was mentioned in numerous trial records through the Middle Ages, particularly those related to Matthew Hopkins, the infamous Witch Finder General. Large numbers of supposed witches were tortured, given a trial of sorts and, in many cases, brutally executed. They were extraordinarily ugly events.

Many witches believe that an animal familiar is not acquired through personal choice, more that an animal will choose the witch to be its guardian and companion. It's apparently no use at all going to your local pet shop and selecting one.

One relatively modern-day English witch who had a familiar, in her case a jackdaw named, for some unknown reason, Mr Hotfoot Jackson, was Sybil Leek (1917–1982) who wrote more than 60 books on the occult and esoteric subjects. She was dubbed 'Britain's most famous witch' by the BBC, probably because they kept interviewing her. She rose to media fame in the 1950s after the repeal of the 1735 Witchcraft Act and she gave impetus to the formation of neopagan witchcraft, namely the modern-day religion of Wicca.

Strong in defence of her beliefs, Sybil sometimes differed and even quarrelled with other witches, probably not something to be recommended. She disapproved of nudity in rituals, a requirement in some Wicca traditions, and was strongly against the use of drugs, but she was at odds with most other witches in that she did believe in cursing – not the act of swearing at someone but, altogether more disconcerting, putting a curse on them!

Leek claimed descent from a long line of witches dating back to the 16th century including Molly Leigh (1685–1746) who was accused of witchcraft in Burslem, Staffordshire but who died before coming to trial. She kept a familiar bird, in her case a Blackbird or a Jackdaw (accounts vary), which perched on her shoulder as she delivered milk from her cows!

In Leigh's case it was the local parson, a Reverend Spencer, who made the accusation. He claimed that Leigh sent her Blackbird to sit on the sign of the Turk's Head pub that the parson frequently visited, and that the bird's presence was responsible for turning the beer sour! Leigh was also blamed for other ailments suffered by the townsfolk.

After her death in 1746, there were claims that her ghost haunted the town. Spencer – along with several other parsons – exhumed her body, opened the coffin, and threw in the still-living Blackbird that had been her companion. Not exactly an act of Christian charity but one hopes that the local beer improved! They then re-buried Molly in a north to south direction, at a right angle to all the other graves in the churchyard.

Wicca is a pagan religion dating from the early 20th century, often referred to as witchcraft by its adherents who are known as Wiccans or witches though it was first popularised during the 1950s by Gerald Gardner, a retired British civil servant. Most prevalent in the US and Britain, there might be anywhere between two and eight hundred thousand of them. Birds – and animals generally – don't figure in their practices and they certainly don't possess familiars.

But feathers do have a role in some Wiccan practices, though only in one form. And that is the so-called 'witch's ladder'.

Seemingly, such a ladder, a piece of rope about five feet long and half an inch thick with a number of male goose feathers on it that had been twisted in sideways to form a series of horizontal 'steps', was discovered in a hidden attic room in a house in Wellington, Somerset in 1878 when it was being demolished.

The ladder might not have attracted much attention except that it was found alongside six broomsticks and a chair! Local people believed that the old woman who used to live there was a witch. It was believed that witches of old cast an evil spell over a person by tying the knots and then hiding the cord, and the only way to undo the spell was to find the hidden cord and untie each knot. The ladder is in the Pitt Rivers Museum at Oxford University.

But this explanation is contentious and the alternative view is that it might have been used to deter animals, deer especially, and was perhaps strung from trees to do that. Intriguingly, though, this alternative use doesn't explain the other objects found with it. Coincidence?

Today, Wiccans use witch's ladders primarily in healing and wish-granting rituals. Although ladders are often created as part of a specific spell, many Wiccans keep a personal ladder, though feathers aren't apparently always part of it. They can also be used to 'bind the 13 moons of the year', purportedly to allow the witch to better work weather and nature magic.

Millions of birdwatchers the world over, though, whether enthusiastic or just casual, talk about a very different kind of magic. Theirs is certainly a magic about spells being cast. But good ones. And the spell-casting is done by the birds themselves!

It's the magic of watching a flock, thousands strong, of European Starlings 'folding and pulsing in the dusk sky like a dark aurora' as Britain's leading nature writer, Richard Mabey once described it. Catching a split-second glimpse of a Peregrine suddenly diving between high-rise buildings like an earth-bound arrow to take the life out of an unsuspecting pigeon below. Or the excitement of seeing your first springtime Purple Martins return to examine the nestboxes in your garden after months of winter cold.

It's the birds that cast a spell on some of us. And even if they haven't worked their magic on you, or not yet anyway, many of them will continue to play a big part in your lives whether you notice them or not.

Further reading

Allen, Barbara. *Pigeon*. Reaktion Books, 2009.

Barker, Juliet. *Agincourt: The King, The Campaign, The Battle*. Abacus, 2006.

Beletsky, Les. *Birds of the World*. Collins, 2006.

Buczacki, Stefan. *Fauna Britannica*. Hamlyn, 2002.

Campbell, Bruce and Lack, Elizabeth (eds). *A Dictionary of Birds*. T & A D Poyser, 1985.

Cocker, Mark and Mabey, Richard. *Birds Britannica*. Chatto and Windus, 2005.

Downer, John. *Lifesense: Our Lives Through Animal Eyes*. BBC Books, 1991.

Elphick, Jonathan. *Birds: The Art of Ornithology*. Scriptum Editions, 2004.

Gibson, Graeme. *The Bedside Book of Birds: An Avian Miscellany*. Bloomsbury, 2005.

Greenoak, Francesca. *British Birds: Their Folklore, Names and Literature*. Christopher Helm, 1997.

Heinrich, Bernd. *Mind of the Raven*. Harper Perennial, 2006.

Juniper, Tony. *Spix's Macaw: The Race to Save the World's Rarest Bird*. Fourth Estate, 2003.

Lovegrove, Roger. *Silent Fields: The Long Decline of a Nation's Wildlife*. Oxford University Press, 2007.

Lutwack, Leonard. *Birds in Literature*. University Press of Florida, 1994)

Martin, Stephen. *Penguin*. Reaktion Books, 2009.

Nozedar, Adele. *The Secret Language of Birds: A Treasury of Myths, Folklore and Inspirational True Stories*. Harper Collins, 2006.

Soper, Tony. *Wildlife of the North Atlantic: A Cruising Guide*. Bradt Travel Guides, 2008.

Stutchbury, Bridget. *Silence of the Songbirds*. Walker and Company, 2007.

Summers-Smith, J. Denis. *On Sparrows and Man*. The Thersby Group, 2005.

Tudge, Colin. *Consider the Birds: Who They Are and What They Do*. Allen Lane, 2008.

AUTHOR'S BIOGRAPHY

Dr Malcolm Smith is an established freelance writer, contributing on wildlife, heritage and travel to the *Daily Telegraph* magazine, *Country Life*, *CNN Traveller* and others. Originally a bacteriologist, he spent almost all of his professional career in wildlife and landscape conservation. Until 2004 he was Chief Scientist and Senior Director with the Countryside Council for Wales, which he left to devote more time to writing.

He has had an almost life-long interest in birds and considerable experience of the interaction of birds with people in a number of countries. He was a Board Member of The Environment Agency, the largest environmental regulator in Europe, from 2004 to 2010.

GROWING BARN OWLS IN MY GARDEN

Paul Hackney

- A 20-year story of successful barn owl conservation
- An informative and entertaining story of one of Britain's most iconic birds

The barn owl is a 'flagship' species, at the top of the food chain, and its presence or absence is a good indicator of the health of the countryside. This is the enjoyable and informative story of the author's success in restoring this beautiful bird to areas of the country where its numbers had catastrophically declined.

The author describes his many encounters with barn owls, from the acquisition of his first breeding pair; 'Barney', a completely humanised owl; to stories of the fascinating array of people involved in releasing, studying, and simply marvelling at this beautiful bird.

After almost 20 years, there is now evidence of a marked increase in barn owl numbers in areas where the author has worked. During this period, he bred and released around 250 birds, put up nest boxes and advised on barn owl-friendly approaches to land management.

The return of the barn owl not only heralds a brighter future for the British countryside, but also shows that the negative effects of human activity on the environment can be reversed with effort, goodwill and determination.

ISBN 978-184995-027-5   240 × 170mm   c.160pp + 16pp colour section   softback   £16.99   April, 2011

KESTRELS FOR COMPANY

Gordon Riddle

- A captivating insight into the world of the kestrel through the eyes of an enthusiastic raptor fieldworker
- Easy-to-read style combining a mixture of facts with entertaining anecdotes and experiences – complemented with a wide range of colour illustrations

An appealing book that rightfully raises the profile of the kestrel. It provides an extensive picture of this delightful falcon, including its lifestyle and the factors that affect its breeding success and survival. This is based upon almost 40 years' monitoring of the kestrel in south-west Scotland and further afield by the author and colleagues, giving a flavour of the integrated approach to monitoring and conservation.

As well as the wealth of factual data, there are entertaining anecdotes and stories both from the author's experiences and from the wider media coverage of this raptor over the years. The reader is taken to exotic locations such as the Seychelles, Mauritius and the Cape Verde Islands to see the endemic island kestrels which have always held a great fascination for the author.

The author reflects upon the political, economic and conservation issues that have dominated this field in the past few decades and through this personal and well-informed account the reader gains access to the world of the kestrel.

ISBN 978-184995-029-9   240 × 170mm   softback   208pp   full colour throughout with over 150 illustrations £18.99   April, 2011

MANGROVES AND MAN-EATERS
and other wildlife encounters

Dan Freeman

'… *In this entertaining book, which is as much about people and places as it is about wildlife, you'll read of hair-raising encounters with giant crabs, lions and killer bees. But rest assured, with Dan Freeman you are travelling with the best of guides* …' Extract from Foreword by Tony Soper

This is an action-packed book full of anecdotal adventure as the author takes readers on his journeys to find wildlife around the world. What makes this book really special is that Dan has also written about the people he has taken with him, the people they have encountered and the histories and politics of the countries in which they have worked.

In 'Bonding with Spiders' Dan meets the original James Bond, the bird-eating spider from *Dr. No* and has his own nightmarish encounter in the Australian bush, sharing his tent with a giant spider! Other stories include filming piranhas in South America, tortoises in France, and wolves, bears and ibex in Italy.

This powerful and evocative collection of stories is the result of 45 years engaging with animals and people on six continents. Dan has observed his subjects with a naturalist's passion for detail, resulting in a book that is engaging, informative and highly revealing. Although some of the creatures would make you want to run a mile, the book will be hard to put down!

ISBN 978-184995-009-1   240 × 170mm   224pp   24pp colour section   softback   £18.99

THE HEN HARRIER
Don Scott

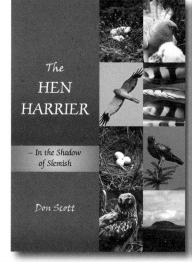

The hen harrier is one of the iconic species of the bird world and its history is a mix of controversy, persecution, and recent patchy recovery. This dedicated study of the bird in N. Ireland for over two decades reveals previously unrecorded facets of the birds' lifestyle, and provides a detailed account of their life, habits and future prospects. The author presents much new information about the harrier in its continuing struggle to re-establish its hold despite high levels of persecution from man or predation by other species.

The author's passion for the bird is obvious as he shares moments of excitement and sadness, and he speaks frankly about the maltreatment and mismanagement of this elegant raptor over the years. This is an unmatched account not to be missed.

A fascinating and detailed study of the Hen Harrier

'*This book is an essential read for all those interested in the hen harrier and the conservation of birds of prey in general, and comes highly recommended*'. Professor John Edwards, **Peregrine**, the Hawk and Owl Trust magazine.

ISBN 978-1904445-93-7   240 × 170mm   180pp + 16pp colour section   softback   £18.99

A LIFE OF OSPREYS
Roy Dennis

Ospreys are one of our best known and best loved birds and the name Roy Dennis is not only synonymous with the successful return of the osprey to Scotland, but is also renowned for his international work with a variety of species. From the time he saw his first osprey, back in 1960, Roy has worked to help this magnificent raptor establish itself once more in a country where it had been hounded and persecuted to near-extinction over hundreds of years.

With many personal anecdotes and insights, the book covers the ecology and conservation of the osprey from Roy pioneering the building of artificial nests to starting the first European translocation of chicks from their nests in the Highlands and releasing them at Rutland Nature Reserve in the Midlands.

Included in this book are Roy's personal diary entries, written at a time when no one knew whether or not his lifetime's work would succeed, and which add a unique sense of history to this personal tale.

'Everything one could ever wish to know about these birds seems to be covered in this book' **John Muir Trust Journal**

'The book is delightful, lavishly and intelligently illustrated containing much factual data and is highly readable. … Buy it' **ECOS**

'… one of the most arresting nature books this year… His book has excellent photographs and also information on where to see the osprey eyries' **The Times**

ISBN 978-1904445-26-5   240 × 170 mm   224pp   liberally illustrated, full colour throughout   softback   £18.99

DAYS WITH THE GOLDEN EAGLE
Seton Gordon

A reprint of this classic eagle book from one of the pioneers of nature writing. Complete with photographs from the original collections and with an introduction by Jim Crumley.

Writer and photographer Seton Gordon was among the first to observe the daily life of this magnificent bird. From life day-to-day on the eyrie, it is all covered in his own inimitable style.

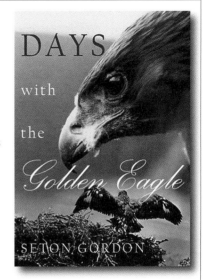

'What readers will find is a factual, yet sensitive and evocative account of events from tiny eaglets to successful fledging. ...It is good to see re-publication ... they will appreciate reading it, seeing his remarkable photographs, and feeling they are on the hill with this timeless outstanding naturalist and writer'. **Birding Scotland**

ISBN 978-1870325-35-6   240 × 170mm   192pp   illustrated   softback   £18.99

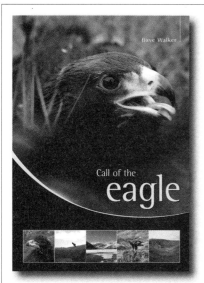

CALL OF THE EAGLE
Dave Walker

One man's efforts over 30 years to study, protect and defend England's rarest breeding bird – the golden eagle

Employed by the RSPB as a senior species protection warden at a secret location in Cumbria, the author was fortunate enough to become involved with this iconic species during their most productive breeding period.

The author discovered and recorded many previously unknown facts about golden eagles. He conducted one of the most detailed and complete study of a pair of golden eagles with, at its heart, the life and times of an eagle he followed from its arrival in 1982 until its death, 22 years later – a bird that would eventually show little fear of him and accept his presence.

Call of the Eagle amply illustrates the close attachment and passion that drove the author to devote so much of his life to this magnificent raptor, famed as the King of Birds.

'...an engrossing account of golden eagle ecology. ...is utterly absorbing. This memoir is packed with details – dates, times and behaviour'. **Peregrine**

'...it is clear that his knowledge of their habits is second to none'. **Birding World**

ISBN: 978-1904445-82-1   240 × 170 mm   176pp plus 4pp colour section   £16.99

FLIGHT OF THE WILD GEESE
Graham Uney

Flight of the Wild Geese tells the story of the winter wildlife of the Solway Firth, that wonderfully wild estuary set between the rugged hills of Cumbria and the rolling farmland, moors and forests of Dumfries and Galloway. It explores the links that these beautiful places share with the most remote islands of the North Atlantic, and with the stunning landscapes of the high Arctic. This is a book of birds, of people, and of places.

Growing up in the flatlands of East Yorkshire, the author yearned to know more about where the winter-visiting birds went during the summer. Later in life and with the Solway Firth on his doorstep, where some of the largest numbers of geese are to be found, he decided to find out.

'a fine travel tale, mixed with natural history and keen observation en route. ... this is the perfect book to read ... ' **Waterlife**

'This is a book written by a birder and a birder's book ... if you enjoy reading about birds and their homes you'll enjoy this book'. **Habitat**

ISBN 978-1904445-54-8   240 × 170mm
liberally illustrated   176pp + 16pp colour section
£16.99   softback

 www.whittlespublishing.com   e: info@whittlespublishing.com
t: 01593-731 333   f: 01593-731 400